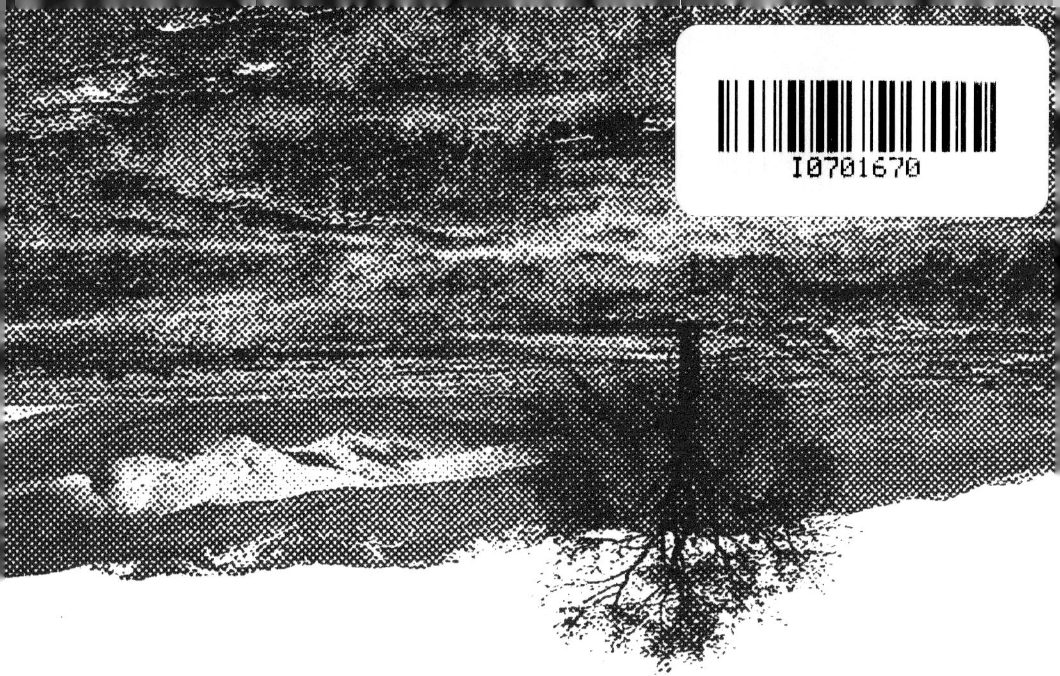

A JOURNAL OF THE PLAGUE YEARS

WORDS AND MUSIC
FROM THE LOST DAYS

EDITORS
SUSAN ZAKIN WITH BRIAN CULLMAN

NEW YORK AND JOSHUA TREE

First edition May 2024

Book and book cover design by Dana Collins
Typeset in Heldane Display and Chronicle Text
Globe image courtesy of Rawpixel Ltd.
979-8-218-15676-3

www.journaloftheplagueyears.ink

Journal of the Plague Years howls with writing (thinking!) that undermines the dumbassness of the excruciating reality we are living through.

Donald Trump et al. won't understand a word of it.

—**Terry McDonell,** *The Accidental Life*

As journalism struggles to find a new voice and American fiction risks irrelevance, *Journal of the Plague Years* appears, speaking a hybrid language, new and creative, urgent yet elegantly rational. Featuring work by some of America's most gifted writers, this collection is the definitive record of the twin plagues of Covid-19 and authoritarianism, offering necessary perspective as the country faces its fate.

—**Alex Shoumatoff,** *The World Is Burning*

We, a people marooned by a mysterious and still unfathomable plague, need a plausible narrative of the future to make sense of the recent past, of what has happened to our world. As these raw and eloquent pages teach us, we'll get through it with our egos intact only by coming together to share our stories and songs, remember our rituals, and reimagine our humanness. These dispatches from the frontlines of the new conditions feel vital and altogether necessary to the task.

—**Laura Kipnis,** *Love in the Time of Contagion*

These are not reassuring times, but when trouble comes you either meet the moment or you become one with the trouble. The writing in *Journal of the Plague Years* isn't only exigent in our moment, it is also making for an historic record that needs to be preserved.

—**Mikal Gilmore,** *Shot in the Heart*

These essays and reports are action-packed with underground ideas, wild adventures, and fresh insights—what journalism used to be before it upmarketed to polishing the common turd. Careful: guaranteed to enrage those choking their algorithms for more confirmation bias.

—**Jack Hitt,** *Bunch of Amateurs, This American Life*

For Ted Mooney. *Covfefe!*

Every existential crisis should be accompanied by music.
At the end of each story click on the QR code for a playlist.

TABLE OF CONTENTS

The Years We Can't Remember

I can remember the beginning. I bet you can, too.

Not necessarily the actual day — March 11, 2020 — that the World Health Organization declared a global pandemic. But the way the novel coronavirus Covid-19 entered our life.

I remember the first event canceled "out of an abundance of caution."

The email from school instructing us to pick up our daughter immediately, as if she were in danger from the moment the administration decided to close.

The *it's really happening* shiver that ran through the public library, four hours before closing time, when a staffer informed us over the PA system that we had 15 minutes to get out.

The last dinner at a friend's house, where some of us hugged while joking about whether we should hug, and others kept their distance (see also: the first social schism along the safety divide). The next night, the last party at our house and then, the day after, the first time we declined an invitation for fear of the virus. (We were also tired. So: the first Covid risk vs. reward calculation.)

I should say: I live in Albany, New York, which mirrored the caution and the closings of New York City, but not its ferocious contagion rate and death toll. I don't have a first morgue truck to remember or a first 7 p.m. celebration of health workers. Nothing so dramatic.

But the beginning was vivid all the same.

After that? It's a blur. We gathered our family on our farm, where we followed the news obsessively and the rules as best we could. Today I can remember, generally speaking, which of my children's milestone events got canceled, which of their friends moved in. But concrete memories from the pandemic era hover just beyond my grasp, like the smiles of masked strangers. Looking back at 2020, 2021 and even 2022, I feel socially distanced from my own brain.

We knew the whole time that we were experiencing History on a global scale. So why don't I remember it?

Why don't we all?

Study after study after study has confirmed what everyone I know has expressed: that the pandemic altered our sense of time, which has in turn warped our memory. One study from a year into the pandemic asked participants to describe their experience of time and then sorted their responses into formal-sounding but utterly familiar categories, such as *temporal rift* ("Everything that happened before the pandemic feels like it happened in some distant era, in the 'Before Times'") and *temporal vertigo* ("The pandemic itself seems to be going on for both 10 years, and two weeks").

The Covid-19 pandemic, which to date has killed between 7 million and 20 million people worldwide, including more than 1.2 million Americans, is almost perfectly designed to be forgotten.

For starters, it had two modes, both of which resist memory. One mode was horrific. People saw loved ones die struggling for breath — or couldn't see them at all because of safety protocols. Front-line health workers risked their lives and witnessed horrors in under-staffed, under-equipped hospitals. For those who experienced the pandemic as extreme trauma, memories of specific events are often too painful to revisit — and acute stress can make retrieving those memories more difficult.

The other pandemic mode was humdrum. Most of us who were spared life-and-death trauma probably experienced the pandemic as featureless tedium: day after day in the same place with the same people and no present or future events to divide the calendar into little memorable bites.

"Gone are the rehearsals that made Sundays Sunday, the town board meetings that made Wednesdays Wednesday," I wrote at the time, in a column about why my family of nonbelievers decided to hold a Zoom Shabbat (essentially, to make a Friday feel like Friday). "Time stretches out, unmarked, unshaped and, therefore, incomprehensible."

That was two and a half weeks in.

Dorthe Berntsen, a professor of psychology specializing in autobiographical memory, told us that monotony misshapes memory. When we experience the same thing over and over, she said, "The memory sort of puts it together as almost one event." She predicted that "we will have quite unclear memories from those specific years."

Unclear and also inaccurate, since we're likely to remember that period as shorter than it actually was. A study from 2023 posits that "lockdowns compressed remembered time" because "restricted movement and fewer context changes led to fewer samples of unique events in memory." In other words, there was nothing to remember, if you don't count endless arguments about who should wear masks when.

To add to our future confusion, all the "context changes" that did occur were cyclical rather than linear. More than once we had a lockdown, then a loosening, then a variant, then a surge. My library closed, then opened, then closed again. Which year was Omicron and which was Delta? When did we get Covid — was that after we got the vaccine the first time or the second? Did we really travel to meet a newborn niece in September but two months later cancel our Thanksgiving trip?

Placing an event somewhere in pandemic time is like trying to attend a Zoom meeting on a farm with poor WiFi and seven people. You give it a few tries and then, half frustrated and half grateful, you give up.

Of course, I could go to the record. Was any historic event better documented, from our TikToks to our government updates to our constant text messaging? Are not all of our takeout orders and e-book downloads and shipments of N95 masks neatly cached for us? I didn't phone anyone when I tested positive; I texted. Which means I could look up for you — for posterity — exactly what I wrote. But I really, really don't want to.

Science writer Laura Spinney told me that one reason we forget pandemics is, paradoxically, because they're so all-encompassing. Her book *Pale Rider* is a history of the 1918 flu, which killed 50 million to 100 million people — as many as five times the number who died in World War I, in half the time. But it gets far less attention, because, unlike in war, with its distinction between war front and home front, a pandemic extends potentially everywhere, threatening everyone. Everyone has "this feeling of you can't get away from it," Spinney said. "Because you're not allowed to forget it in any waking minute, there is this greater pressure to want to leave it behind as far as you can."

Another peculiarity of a pandemic is the lack of a definite ending. The beginning was concentrated and palpable: within a single week in March 2020, the World Health Organization made its announcement, President Donald Trump declared a national emergency, schools closed, Tom Hanks got Covid and the NBA suspended its season.

But the ending? No single week or month or even year neatly marked the pandemic's outer edge. As risks abated and the rules loosened and public life gradually restarted, we each more or less declared our own ending, whether or not Covid had actually disappeared.

"Basically, a pandemic looks like a bell curve," Spinney told me. "Everybody just decides where on that curve they decide the pandemic is over."

For me, it was early in 2022. My mother — in her mid-70s, with a history of asthma — called to say she'd tested positive for Covid. But she was vaccinated and Paxlovid had just become available, and I realized I wasn't afraid anymore. Which meant *my* pandemic was over.

Obviously, Covid wasn't. It would be another year before the WHO officially declared that the virus was no longer a global public health emergency. Two years after that — that is, now — Covid-19 still kills a few thousand Americans a month; we still have new variants and new vaccines. Millions of people live with long Covid. And as a society we are all living with long-term Covid damage: higher housing prices, persistent adolescent mental health issues, a nursing shortage that is both chronic and acute.

If we were, as Jonathan Freedland wrote in *The Guardian* in 2021, "delaying the moment of collective mourning until we can be certain it's all over," we're still waiting.

Even if we had a chance at an end, we've lost hope of the "collective" part, at least in America. Freedland argues that a pandemic is forgettable partly because it lacks "clear heroes and villains with intent and motive." It's true that pathogens themselves don't make great protagonists. But the Covid pandemic *did* have heroes; we just don't agree on who they were. To me, infectious-disease expert and chief medical adviser to the president, Anthony S. Fauci, is a hero who did his best to keep Americans informed and prepared throughout the pandemic. And yet Fauci is now so demonized by the right that President Joe Biden issued him a preemptive pardon before he left office.

What about the scientists who, in record time, developed a vaccine that saved millions of lives? Good choice — unless you believe that the vaccine kills people and/or alters their DNA. Depending on your politics, officials who implemented lockdowns and mask mandates are public health heroes or deep-state villains.

Traumatic and tedious, cyclical and endless, an experience we universally wish to forget, with a meaning we collectively dispute. We've had pandemics before, but in Covid-19 we've discovered a truly memory-resistant strain.

In her review of a book about the first year of Covid, Spinney wrote, "pandemics tend to strike when both the human body and the body politic have forgotten the last one. Vaccines address the immunological amnesia, and it shouldn't be beyond our wits to inoculate ourselves psychologically too."

But our public discourse is not moving nearly as fast as science did — or even necessarily in the right direction.

Scientists at a global Covid conference recently expressed concern that by forgetting the lessons of this pandemic the world is failing to prepare for the next one. That's especially true in the United States, where, as if we had totally forgotten Trump's behavior during Covid, we have elected a new and more virulent variant of the Trump administration, which ordered the country to withdraw from the WHO even as the avian flu threatens.

Our new secretary of health and human services disdains vaccines and has implied (and denied that he implied) that the coronavirus was engineered to spare the Jews and the Chinese. A week after Robert F. Kennedy Jr. took office, the Centers for Disease Control and Prevention aborted a flu vaccine ad campaign; two weeks later, the FDA canceled a meeting of a vaccine advisory group. In the clash between personal liberty and public responsibility that characterized the pandemic discourse, personal liberty seems to have won — and the casualties continue to mount.

"Memory is an active process," Spinney wrote in the epilogue to *Pale Rider*. "Details have to be rehearsed to be retained, but who wants to rehearse the details of a pandemic?" Nobody I know.

But given the new administration's aggressive assault on truth, memory, history, and — above all — science, we don't have a choice.

Fortunately, we have *A Journal of the Plague Years*. The poetry, prose, and photographs that follow may remind you of your own experience of Covid. Or they may alert you to a Covid you did not experience — in Portland, Vietnam, Montgomery, or Navajo country, New Mexico. But one thing they are certain to do is revive that sense of fellowship that was one of Covid's great gifts: the sense that we are all connected even in our moment of deepest isolation. The wonder of sharing across the thin and endless membrane of the internet what we have seen, read, thought about, and remembered during this plague. This collection widens from the personal decisions — adopt a dog? Move to Serbia? — to the political events that shook an already shaken world — the Black Lives Matter protests, the 2020 election, January 6. Withdrawal from Afghanistan, invasion of Ukraine. And it reflects: on other plagues, on other cataclysms, on art and literature and history. During Covid, "real life" may have chilled to a sluggish crawl for many of us. But oh, the life of the mind was ablaze!

A Journal both answers the call to remember and repeats it like a mantra. The crackdown on dissent, the distrust of government, the desire the expel the "other" — we must remember not just to recover that time but to make sense of our current moment. Maybe you don't want to, just like me. But at this book's urging, fortified by its companionship, you may find the courage to look back.

***

I search my texts for the word "positive" and I find it: the day I got Covid. It wasn't 2021, as I had thought — it was 2022, a few months after I'd declared my pandemic over. April Fools' Day. (How could I forget that?)

I had come home from the library because I felt sick and — I remember now — finally let myself realize that my two-day headache and my urgent need to sleep might be connected to the pandemic. I took a test: the "positive" line went dark the instant the reagent droplets wicked across the testing strip.

Being sick halts the forward motion of your life and snaps the tethers to linear time — in this way *having* Covid, the disease, was much like *living through Covid*, the era. I slept, I woke, I slept some more. Somewhere in there, masked grown children brought me tea.

Canceled: a gig as a moderator at a feminist conference, an overnight with friends in the Poconos, a movie date, a birthday potluck. Infected: every member of my family.

Someone from the Albany County Health Department called to tell me my five-day quarantine was over. I laughed, I coughed, I took another test, although by then we were rationing those little boxes with their elaborate packaging. (Oh! The *trash* of Covid — remember that? The single-use plastic bags carrying plastic takeout boxes, the masks each in their cellophane wrappers?)

Another instant "positive." Felt: relief, dismay, permission to return to bed. (Acknowledged: the privilege of resting when sick.)

Recommended: "Free Love" by Tessa Hadley. Nasal spray. Hot and sour soup. Friends who check in. Friends who bring groceries. A husband who, slightly less sick, sleeping in the guest room, gets up at 7 a.m. to decide whether to take our daughter to school for a PCR test. I see from our text chain that I tried to participate, from bed, in the complicated risk calculations that characterized all our Covid-era decision-making.

"I fell asleep again," I texted, at 8:42. "What happened?"

What happened?

Read this remarkable collection and when it has inspired you, pick a day and try to remember.

THE SHOCK

The first stirrings were faint. Little-known diseases had reached our country before but like so many of the world's ills, barely touched us. Legionnaire's disease. SARS. Ebola. They came and went, not changing the way we lived. Or died.

By March, we were paying attention. We didn't know how worried to be, but we asked friends: "Do you think I should make that trip? Get on a plane?" The mysterious disease factored into our decisions. It didn't change them yet.

Then some of us got sick.

The Music of Shelter

BRIAN CULLMAN

THE TRANSVESTITES THAT GATHER ACROSS THE STREET by the gates of the school don't look the same with their N95 masks on. They huddle together, much too close, with oversized handbags & cheap cigarette lighters and keep their heads down. They're in tight pants or miniskirts, heels way too high, and they pass a blunt back and forth between them. I try to imagine the lipstick they're wearing, purple or shocking pink. I can't.

I nod my head as I pass.

"Stay safe, Daddy," one calls out. "Stay safe. Ain't nothin' good comin.'"

I came down with the virus about six weeks ago. Maybe more. There was no fever, no sore throat, but I had a dry and constant cough and was exhausted all the time. I'd sleep for nine or ten hours, get up, get dressed, and then go back to bed. I had no sense of smell and there was a sharp metallic taste in my mouth, like I'd been chewing on rusted hubcaps all night.

Everyone I know who's gotten sick with this complains about that taste of metal. That's the constant. Apart from that, all our symptoms are different, but the metal taste is there for all of us, and for all of us the air tastes stale and secondhand.

Years ago, I lived on 16th Street and Third Avenue, across from Joe Junior's, and just below 15th Street, there was a secondhand cheese store. For a few dollars, you could buy an enormous wheel of cheese that was a few hours, maybe a day away from going bad. If you were having a party in, say, 20 minutes, it was the place to go.

But the air in there had that strange smell of something turning, something in transition. It smelled of long-gone locker rooms and of butter and death.

It wasn't unpleasant.

A friend died of Covid-19 last week. He couldn't get an ambulance to take him to the hospital, and his lungs gave out. He'd been ill for about 10 days, maybe 12. He'd start to feel better, like he was on the mend, then the virus would sneak up and knock him down again till there was no breath left in him.

He died in a small apartment on the Upper West Side with his wife and daughter around him. The ambulance that wouldn't pick him up and take him to hospital also wouldn't pick him up and take him to a funeral home or morgue. There were no cars available. His wife and daughter were alone with him, and the hours went by. They covered him with an old gray blanket, but his feet stuck out. They worried that his feet were cold, so they found a green towel they could cover them with. And they waited.

Sometime that night, an artist they knew offered his help, and one of the art vans that usually transported his work to MOMA or the Whitney or to art storage in Long Island City was hired to transport the body to a funeral home on the Upper East Side. There was still artwork, wrapped and stored, in the back of the van, an early Basquiat or a Wayne Thiebaud. He'd spent his life surrounded by art of every description. He was right at home.

Except maybe for the green towel.

Once you've had this virus and come out the other side, once you stop sleeping all day long, once the air stops tasting stale, and once that metal taste goes away, no one knows if you're really in the clear, whether you can come down with it again or with some variation of it. No one seems to know anything.

All we know is the ambulance isn't coming.

An Epidemic
of Love and Worry

THRITY UMRIGAR

THE DAYS HAVE NEVER BEEN FULLER.

All day long, the phone rings and buzzes. Friends checking in to take the temperature of our emotional lives. Asking if we need masks or whether we will add their grocery requests to our delivery lists. We give someone a bag of rice from our stock; another friend texts to say she's on her way to drop off some muffins that she's baked. I stand on the porch, she in the driveway. The plan is to talk from that distance. What I'm not anticipating is my bursting into tears upon seeing her bright, cheerful face, at the sheer normalcy of a friendly visit.

For 21 years, we were the couple who hosted dinners every Saturday and frequently threw parties. It was our thing, what we did together—feeding people. Bringing different groups of friends together. Throwing large bashes and quiet dinners. Now, on Saturday nights, we talk on the phone to those friends. Now, we marvel at how our grocery bills are shrinking since we're only feeding ourselves.

I have a friend in Japan who never sleeps. We text each other at any old time. Before Japan went into lockdown, she offered to mail us toilet paper and hand sanitizer. I refused, unable to deal with this new, depressing reality. But I have never felt more embarrassed about being an American.

And because I have family in India, my phone buzzes with WhatsApp messages day and night. Often, it's memes about the virus whose veracity I have to check and sometimes refute. But mostly, it's news from afar and most of it worrisome: A close family member who still, despite my strongest protests, allows her cook into the house daily. A cousin whose husband is stranded at his farm, three hours away from Bombay, haplessly watching his fruit rotting on the vine because of lack of farm labor. A relative of a friend complaining about food shortages in her affluent neighborhood. A close friend railing about how all the precautions one is asked to take—hand-washing, sheltering in place, social distancing—are symbols of privilege, unavailable to millions of working-class Indians living in crowded slums.

It's a daily swirl of anxiety, worry, love, helplessness. Through it all, I keep marveling at how this one little virus has laid bare all the other, chronic viruses of the world—poverty, homelessness, income inequity, lack of health care, the climate crisis.

The particulars differ from nation to nation, but the issues are the same. It's humbling to realize how ineffectual one's own desire to help can be. My superhero complex has made me rush to India time after time to tend to an ailing family member. If, God forbid, someone I love takes ill with the coronavirus, what then? There are no planes to catch and the borders are sealed. This fucking illness is an immigrant's worst nightmare.

In my own life, in my own home in suburban Cleveland, all I notice are things to be grateful for: a beautiful backyard where each day the birds and flowers announce the arrival of spring; unlimited hot running water; technology at my fingertips; a loving partner who does everything to make my life easier; a home filled with books and music; and (so far) avoidance of the virus. Blessings everywhere I look, tinged with horror and guilt about what is happening elsewhere—the carnage in the hospitals in New York, the shuttering of beloved local businesses, the terror of friends facing unemployment. An elderly friend whose cat-sitting business has come to a halt because none of her clients are going on vacation. Another friend who has lost the little money she made working under the table. Friends whose small businesses have been upended. The omnipresent question, hovering above us all: How will we ever come back from this? Who will survive this wipeout? What happens to those who don't? Who will live and who will die before this nightmare ends?

And then, the thing that keeps me up night after night, bug-eyed and wide awake: the November election. The fact is that one of the two major parties knows that it can only win through massive voter suppression. Wouldn't canceling the election be the ultimate trick, the biggest voter suppression of them all? In Milwaukee, Wisconsin they were willing to sacrifice the lives of black and brown Democratic voters by cramming them into five polling stations, down from the usual 180. The conservative majority on the Supreme Court revealed its true, ideological colors—MAGA Red—by not allowing the state to extend voting by mail. We've spent four years deluding ourselves daily—oh, they can't go any lower, oh, they can't shatter this norm, oh, they can't do that, can they?—only to find out, Oh, yes they can. Yes, they did.

Watching those Milwaukee voters, gloved and masked, stand in lines for over five hours, I was reminded of the old footage of the everyday heroes of the civil rights movement, and I felt the same mix of emotions—pride at their heroism and patriotism, and outrage that it had to be tested in these ways.

Sometimes, after I see videos of hungry, impoverished day laborers in India trudging for 150 miles to make their way back to their home villages, I get irritated at the endless Facebook challenges to post pictures of beautiful places we have visited, or the pictures of perfect loaves of bread everyone is suddenly baking. That's when I am most acutely aware of my immigrant self, hopelessly divided.

Then, I remember that I love the people posting these pictures and that they're doing this to keep our spirits up. Then, I remember that we are all scared and lonely, that most of us are not sleeping well at night, and that the only thing we have in the face of this ugly virus is one another. That people are offering beauty as a rescue, as an antidote to suffering. That, despite my best efforts to be grateful and positive, I, too, throw my middle-class tantrums that reek of privilege. Just three days ago, I turned to my partner and said, "You know what I miss? Wearing earrings. Dressing up and going to the Cedar Lee for a movie. And then, meeting friends for dinner." We stared at one another for a long while, mute with longing and nostalgia.

But I snap out of these moments of self-pity rather quickly. Then, I pick up the phone and call friends who are sheltering in place alone. "Hey. It's me," I say. "Just wanted to see how you're doing."

"Oh, you know," they reply. "Okay, I guess. And you?" Thus, we save each other, day by day.

The Enigma Variations

STEPHEN PAIN

THERE IS A NOVEL BY RICHARD WRIGHT IN WHICH a character is thrown into an existential terror after a door is locked and he is outside. When I first experienced something similar, all I did was walk and walk until it became daylight and I negotiated to be let inside. I remember it well because it was in Denmark and I had never seen so many hares in my life.

A few years ago I found myself outside in Paris. I looked for somewhere warm to stay. I stayed in an accident and emergency waiting room. Sat in a metal chair. I could not sleep because every few minutes drunks were being admitted. A big man was brought in once, then the second time the police had pepper sprayed him, and he counted the steps from the door, and while waiting for a doctor, still blinded, he made his way to the reception desk and took his wine and made his way out. I thought he should be on a talent show.

After my girlfriend died, I was penniless and spent several weeks sleeping on a bench in a sleeping bag with a view of the Little Belt, a strait between the island of Fyn and the Jutland Peninsula in Denmark. Each night I heard and saw porpoises only a few metres away. I felt blessed as I was still grieving for my love. This form of homelessness was made possible by collecting empty beer cans and plastic bottles which I recycled in the supermarket. In the day I stayed in a wonderful library. A toilet facility is heavenly. When it rained heavily, the large tree above me sheltered me. I love trees. I touch them when I can, just to signal "Hey cousin, how are you?"

In Firenze I slept in the doors of the most magnificent example of humanist architecture, the Santa Maria Novella Basilica. I made friends with a Latvian and others. The life is hard. Wine figures heavily in life on the streets. It is very easy to become an alcoholic when wine is just a euro or little more. I however managed to control the devil. I thought it crazy sleeping in the doorway. But I did. My friend has done it for seven years.

There is a world unknown to tourists. A dark and yet sometimes comical world, populated by drunks, thieves and people who have lost their way. You hate them. Then you love them. Then you are not sure because you become one. To become homeless, a man or woman of the streets, is not romantic.

Each wears a scar or something as a badge of courage. I have six dislocated fingers because I had blocked punches from drunks. You learn to watch for signs. In Britain the equivalent are more aggressive and violent. In Firenze I understood the Arabs and Romanians, as well as the gypsies. I went to the same church. Listened to the same sermons and collected the one euro fifty afterwards. Enough for a vending machine coffee and a vino Rosso.

I learnt so many things. Firstly you must trust people who sleep near you. I trusted my friend Samir who is Syrian. I trusted Renato who came from Napoli. I trusted Gloria. Beautiful Gloria. A fallen angel. I slept under the arches of the Palazzo Pitti, always waking up at 6:30 a.m. To sleep there became normal. I had cardboard for a mattress and a sleeping bag. In Firenze there is a whole system of Catholic charity and help organizations, I love them all. If I could I would be a vegetarian and Catholic; I cannot, but I sure want to be. The sisters were unbelievably kind. Really. We did not starve or die from the cold because millions believe in God. In these times, of the novel virus, I wish for God/s to look after them all.

It seems strange that every day I walked over the Arno. Every day I noted changes. Saw the nutria, the catfish, the herons and egrets. Every day I walked over the old bridge, and every day I saw the Duomo. I felt a kind of cultural vertigo at times. All this art and culture, but then I watched thieves and scammers in action. I felt sorry for the tourists, yet like Camus perhaps, I understood what made the boys tick. I was robbed five times, until I knew what to do. Have nothing. A more recent experience in England was very different. I could not trust anyone. Everyone wanted something. I felt a foreigner. I slept near McDonald's and as hundreds of nightclubbers passed, I discovered in the Millennials a sense of compassion. They donated food and money. Enough so that I could breakfast in McD. I dearly wanted to use the toilets! Then finally I arrived at a bus stop with a view of the Malvern Hills. I huddled in the shelter and looked at those hills. I saw Trinity Church where I was baptized. I heard sheep grazing on those hills. The hills made famous in Elgar's *Enigma Variations*, and walked upon by every writer from Langland to now. I was homeless but at home.

In times of the pandemic, there was an initial transition period. One by one the World of homelessness became grayer and grayer. In England there were clearly mixed signals. Will they go for herding or quarantine? Gradually, as the tragedy of this pandemic became a reality, services and places to sleep and rest dwindled. The most telling was McDonald's where they cordoned off the eating area like a crime scene. Takeaway only. The buses became like flying Dutchmen. Few took buses. Eventually only the homeless roamed the street, until there was an order. They must be isolated. Not everyone has obeyed. They would lose their revenue of "donations" and access to drugs.

I found myself suddenly going from sleeping in a bus shelter to living in a three-star hotel. It is like a deep sea diver coming up too quickly. It feels strange in a way, even though I had some breaks at friends' places and slept in real beds, this was by myself, as a free individual, and very odd. It was like moving from one culture to another. Becoming them. The bed is too comfortable. The shower perfect. The food rich. The Wi-Fi great. It is pretty silent. Everyone has been so nice and supportive. I think of *Trading Places*. Yes, that movie. What is odd is that outside there is the sci-fi world of death and anxiety. H.G. Wells long ago wrote a short story entitled "The Stolen Bacillus," all about bioterrorism; in a way, this is like that. One can think of short stories in a collection called *Love and Death in Isolation*. Scary that there is a big flat screen which will reveal like a window, all this horror.

I just want comedy. A Cary Grant movie will do.

Quagmire Days

J.C. HALLMAN

THERE WERE NINE OF US AT THE START, nine artists of various stripes. We had gathered for the artist residency program of the Ucross Foundation in Ucross, Wyoming, on March 2. We were actors, composers, painters, writers. For a time—a week, say—we shared meals, played poker, took walks, made art. Then the world began to fall apart.

There's something Pinteresque about artist residencies to begin with. The director of another residency (also in Wyoming, as it happens) told me that she thought of it as the three-week rule: after three weeks, fissures begin to form in artist residencies' miniature civilizations. Personalities fray. There may be feuds, scandals. In our case, it was not our little world that crumbled—it was everywhere else.

As the outbreak began, stateside, in Washington, word arrived that other artist residencies were shutting down. Yaddo in Saratoga Springs. MacDowell in Peterborough. Many others. After two weeks, two of us at Ucross returned home, amid a bit of uncertainty about travel. Then there were seven, we joked.

The art stopped, but the walks continued. Soon, every day seemed like a month, even as a week passed in an instant. After some initial hesitance, a decision was made to shut Ucross down, as well. We needed to leave.

To be clear, the staff of Ucross are some of the best people in the world. Every accommodation was afforded us as we changed plans. As with medical personnel and first responders, the staff delayed their own journeys home, and likely incurred a degree of personal risk, to ensure that we embarked safely, outfitted with masks and gloves, wherever we were going. For me, there was just one problem: I didn't have anywhere to go.

More than two years ago, I gave up my apartment in New York—dragging all my furniture to the curb, putting my library in storage—to embark on an ambitious book project. I haven't had a fixed address since then. Hence, a problem for the modern world: What does an itinerant writer, or a digital nomad, do when the order arrives to shelter in place?

This might be the heart of what we're confronting: just at the moment when the world needs to think globally, to recognize that the welfare of others, even strangers far away, is in our own best interest, we discover that it is our instinct to think locally instead, to build walls, to stockpile drugs and supplies, to go home, to return to our country, our state, our town, our house, our room—if we're fortunate enough to have one.

I got lucky. Again, with thanks to the Ucross staff, I rented a tiny home 20 miles away, at the end of a dead-end street in Buffalo, Wyoming, population 5,000. I had never before been to Buffalo. A sign just across from my mailbox reads: End of the Road.

The most prominent feature of Buffalo's one-street downtown is the Occidental, a classic Western hotel doing business since 1880. The Occidental has hosted the likes of Teddy Roosevelt, Buffalo Bill Cody, Calamity Jane and Butch Cassidy and the Sundance Kid. There's a saloon featuring a zoo of taxidermized heads on the walls, a long-running Thursday night jam session for local musicians and a café called the Busy Bee. The Occidental's owners are my new landlords, actually. Thankfully, they were willing to take in one more traveling stranger at a time when strange travelers might be vectors.

I arrived in town a day before the governor of Wyoming closed bars and restaurants for two weeks, until April 3. On that first night, March 20, I hopped from the Occidental saloon to the local dive bar, the Century Club, where social distancing was still a bit of a joke. Business was good. I met a couple of graybeards, the type of men who are suspicious of book learning, but who have a particular genius for engines and an encyclopedia of knowledge locked away in their heads. It was here that I first encountered what would prove to be a widespread and persistent belief. That whole pandemic thing? Overblown, exaggerated. In the dim light of the bar, I could barely read the faded lettering across the brim of one of the graybeard's camouflage baseball caps: "Trump."

It was the first day that more than a thousand people died worldwide of Covid-19.

On the last day that bars and restaurants were open in Buffalo, I ate breakfast at Main Street Diner. I watched the cook, also the owner, slap my rye toast barehanded down on top of my corned beef special. A short time later, I heard him announce that the only things that could close his diner were an absence of customers, or a man with a badge. The latter obliged him the following morning. The sign he put in his window—"Forced to Close, Not our Choice"—made the front page of the local weekly, the *Buffalo Bulletin*.

There's Wyoming precedent for suspicion about pandemics. At the midpoint of Steven Spielberg's *Close Encounters of the Third Kind,* a group of men gather around a table to brainstorm a way to clear a wide swath of land around Devil's Tower, about 120 miles from where I sit. They settle on a fake epidemic, and from this the film cuts directly to product placement. False Piggly Wiggly, Coca-Cola, and Baskin-Robbins trucks—you know, the deep state—sneak government personnel and supplies into Wyoming to scare away locals. Then aliens swoop in to swap Amelia Earhart for Richard Dreyfuss.

Buffalo has other literary analogues. The city motto, "A creek runs through it"—printed on a downtown mural—is a coy reference to Norman Maclean's paean to Montana, *A River Runs Through It.* Annie Proulx's story "Brokeback Mountain" is said to be set not far away, where sheep graze in the Bighorn mountains. And the hit television series *Longmire* is based on Buffalo, Wyoming.

Since 2011, thousands have descended on the city every July for a long weekend to celebrate Longmire Days. The population of Buffalo triples overnight, upsetting the town's calm idle. The graybeards at the Century Club told me locals call it Quagmire Days.

Small American towns often feature that sort of coy wordplay. In Buffalo, there is Pie Zanos, the Italian eatery. Un-Wine'd, the wine bar. Floor'd, the carpet and tile place. The city is middle-class, but lists downward. Local architecture is either prefab or ad hoc. When I first rolled into town, I smirked at a schlocky statue of an eight-point buck in someone's front yard, a crass lawn ornament.

Then it moved.

My little house—a cozy studio with a roof—stands along Clear Creek, near where old Fischer Brewery used to make wine and beer, and where George Beck's mill produced award-winning flour for more than 20 years.

I take daily walks. One Saturday, I stopped by all the local churches to see what notices had been posted about morning services. John the Baptist advised staying home—"We're going to get through this." First United Methodist would have no meetings until March 31 (later it changed to May 1). Others curtly noted that activities were suspended only because of the ban on public gatherings. The evangelicals had it covered: services would be livestreamed tomorrow at 9:30 a.m.

I passed a smiling woman outside one of the local liquor stores. Business was good, she said. People were buying in bulk. It's a weird sort of apocalypse that compels you to do a lot more of what you were shamefully doing too much of already: staying home, avoiding people, binging Netflix, obsessing about things online, and day drinking.

Every day, I get a cup of coffee at the Busy Bee. Restaurants still do take-out, and for a time you could still walk inside. Now all delivery is curbside. Buffalo's neighborhoods were always quiet—small American towns often have a lonely, deadened quality that feels eerie even in normal times—but occasionally I see kids wandering on bikes and skateboards, and once I heard a circular saw in the distance. The "Covid Spring" is the season of wondering whether there will be any more seasons, but for some, workaday life rolls along as always.

Occasional chats, conducted at a distance—preceded by an up-and-down scan that would be appropriate at a singles' mixer, but is actually a quick visual diagnostic—reveal peculiar fragments of news. The best day for toilet paper at Dollar General is Monday, when the supply truck arrives. A distillery in Casper is retrofitting to make hand sanitizer. Gun and ammo sales in Billings have surged past even the days following the Sandy Hook massacre, when everyone thought they'd be forced to turn in their guns.

In this part of the world, self-reliance is practically a Commandment, and I heard rumors of civil disobedience if Buffalo didn't open up again on April 3. A short time later, the statewide order banning gatherings of more than ten people had been extended to April 30. The streets of Buffalo remained quiet, apart from some bikers who cruised the town one Sunday, blasting the horns on their hogs.

Parks across Wyoming remain closed. Yellowstone, Teton—and, yes, Devil's Tower.

Inside of a week, animals began to figure it out. A small flock of turkeys wiggled right past my front door. I heard owls downtown. And the neighborhood deer have stopped being afraid. A buck once paused in his tracks and gave me a good long look, as though deliberating whether to charge. It's as though, all along, animals have been waiting for the whole civilization thing to implode.

There's a small mobile home park not far from me called New Dawn, because of course it is. For several days running, I walked past a single-wide with a tattered American flag outside on a post, and a sign that said "REPENT" in a window. One day, I saw a woman out front and asked her about the sign. She found it at a rummage sale in Cody, she said. Her name was Jan Weigel, and she lived here in Buffalo with Alan, her husband of ten years. She was of two minds about Covid-19. The fleshly part of her knows it's all a scam, she said, a trick to keep Republicans from voting in November. But she was Christian, too, so she knows that people must be prayed for, and that she must listen to the president, so long as the president is a godly man, like Trump.

I'm curious as to why Jan does not recognize the irony. A man who fashioned his entire career—to the extent hucksters have careers—on a dastardly and dubious use of hyperbole, concluded, for months, that the fears of experts were all wildly exaggerated. Just at the moment when a little hyperbole might have saved lives, Trump flailingly strained to cast himself as a voice of common sense and careful measure.

I realize that when I say that the world began to fall apart mid-March, I'm guilty of thinking only of the American experience. China had already happened. Italy had already happened.

But here's the thing: Buffalo, Wyoming, hasn't yet happened. Or, rather, it's just starting to happen. Wyoming recorded its first official Covid-19 death just the other day, on April 13, more or less exactly in line with the state-by-state projections of the University of Washington's Institute for Health Metrics and Evaluation. The death came at the Johnson County Health Center (JCHC), about a mile from me.

Two weeks ago, the press releases from JCHC concluded sweetly: "We are so fortunate to live in this community, and we feel blessed to serve you during this unsettled time." Now, they simply advise citizens to go on wearing face masks and washing their hands.

Yesterday, I walked to the Dollar General and asked the cashier why she wasn't wearing a mask. A different employee stopped in his tracks, and he explained that management had instructed them not to wear masks, as it would create panic. At Reese and Ray's IGA, a grocery, another cashier told me that wearing a mask "felt weird."

My life now is exactly like an artist residency—except for the loneliness. I haven't seen anyone in three days. Easter came with a blizzard, and left behind six inches of snow. I stay at home. I drink boxed wine. I watch shows, and I surf YouTube, where Buffalo poet David Romtvedt is recording a new poem for each day of the quarantine. Romtvedt's "Things to Do in Buffalo, Wyoming, While Waiting out the Corona Virus" meditates on a plant he found growing in a garbage bin:

But it turns out

this poem's about compost, that is to say

about transformation, how we change

moving through the days, and the days,

how they change moving through us.

Rounds

ALBERTO MONTERO

I WALK TO WORK. I DO THIS EVERY DAY NOW.

I have 20 minutes before my morning rounds start. Duty and caffeine propel me. It's still summer, but there is a subtle coolness in the air. The trees look weary, the leaves ready to cast themselves off to a cold ground.

I think of my dream last night. I can't remember much other than it involved not being able to breathe. This has been a recurring dream of mine for the last few months. It's happened so often that it no longer terrifies me. Like my morning walk, I have become accustomed to it. Last night, a translucent hand covered my mouth. Was this God's asphyxiating palm? In the dream, my skin was darker than my usual light-brown farmer tan.

My 49th birthday is in less than two months. How have I used the years? I try to think back to what I dreamed of being when I was a child. Not a doctor. I don't remember much. I do remember that I wanted to write books. My grandfather bought me a typewriter when I was nine, and I wrote my first nonfiction book. It was about fish. I copied a passage from one of my animal books, typing out what seemed to be a rather hefty manuscript. It took me a while to figure out how to type all the words, since the letters were scrambled on the keyboard. After I wrote, I traced out a shark on a sheet of paper and put my title and name underneath. I vaguely remember punching holes and tying the pages together with a red string. It was probably only ten pages but I felt as if I had completed a mammoth undertaking.

There was a sense of completion.

I am not nostalgic for the past. If I am nostalgic for anything, it is for the greater simplicity of my earlier adult existence. Teleological living is exhausting. Mapping out life is becoming a series of tentative equations linked to one another, and too many of the numbers are so light as to be indecipherable.

Robert Sapolsky, the Stanford University professor who has made a career of studying human behavior, wrote that ambiguity is what distinguishes the time of Covid. Ambiguity, he explains, is quite different from risk. Some people thrive on risk, but people, all people, consistently hate ambiguity.

We are accustomed to evaluating risk. We figure the odds. We utilize our executive functioning. If it works, we feel rewarded. Smart. This is especially true of physicians.

"In contrast, when we wrestle with ambiguity, we activate brain regions central to anxiety and revulsion, and if there's a good outcome, we mostly feel less dread," Sapolsky writes.

We can reason our way to a logical response when it comes to health issues, at least in the developed world. We don't necessarily make good decisions—we tend to rationalize our impulsive behavior—but we know the terrain.

But Sapolsky says, "our brains unravel and run amok in the empty moonscape of ambiguity. And that's what our pandemic world is now."

There are questions, none of which come with answers.

Can airborne coronavirus infect you, even if you are appropriately socially distanced?
Still not clear.

When will there be a vaccine?
Too early to say.

How long do you make antibodies after surviving Covid-19?
Researchers are only in the preliminary stages of understanding that.

Will a second wave of sickness this winter dwarf the first wave (as with the 1918 flu pandemic)?
This appears likely, but there is no way to know.

Why does Covid-19 kill a perfectly healthy young person and spare those who are compromised?
Perhaps there is a genetic component but we are miles away from knowing.

In response to the unpredictability, some people ignore the whole thing and ride their Harleys to Sturgis while others refuse to leave their house, for anything, under any circumstances. This, too, is hard-wired, it seems.

"A time like this can make us gyrate between paralysis and impetuousness; blind us as to whose well-being matters; drive us to a frantic search for attribution that leads us to scapegoating. We must guard against how ambiguity can bring out the worst in us," Sapolsky writes.

As a physician, I treat women with breast cancer: a known phenomenon. But I realize that, in a deep way, all disease carries the same sliding terror. I comfort my patients with my knowledge of risk: for some this means estimating the probability of a cure with current treatments, for others estimating their chances of living another six to twelve months.

But this? This is outside my statistical knowledge. Just as I did as a child, I type, organizing the letters of the alphabet.

I trace the picture of the shark. I name sea creatures, copying words from one book to another. When it's all done, I tie the pages together with red string.

The uncertainty of where to go next, of not knowing whether to turn left or right, swims beneath my words. At certain times, it is paralyzing. I'm no different from anyone else.

On my way to work, I pass small blue flowers growing out of a crack in the sidewalk. I don't know their name, but their color and delicacy strike me as stunning. I stop to snap a picture. Under the elevated tracks, a train barrels off eastward. I am near the hospital now and the sound of the train grows fainter.

On Fear

STEVE ERICKSON

THIS MORNING HE WAKES UP SO FUCKING TIRED of being afraid. He's tired of the knot in his gut that's there when he goes to bed at night and still there in the morning. He's tired of being afraid of his family vicissitudes, of being afraid for his kids & his wife & his 92-year-old Mom. He's tired of being afraid of the very air he breathes, he's tired of being afraid of tomorrow and of tomorrow's tomorrow. He's tired of being afraid of getting old, even as he's already old—he's tired of being afraid of being alone. Does everyone feel this much a coward these days? More and more he blurts his fear in the static of his stutter—he keeps trying to will the fear away. He's tired of trying to will his way thru the fear and then when he gets to the other side of it, it's still there after all. He's tired of being afraid of the bad faith of "friends" who aren't that friendly & enemies who have been waiting years to jump to the worst possible conclusion about him. He's tired of being afraid of his failure, of being afraid that everything he's done has come to nothing. Well, actually he's gotten used to that fear, he used to be more afraid of his own personal oblivion before it became wrapped up in everybody else's. He's gotten used to the fear of having made no difference or impact, the fear of his disappearance from whatever small place on the mass consciousness he ever occupied. But these days he doesn't really think as much about that in the face of the things that really matter, looming plague & economic upheaval & secret police & democracy's dismantlement, when all he can do is flee to his writing which is the only place he's never been afraid even when he should have been. He's afraid for the country where protesters against masks carry signs that read SELFISH AND PROUD. He's afraid that the America of the moment, an American Reich where Baader-Meinhof patrols the culture, isn't an aberrational one but the true one, and that it's been the true one for a while. The precipice of everything is right there at everyone's feet like never before. There's no getting over the fear, there's only living with it like you live with a virus that the body accommodates but never defeats. He's tired of being so afraid he can't even choose between the first person & third, so he keeps vacillating between the two, selecting the third for however long it can protect me.

THE RESPONSE

Then we knew. The pandemic was like nothing in our lifetimes. So sudden, so elemental, mortality staring us in the face in the mundanity of the supermarket, at a gas station, a restaurant. At Christmas or a July 4th barbecue.

There had been 9/11 but while the attack made Americans feel vulnerable in a new way—a way many people in the world had felt vulnerable all their lives—the real effects, like cracks in glass, spread slowly. Some would say we learned all the wrong lessons or didn't learn any at all.

Later, we survived the economic shock of 2008. But that was money and a slow roll. When the crash came, what we felt was mostly a distant cruelty perpetrated by banks and bad policy. We had grown accustomed to that kind of betrayal. That year was seen as a stochastic event, but it was a piece of that larger whole, a half century of inequality's tightening screws.

But this? This was the irrationality of death and it traveled in the air. How much adrenaline can a person tolerate? More to the point, what does all that adrenaline, all that fear, do to people? What do they do to each other? We were about to find out.

To Them I Whisper Either/Or

LAUREN CAMP

It all happens in slow motion.
Every person eats and belongs
in their minutes of song and blood and the naked
wind. If there is a welter
of doubt, we figure to keep
to the screen. If one
rants about dirt, another makes an issue
of the dark sign of leaves. The air porched
or frozen. We throw back
concerns about what we'll do next
until something notches up as it always does
and margin to margin, we repeat
some part of any routine. We prop up our grammar
to ask questions that turn the dark home.
It's not that I mind kneeling
into each bend of the future
for a theory of how to adapt,
it's that now we talk
only of the center
of doors. A century ago
there were twenty-three
unsolvable problems
and men who cinched in and studied
obedient until they knew
with deliberate skill what needed
to be known. Look at us today. We feel only
the smallest logic. My god,
we can't figure anything but what to exclude.

It's Always Now

BLANCHE MCCRARY BOYD

THE PANDEMIC FINDS ME DROPPED OUT once again, less advertently than in the Sixties and Seventies, staring at these spring birds flitting around, these quiet trees growing, these flowers popping forward with no notion of a world medical emergency. I've been thrown back anew onto my in-breaths and out-breaths, thinking only occasionally about dying on a ventilator and the great big meaning of it all.

I never imagined I'd live to be 75 years old, never even imagined I'd make it through my thirties because of my addictions to alcohol and drugs, but here I am, 38 years sober and still breathing—somewhat uneasily—inside my layer of middle-class comfort with a wife and children. When our kids were small, we even had a minivan. This is what love has reduced me to: Although I am stalked by a lethal virus, embedded in a society where blacks can be killed at will and the streets are on fire, although we are led by a president with the mien and brain of a peacock, I seem to be happy.

Falling in love and having children changed me. I was 54 years old when James and Julia were born, and, in a flash, the world became intelligible. Because here they were, these twins sliding sloppily out of my wife's vagina, James first, and it was like, Oh my God, it's a new person! It's somebody else! And these were not composites, these were not anyone else who'd ever arrived on this planet before, and my revelations through psychedelics, which I still occasionally mourned, were instantly rendered silly. My shrink (brain doctor is the term I prefer) said, Well, you've never imagined what you've never imagined.

I'd known about children, of course, had even been one, and I'd seen those films of childbirths, but seeing a child born on film and seeing it happen in real time is like the difference between kissing your arm and marrying someone. These events might be mildly related, but one certainly does not prepare you for the other.

I hadn't wanted children, I was just accommodating this woman I had, against my better judgment, fallen in love with, and she kept insisting. These two lumps of flesh were each about the size of a roast beef and nearly as red, and they arrived entirely helpless, yet with personalities intact, James so calm he didn't cry. Is he all right? Yes, the doctor said, he's just a laidback little dude.

Six minutes later Julia screamed through, and she might as well have been carrying a scroll of nonnegotiable demands. I hadn't quite figured this out yet, but within months I realized that, after all those years of therapy in which I'd been hoping to change, to become less urgent, less difficult, less combative and unhappy (and maybe even not really an alcoholic addict or lesbian), I'd been born the way I am.

Getting born is a chancy matter. Within one week a healthy male can make enough sperm to double the world's population of seven billion (that's a lot of sperm), and every woman has 350 to 400 eggs. So it's just a big crap shoot, and everyone who takes a first breath here arrives as a unique confluence of genetics and circumstance. We are all entirely unique, but only as unique as everyone else, which has the unfortunate consequence of rendering uniqueness ordinary. This thought may seem confusing, but it's at the root of art as well as conflict.

When I'd been sober a few years, I had the good fortune to become friends with the writer Annie Dillard, and, after she read a piece I'd written about my friend's shotgun suicide, tears formed in her eyes. "You have no idea how moving you are." I wasn't sure what she meant, so she said, "All of those years you spent suffering, when you could have been reading."

I could have been reading. I so admired the fact that Annie loved original sources, 19th-century accounts of pioneers, religious thinkers, science, and had produced the brilliant *Pilgrim at Tinker Creek*, but I'd always placed my own bets on original experience. I'd spent many years not only drinking and taking drugs but getting initiated by a shaman in Peru, traveling through the abandoned peninsulas of upper Iceland, letting an Indian guru give me *shaktipat* trying to zap awake the light of God inside me.

I'd written about stock car races and tough man contests and hurricanes and growing up in the Deep South during American apartheid on a fucking plantation, and I'd acknowledged my redneck contempt for the pretentiousness of high art and classical music and modern dance and even tennis. I'd written about growing up racist, interviewed a KKK Grand Wizard, covered the Susan Smith murders, and recorded "Hot Rod Lincoln" with the Rock Bottom Remainders. I'd also helped found an independent institute for the study of radical feminist thought named Sagaris Institute and then, two years later, abandoned it.

Now, at 75, our kids are 20, and I spend a lot of time reading. Or, more often, listening to books, since my eyes don't work the way they used to, because of the planned obsolescence of our bodies. How does my physiology know this process, making these spots and wrinkles and these other, deeper changes? I do understand that whatever force breathed me into this world will breathe me out, but I'm in no hurry.

After the kids were born, my writing career seemed to disappear, because it's very hard to keep small helpless creatures alive. Leslie could only nurse them both for a brief time, and when I first put a bottle's tiny nipple up to Julia's mouth, she seized it ferociously, and I had this desperately relieved thought: oh my God, she's going to live!

Years of happiness and exhaustion followed, while we tried to figure out how to raise and support our children. We both had good paying jobs, Leslie as a psychotherapist, me as a teacher of creative writing, but what on earth were we going to do about global warming?

Like all parents, we had to make constant, calculated choices, because it's frightening to let children out of one's direct sight and keep all those electric sockets covered and figure out what the little fuckers will and won't eat. And what did they mean with those grunts and gurgles and meaningful looks? Why did they smile and hug us and let us kiss them? Why were they crying?

Risks may have been my chosen path, but those risks had been about myself. It takes one kind of courage to jump out of a plane, a much different sort to let children cross the street for the first time, or to leave them at a daycare center. Will they ever forgive us? I was actually crying. But they liked daycare, although Julia refused—and still refuses—to drink milk. After sitting stubbornly in front of a full glass through many play periods, we finally had to get a doctor's note saying she was allergic, although she's not.

Having children is a lesson in immediacy, a Be Here Now that LSD guru Timothy Leary didn't seem to know about, or about the demands and exhaustion that come with all that immediacy. I used to stop in a parking lot on the way home from work and read *The New York Times* and sob into the steering wheel.

I had never planned to love anyone this way. I'd always assumed love had to do with sexual attraction, and this was a mistake I had carried through many years of lesbian serial monogamy. But when I met Leslie, love was like a bowling ball sinking deeper and deeper into my gut, and bringing with it an unfamiliar peace. Still, when she said she wanted to have children, I was like: no, no, no, I am not parental material!

Leslie was 39 and I was already in my fifties. She would be their mother, their blood, but who would I be? And I felt homophobic about whether lesbians had the right—or the chops—to raise sons, if that's who showed up in the birth lottery. Also, I would have no legal rights, and if a child were in an intensive care situation, I wouldn't even be able to enter the room.

Leslie comes from a strong and supportive family, and I said, If something happens to you, you think your mother and brother would leave our children with big bad me? Now Leslie's mother lives in the house behind us and we see her all the time, and when the kids were little, they could run through the woods to grandmother's house, haha.

When we learned that Leslie was pregnant with twins, a boy and a girl, it was a jackpot, and I gave in. I'd become increasingly involved in the process of choosing her sperm donor because it turned out I had strong opinions (no surprise there), and soon I found myself writing x's with magic marker on her butt and giving her hormone shots. I was surprised that, unlike other women I'd been sexually involved with, she took no pleasure in my inflicting pain and that I hated causing it. But this wasn't sex, it was something deeper.

I was still refusing cohabitation at that point. The old joke that what lesbians do on a second date is rent a U-Haul mirrored my history, or, to be more accurate, I'd always either taken a hostage or been one, but now I lived alone and owned a wonderful condo in a building so eccentric I laughed out loud the first time I saw it, and everything seemed nearly perfect.

I'd written a good novel, just been 'on tour,' been awarded a tenure I hadn't sought, and then I went to a party at the writer Amy Bloom's house and saw this woman sitting on the grass (who's that?) and talked to her for five hours and, without knowing I was going to, invited her to go to Greece with me in the fall, because there it was, this bowling ball sinking slowly through my heart.

I even called my mother the next day to say I'd met someone. She asked these three questions: Is she white? Is she a prostitute? Does she own her own house? I said she had a job and owned a house and was not a prostitute, and I finessed the whiteness question by saying, she's Jewish. In retrospect my response is shabby and condoning, but I thought my mother was doing pretty well for someone whose first response to my being gay had been to say, It makes me want to throw up, and we'd already had the race fight too many times to repeat it.

I kept saying to Leslie, you don't want to live with me, I'm an asshole, I'll give you a list of women to confirm it, but when she tried to buy the house across the street from me, I finally realized that, if I wanted this woman and these children in my life, I'd have to change. So I did.

I was the first person, other than the doctor who delivered our children, to hold them, and, a little later, when they were taken to the nursery to be cleaned up and checked out, I followed down the hall as if they were magnets. Our doctor walked behind me.

When I opened the door to the nursery for the newborns, the nurse in charge looked me up and down. Who are you? Only new parents were allowed in this room, and I looked too old to have given birth any time recently. I turned to the doctor, half-smiling, half-panicked. You're their mother, she said, and don't you ever forget it.

But it wasn't that simple and still isn't. The law in Connecticut changed while Leslie was pregnant, which would make it possible for me to adopt James and Julia, but Leslie and I first had to be interviewed by the Department of Children and Family Services, and letters attesting to my character had to be written by her mother and brother. My history of drug addiction was confirmed but dismissed, because I'd been clean and sober more than 15 years at that point, and we both looked breathtakingly healthy and middle-class in our big house that Leslie's mother had helped us buy. (I know, I know, I know.)

After the adoption was approved, I carried a laminated card to prove that I was their mother because I have a different last name, and we paid a lawyer to set up wills and powers of attorney, and we did a lot of other establishment stuff I never thought I'd have to face, like that minivan, and the Rosie O'Donnell gay family cruises, and getting flu shots and even a retirement plan. I didn't know if I was being compromised or made whole.

Leslie was seven months pregnant when we finally moved in together. She had never lived with anyone, and I was, as my mother succinctly put it, a six-time loser. But this was a crazy, wonderful time for us, like shooting rapids through rivers we'd never seen.

During my drug years, I'd spent lots of high time contemplating my hands, because I'd understood that, scientifically speaking, we are all just a series of electrical valences and are composed primarily of space. So, druggily, I'd kept wanting to see through my hands. Now I wanted to understand the mystery of these fleshly arrivals as our lives became exercises in changing diapers and trying to get a little sleep and eat and feed them and keep them safe and still get to our jobs, and always the task was: What is the next right thing? Fear and responsibility could not be separated from joy and exhaustion.

AA has given me a certain kind of training about how to stay in the present: look down, there's your feet, this is where you are, get in the minute you're in. So this is where I am, sitting on my porch, immersed in my white American ordinariness, aging and with a younger wife (yes, we did finally get married) and these grown children who have been sent home from their colleges by the pandemic.

Until a few weeks ago I was teaching on Zoom, the kids were completing their coursework online, and Leslie remains in her home office daily, trying to help others. Nevertheless, there is a lot of leisure for us, meals together once again, walks on the beach or in the woods. Last night I watched two episodes of *Avatar* with my daughter, and the night before I sat with my son while he played Fortnite on the television in the basement. I'm too chicken to try it because I hate being bad at anything.

At first I hadn't believed it about the pandemic, and it's worth admitting that my first response had been to fly to Florida to buy an old convertible. I like cars, I'd already made these plans, and I was unwilling to forego them.

But on March 9, in the airport and on the plane to Fort Lauderdale, everyone looked nervous and embarrassed while we wiped down our seats and food trays. (I did as Leslie had instructed me.) I'd planned to leave the Solara in Florida with our friends and return in the winter, but, once there, I found myself cautious about flying again, so I drove the car back to Connecticut, and I could feel the tensions accumulating as I headed north.

Traffic out of Florida and through Georgia was heavy because the snowbirds were heading home too, but then the highways became increasingly deserted, and the hotel I stayed at in Virginia was nearly empty. I was the only person in the restaurant where I grabbed dinner.

"When you get here," Leslie told me on the phone, "drive straight into the garage and take off your clothes and leave all of your things out there. I'll have a robe for you, and you're going straight into a shower." She and the children were worried about me because of my age group, but I was more concerned that I had scared them, or, as I finally understood, possibly exposed them. Apparently I remain an iffy judge about my responsibilities to those I love.

I do know I've finally gotten old enough to let go of the things I can't change.

Eudora Welty wrote that a child feels indelible in the world but learns it is the world becoming indelible on her, and I've let go of most of my fears and even my ambitions. I play mostly in the shallow end of the pool, and I don't even think it's the shallow end anymore. (We don't have a pool, by the way.)

I understand that I can't fix global warming or cure this virus or get that peacock out of the White House, but the future belongs to the young. Or, as I tell our kids, it's your problem now. And when your future gets here, it will still be today.

Frontline Diary

HAILEY NICOLE WARNER

WHEN I WAS IN JUNIOR HIGH AND HIGH SCHOOL, my dad drove for a Yellow Cab company in Chico, California. He worked 60 hours a week, sometimes more, with a side hustle playing keyboard in funk bands, mostly casino gigs and concerts in the local plaza. He even picked up a few students on the side, young pianists looking to play charts or have the classical stiffness banged out of their fingers. He was a regular at Angie's poker club on and off for years, and though he never spoke about it to me, my mom hinted that he wasn't half bad. According to her, some months he made enough for bills and child support just from playing poker.

My dad had a way of turning his talents into money. He improvised until he had something that worked, and he was good at it. For years he cycled this strange work clock, driving nights and dedicating his days to the odd jobs. He was always tired. I never saw him without his travel thermos of coffee, and his kitchen table was cluttered with cabbie dispatch notes, sheet music, fast food wrappers, and coffee-stained napkins. The table of a working man.

I couldn't live like that, but now I understand his brand of proud tiredness. For wage workers, the day really begins when work ends. Only so many hours truly belong to us. So they count.

This year, as Covid shook San Francisco, I worked two jobs in the Mission District while I finished my last year of college. For five months I hopped from the opening shift at a café to the closing shift at a small retail shop.

In the beginning, people were overly nice. We were all in shock, and the initial fear made us careful. People saw a glimpse of normalcy in the café. In March and April that seemed like something sacred.

Summer was a different story. People felt pent up. In October, I watched a lady throw her smoothie at a man who had wronged her in some way that I didn't catch. Her exact words when she did it: *I'm more of a man than you'll ever be.* Damn.

The squabble fizzled out from there, but still, these were complete strangers. I was taking an order when it happened. I mentally checked out for a second during the transaction to keep from laughing or screaming. We all wanted to scream by then.

The café was located in the kind of tech-dominated, eight-dollar-chai-latte gentrified block that makes me want to set San Francisco on fire. It's in close proximity to Dolores Park, one of the city's most notorious party parks. When Pride season came in May, we had lines out the door, and the park looked just as it had the previous summer—packed to capacity. Aside from masks and stickers showing customers where to stand, it seemed nothing had changed, which was good for the owner, but it made me nervous as hell. Even without tourists, the café was almost back to normal capacity, but with half the staff.

When we opened our patio for outdoor dining instead of takeout only, my manager sat me down for a serious chat. We'd become close over the two years I worked there. I knew both her daughters, and her husband was a chef in the café's kitchen. Her youngest son was just starting junior high. The mother in her told me to be careful, to sanitize everything, and we hugged with our masks hiding something we wouldn't say. We were terrified, but that feeling was muted by routine.

In the mornings we'd help ourselves to coffee and our greeting was always the same: *How are you? Tired, but good.*

When fall came, I knew I couldn't work at the café anymore. I wanted to scream every day, but at who? Maybe not at the people leaving crumpled napkins on their table, or people who pulled down masks to order, but it was heading there.

So I quit.

My second job would be enough, I thought, and I was at a much lower risk of infection there, working at the same small retail shop located deeper in the Mission, further away from Dolores and its foot traffic.

Maybe I needed to run around less, too. For the entire year, I've felt like I was in motion. Since July I've lived in three different districts of San Francisco, though my bus to work hasn't changed. In September I moved into a studio in San Francisco's Outer Tenderloin. That means it's on the edge of what remains one of the city's few seedy neighborhoods. From the fifth floor there's a view of the taller brick buildings and hotels that make up the block.

The first night was like a scene straight out of a sitcom: two small-town best friends turned roommates finally have their own little piece of the city. My roommate and I were exhausted from moving. We pushed our mattresses together to make room for the boxes we couldn't deal with. We ordered pad thai and popped a bottle of champagne. It had been a long time since we were excited about something. Our apartment in this city of insanely high rents was a small victory to hold against the year of losses.

We opened the bay windows and listened to the sounds of the city below us. Then, like an emaciated Gandalf, there he was. In the window directly across from ours stood an old man wearing only a T-shirt. He was trembling slightly, looking right at us and jerking off shamelessly.

We laughed at first. How could this be happening? But it did. Constantly. We realized that the more we reacted the more excited he became. He haunted us day and night. He was there so often I wondered how it was even possible—physically, I mean. We were dealing with a serial masturbator, so we called the cops.

That got him to stop—for the most part. And I didn't notice as much, for a while, because I wasn't there.

A month after I quit my job at the café and a few weeks after I moved into the apartment, I tested positive for Covid-19. I am grateful for early detection and for symptoms so mild that they almost went unnoticed. The city of San Francisco put me up in a hotel. For two weeks, everything stopped. No bus rides. No need to act cheery to customers.

No Gandalf.

Since then, I've fallen back into the routine of work hours and free hours. I'm resigned to it, but sometimes I still get that urge to scream. I don't have the temperament for poker, I guess.

I'm still keeping it together at work, but whenever I see the serial masturbator any modicum of sanity disappears. I'll come home and not always, but still, often enough, he'll be there. It's a little different now. Since the cops talked to him, his retreat is easily won by me leaning out the window and screaming as loud as I can:

"Knock it off buddy or you know who I'll call!"

Maybe that's the silver lining of all this. That's the kicker. Now when I come home, tired and ready to scream, I have a target.

I'm still not poker-faced like my dad, but it does feel like the cards are starting to line up, in their own peculiar way.

A housebound elderly woman
watches television in her
Navajo Nation house.

The Elders

SUNNIE R. CLAHCHISCHILIGI
PHOTOGRAPHY BY DON J. USNER

ON A RECENT VISIT TO THE NAVAJO NATION, I sat with my parents in their
garage while KTNN, a local Navajo radio station, played in the background. I
listened to the beat of Navajo traditional two-step music and skip dance songs,
thinking about the time in elementary school that my late grandmother stayed
up all night to make me a traditional Navajo outfit for a fundraising event. In
between songs, messages in Diné encouraged listeners to stay home, pleading
with the public to think of the safety and well-being of the Navajo Nation's
most vulnerable people—our elders.

Since the pandemic hit, memories and thoughts of my grandmother are
ever-present. The coronavirus, as of Aug. 4, has infected 9,139 people on the
Navajo Nation and killed 462, many of them elderly.

What would it be like if my grandmother were here during Covid? I wondered. Could I keep myself from visiting for months? What would my family
do to keep her safe?

When you grow up Navajo, at least for me, you are taught that elders are
the pillars of the family, especially grandmothers. They are the keepers of our
stories, history, traditions and culture. They connect us to our ancestors. They

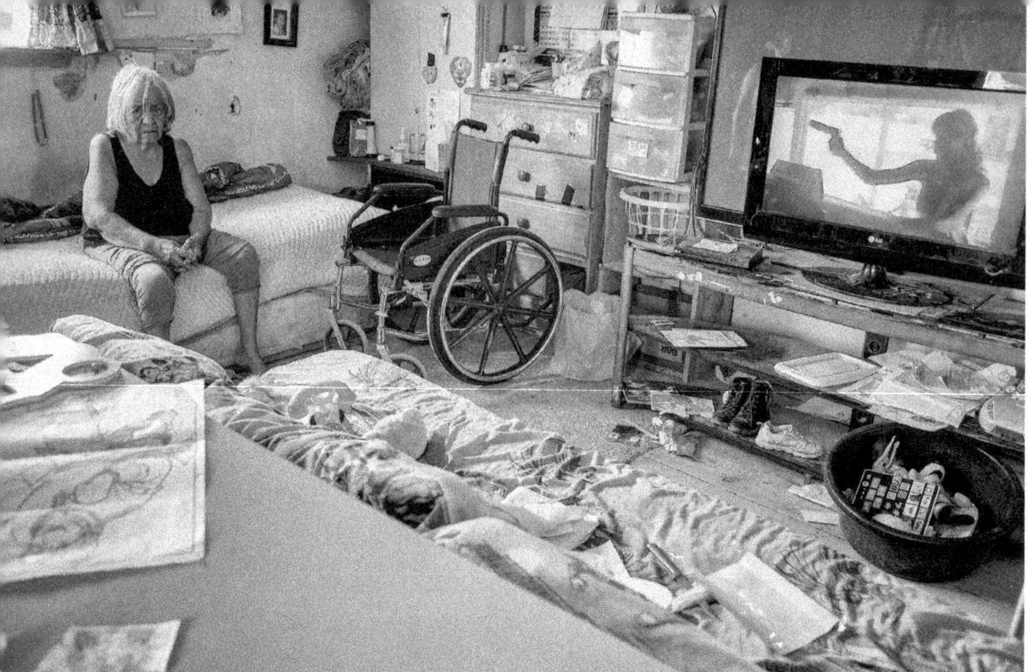

take care of us, and in exchange, we're taught to look after them. When my late grandmother started to show signs of old age, I drove her to doctors' appointments, cared for her on weekends, and made sure she yearned for nothing.

Are elders around the reservation getting the attention they need during the pandemic? And, most importantly, do they have enough water and food? I decided to find out.

I began by interviewing people who live in the Northern Agency in northwest New Mexico, where my family is rooted. A large number of people over the age of 65—nearly 350, according to Navajo Nation data—live in four remote communities along the foothills south of Shiprock. Dozens are 75 or older.

My first interviewee, a grandmother in her seventies, lives with her young granddaughter along a winding road in a small Navajo chapter in the rugged hills. When I arrived, the girl came running out of their cement home to greet me, then led me inside. Her grandmother sat slumped over the edge of a stained mattress. I crouched nearby in an effort to maintain eye contact, taking care to maintain a safe distance. We talked about the pandemic, about life and death, and about her granddaughter. The girl had survived cancer and had lost her mother, while not yet ten years old.

"I'm worried about my granddaughter," the grandmother told me in Diné. Tears ran down her cheeks.

Sisters Elizabeth Woody and Mary Beach outside Woody's home
on the Navajo Nation, south of Shiprock.

On this hot summer day, the two were alone, left to look after one another, something the grandmother takes pride in, and something they are used to. They have no running water or indoor plumbing. The grandmother has to trek to an outhouse, built on such uneven ground that she has tripped and fallen on numerous occasions, leading to a hospitalization. Now she has a wheelchair, which she has to use more and more often.She is barely able to stand to make a meal. Her salvation—the only reliable food she and her granddaughter can get—comes from the local senior center, which delivers a lunch they share Mondays through Fridays. On weekends, they fend for themselves.

Other than a ripped couch, the home has little furniture. The girl has few toys. Her prized possessions are a few notepads, which are completely covered with drawings, one on top of the other, because she's used up every last page.

The grandmother said she and her son have taken care of the child since she turned four. When her son is away at his job, which is often, she is responsible for the girl.

"She's the only one that takes care of me," the grandmother said. "We take care of each other."

Tears flooded my eyes behind the surgical mask and Navajo scarf I wore. My voice turned shaky as I complimented her efforts to look after her grand-daughter and thanked her in Navajo for sharing her story. I've been a journalist

for almost 20 years, and this was the first time I cried on assignment.

I visited three other elders that week, at a peak of the Covid-19 crisis on the reservation.

Edison Johnson, a man in his sixties, lives in a dirt-floored shack with no running water, toilet, sink, kitchen—or electricity. He stores food in plastic coolers; he has no access to ice, so they keep nothing cool.

Eating fresh food is almost impossible because there is no way to keep it from spoiling. He lives off of processed foods that keep without a refrigerator.

When he needs electricity, he runs a series of extension cords from his son's house to his own, at the top of a hill. "I wish I had an oven so I could make biscuits," he said.

Elizabeth Woody, 70, gets her water from a faucet outside her house. She has no indoor toilet. If she needs to bathe, she explained, she fills a bucket with water and gives herself a sponge bath. Like the others I spoke to, she has no vehicle.

The elders complained very little. It was as if they had accepted this way of life—living in desperate conditions, largely ignored by their community and political leaders. They were used to not being taken care of.

And the few people in the community who advocated for them faced retribution, I was told. If people talked to the media, they feared they would lose

(Left) Edison Johnson at home on the Navajo Nation south of Shiprock.

(Above) Elizabeth Woody stands in the shade with her dogs, by her home on the Navajo Nation.

their jobs. (Tribal employees and others remain anonymous in this story to protect them.)

The grandmother said she had asked for assistance from her chapter, as local communities are known. Little help came. Some people advocated for her when she fell and injured herself: They demanded that the chapter build a level ramp to her outhouse. After a hard fight, she received an uneven slab of cement that was hardly better than the dirt she had before.

She did receive barrels of clean drinking water—but not from her chapter. Instead, it came from Water Warriors United, a Native-operated nonprofit organization that delivers water to those in need.

Numerous other nonprofits—some from as far away as California—have donated boxes of food to the chapters. The Navajo Nation, it is widely known, has some of the highest rates of hunger in the country; with a pandemic at hand, action was clearly needed to prevent a catastrophe. Throughout the past four months, Navajo Nation President Jonathan Nez has handed out free food at most of the 110 chapters around the reservation. But none of the elders I spoke to had received a food donation. They lived too far away. They had no one to pick up the boxes for them.

"All in all, no one is caring for anyone. They're just thinking about themselves," a community worker told me.

(Left Page)
Edison Johnson steps outside his home on the Navajo Nation, south of Shiprock.

(Next Page)
Leo Taugelchee receives a hot meal from a senior center on the Navajo Nation, south of Shiprock.

Some elders weren't even aware the free food deliveries were happening. They had no phone, television, or computer. Their contact with the outside world came from Navajo radio stations like KTNN. Some had no contact at all.

Even people who did manage to get a food box might go hungry. Some boxes only contained apples, oranges and onions, I was told. Others contained hard foods that elderly people couldn't eat because they so often had missing teeth. The boxes were supposed to feed people for a week, but some only held enough food for two days. Others included toiletries that had expired in 2010. One source told me that she was so worried about the elders in her community, she often bought food for them out of her own pocket.

Who was responsible? Chapter officials, neglectful family members, the community and—most of all—the Navajo Nation leaders, sources said.

And so I called the leaders. The only person to respond was Navajo Nation Council Delegate Amber Kanazbah Crotty, who represents seven chapters in the Northern Agency. She's known as an advocate for senior citizens.

Crotty said she always has elders in mind, especially when looking at legislation. She asks herself, "How is this going to support our elder population?" She said she makes a point to focus on elders because she believes that the way elders are treated is a reflection of how all Diné should be treated.

Some elderly people do fall through the cracks, she said. She was working on a long-term solution—a case management system that would closely track elders' needs. But to the best of her knowledge, food and other resources had been available to the elderly, even in remote areas.

"We had food available for families in crisis or families that are testing positive while they isolate," Crotty said. "That would help elders with limited income, just making sure they're not exposed. So those are some of the immediate steps that we're doing."

Less than 24 hours after my interview with Crotty, one of my sources called me to say she no longer wanted to be named in my story. Her supervisor had spoken to her, and she and other employees were told to refrain from talking about the food shortages, especially to the media. "We could lose our jobs," the source said. Within the day, two community workers I'd interviewed also backed out of the story.

Repeated follow-up calls and emails to Crotty went unanswered. My calls to local chapter officials also went unanswered. Attempts to reach Navajo Nation President Jonathan Nez failed.

Throughout my time as a Navajo journalist, I've heard many stories of Navajo officials who stonewalled reporters or intimidated people who spoke out. Navajo Nation leaders often refused to answer questions from Navajo reporters and local media (although they showed little reluctance when it came to giving quotes to national media like CNN and the *New York Times*).

I was aware of the frustrations. But to be shut out for a story about Navajo elders? That was something I never expected. I especially didn't expect it during a pandemic, when protecting elders lies at the heart of a public health campaign to slow the surge of Covid-19. I didn't expect it amid the constant messages to take care of our elders, which appear in Navajo Nation virtual town hall meetings, on Twitter, Facebook and television.

The reservation is my home. I have a deep connection and admiration for where my roots are planted. But it's hard to ignore the darkness that coincides.

Now, when I listen to KTNN, I think of the elders I met, and wonder if they're listening, too. I think about the little girl who survived cancer and wonder what to send her for her birthday. (She wrote the date on a slip of paper and slipped it into my hand before I departed.) Five weekends have passed since I bid the grandmother and girl farewell. And every weekend since, I've wondered whether they have enough to eat and whether anyone's checked in on them. I've wondered if anyone else is wondering about them.

Dragon Bridge

BEN QUICK

THEY KEPT US LOCKED UP FOR SO LONG THE first typhoon of the season rolled in from the East Sea. Tugboats pulled homes upriver from fishing villages. Long white boats used in better times for nightly Han River cruises could be seen sailing alongside them to the inlet where one branch of the Han narrows until it disappears.

The day before the storm I made a break to an ATM outside a hospital. My ward volunteer sent me a map of a route with no checkpoints. Off I went into the rain. I returned wet but 5,000,000 Dong heavier and with the sense of security only money can bring. The storm turned out to be a lot of rain but only a little wind, not enough to cause much damage. The 600 checkpoints that had come down in anticipation of a deluge went back up before the city had dried out. I couldn't help noticing that the police working the checkpoints didn't seem to have quite the same enthusiasm for the job.

My cash turned out to be more than enough for next few days. But we worried that we'd be stuck in our homes for even longer, so the need to stock up felt urgent. I applied for a travel pass to drive to the largest pharmacy in town, a one-stop shop that supplies hospitals and individuals and would have everything I might need. I wanted to access my bank's ATM, the only one where I would be able to withdraw enough money for the coming month.

The travel permit took 24 hours to process and would allow me two-and-a-half hours to take care of business. It also required the signature of my ward boss, the man through whom all requests for anything in my small part of the city had to go. Not an easy man to track down even under the best of circumstances, and the task was even harder at a time when nearly every household needed something urgently, things like diapers, sanitary napkins, drinking water, rice, things like protein, things far more important than a foreigner's blood pressure meds and money.

But I was positive that I couldn't work my way out of Khue My Ward—the neighborhood where I live—without it. The city center was seven kilometers away and the barricades on the side streets and alleys had been fortified in such a way that made them impossible to drive around. I'd seen a newspaper article that featured the chief of police bragging about the ability of the street cameras to catch anyone doing anything. Every square meter of the city could be viewed by police, he'd claimed. I believed him.

I drove my motorbike slowly up the nearly empty pavement of Bui Ta Han, the main north-south artery near my house, the end of which had been turned into a security outpost checking all traffic coming or going from the ward. The road was empty except for a few ward volunteers. I did my best to avoid eye contact.

When I pulled into the shade cast by the tarp of the makeshift shelter and stepped off my Honda, a cop in starched olive clothing and an official hat stiffer than his pants looked at me suspiciously. But when I said "ngay hom qua," meaning "yesterday" in Vietnamese to indicate I'd been there the day before to fill out an application, he relaxed, reached into a cardboard box, pulled out a folded slip of paper with a QR code, my name, the date, and a few other details, awkwardly recited my middle name, and waved me through. No documents needed.

It's one of those things that can make you laugh during a lockdown, even if it signaled an inherent human disorder that could be fatal under the circumstances. Try unsuccessfully for days to drive across town to access something important. When you finally succeed, the word "yesterday" is enough to get you there.

∿

Most Americans don't realize that Vietnam has successfully fought off invaders for centuries: first the Chinese, then the French, and then, of course, my father's generation. In the late summer of 2021, a different kind of invader came to Da Nang. They came not from a foreign land, for these were members of Vietnam's land speculator class coming to take advantage of local business owners in the midst of the worst financial conditions of the century. And this time the invaders will win.

I'd seen history turn in Da Nang before. When I moved here in the summer of 2017, the city was booming. Before the pandemic, Da Nang was considered by many to be Vietnam's most livable city. Buffered to the south and east by hundreds of miles of pristine beaches, to the north and west by tropical mountain ranges, Da Nang is nearly equidistant from Ho Chi Minh City and Hanoi, the only two cities surpassing its significance to the country.

Thriving because of its proximity to the Han River, Da Nang is within one hundred kilometers of UNESCO World Heritage Sites that span the country's recorded history: Hue, the formal imperial capital of Vietnam, is a city built on and around a castle; not far away is My Son, a looming relic of the Cham civilization descended from Polynesian migrants who arrived from Borneo two millennia ago which is that culture's only significant structure in Vietnam to survive the bombardment of the American War. (Think a smaller version of Angkor Wat.) Not long after my arrival, I found my way to these and to the third: the city of Hoi An, until the mid-19th century the busiest port in the region, now a bustling tourist town of 100,000, 20 minutes by motorbike or car from the south of Da Nang.

When I thought about a life in Vietnam, the country that my father, like so many other young American men, shipped off to during the war, Da Nang was the only place I considered. When I moved here, the economy was booming, yet the city offered a life apart from the country's endemic traffic congestion, a rare combination anywhere. Da Nang had begun to appear on many travel magazines' best-of lists for Southeast Asia. Best beaches. Best golf courses. Best cities for families. It was safe, clean, and there were enough expat families living in Da Nang for my son to have access to international schools.

I wonder now if it was it history that drew me. Mine or perhaps my father's. My country's. Theirs. Like the children of so many other veterans—American and Vietnamese—I'd felt the effects of my father's exposure to chemical warfare waged by the American and South Vietnamese military. So much of my own story is tied up with Vietnam.

If history was my objective, fixing the series of events that led me to this place, that was a fantasy destined to be thwarted. My Da Nang would erase history. But at the beginning the city felt like the best of both worlds.

In mid-September, following more than 60 days of the strictest lockdown in the world including a month of what authorities in Da Nang called "radical social-distancing measures," the city began settling into what is being called the new normal, two words heard around the world in the ongoing global Covid-19 pandemic.

For those unaware of exactly what was meant by the term "radical social-dis-tancing measures," it constituted a lockdown on top of another lockdown called Directive 16, which was also a lockdown on top of another lockdown known as Directive 15.

For the residents of Da Nang, it was hell. Worse than the fact that the damage it has done to the de facto capital of Central Vietnam will surely be felt for decades, it was a hell that nobody outside of Da Nang realized existed. And now that we are seemingly on the other side of that tangle of words and numbers, the story of the Vietnamese Covid response, still ongoing, is being written and revised. The story of Da Nang, where the lockdown changed everything, has been left off those pages.

∾

For much of the first year of the global Covid-19 pandemic, Vietnam was held up as an example of what to do right. We had very low case numbers and few deaths compared to other countries. The country's fight against the Covid-19 virus provided a lens to the world through which the benefits of an ideology that values individual sacrifice for the greater good shone brilliantly.

After an initial six-week lockdown with only shops selling essential goods allowed to operate, the country was Covid-free with the exception of a few quarantine zones—mostly military barracks and luxury hotels—holding passengers of inbound flights for mandatory 21-day entry quarantines. Two negative tests and you were free to go about your business.

There were a few spikes in case numbers resulting in subsequent lockdowns—the second one originating in Da Nang—but by and large, unless you were dependent on the hospitality sector, life went on, even if it was mostly online. Restaurants, coffee shops, and bars were not allowed to seat customers, but they were free to serve diners via delivery and takeout. Grab, the largest ride-sharing and food delivery app in Vietnam, was booming. All we were missing were the tourists.

By the end of May 2021, 14 months after the pandemic had been identified, there were good reasons to believe that Da Nang would soon be completely open and the rest of the country would not be far behind. Hotel workers and tour guides and laid-off baristas radiated optimism. Schools had been teaching students in person since the middle of January.

On July 10th, Da Nang's beaches, important drivers of the local economic engine, the reason many expats and Vietnamese from the two big cities relocated, designated by the Vietnamese government as national treasures never to fall in private hands, miles and miles of uninterrupted stretches of sand and surf that had graced covers of the world's most glamorous travel guides, reopened. People were giddy.

By late summer of 2021, after the initial success story, despite public support and national celebrities making viral YouTube videos about using hygiene to protect yourselves and your loved ones, schoolchildren posting millions of imitation videos, citizens and expats and seemingly everyone in the country cheering each other on—"We can do it! Yes, we can!"—after the glowing articles in the international press about the almost magical powers of the contact tracing program, the hundreds of days without a single Covid-related death in the country, evidence of overconfidence began to mount.

Especially troubling was the lack of evidence of a large-scale vaccination program. It was starting to seem as if Vietnam's leaders might actually believe they had the ability to wipe this virus out for good. As in zero cases going forward. No vaccine needed.

In this atmosphere, it is not entirely surprising, nor, considering how successful sealing borders, testing, tracking and tracing had been before the Delta variant of the virus appeared, was it entirely irrational that until the beginning of September 2021, the official Vietnamese policy, though never broadcast as loudly as the YouTube songs, was to insist on total eradication of Covid-19 from the motherland.

For Da Nang, the question was, at what cost? How much was willing to be sacrificed to exterminate the enemy? People were running out of food and potable water, the basic things needed to survive. Da Nang was at its darkest, in a stay-at-home lockdown for nearly a week, leaving many of us without access to money, food, or medicine. The week would become ten days. The ten days would become 20.

Simply to pass something like hair clippers or bread to a neighbor, we tiptoed around the narrow spaces between homes in the dark, doing our best to avoid the cameras on the street. I was lucky. I'd become close with one of my neighbors over the past year, and he knew how to cook. Very well. And he was one of the smart folks who had stocked two freezers full of food before the lockdown. Even though it was technically a crime, he would send me a text message most nights around six o'clock. "Thanh's on his way. Can you give him back the containers?" His ten-year-old son would scamper down the sidewalk under cover of trees and hedgerows and wait for me at my gate with a container of curry and a baguette

or fried rice and French fries. He'd pass them to me and I'd pass the empties to him, and he'd scamper back home.

I knew things were becoming desperate when even Thien began to run out of things. First it was ketchup. Then potatoes. Before the 7-day/24-hour curfew had started, people had been given a short reprieve. Stock up for seven days. These were the orders from the Da Nang people's committee, essentially a city council. Seven days.

On the fifth day, we were told to hang on for three more. As this point, as you might imagine, scarcity became a problem. Price gouging by the few authorized to sell food through official channels set in. You may have been able to order a box of meat and veggies last week through your ward volunteers. It would take three or four days to get to your house. It might have cost you 30 dollars. Several days later, were you able to even locate one, that same package might cost twice that. And it might take twice the time to arrive.

My girlfriend, like many others, began looking for ways of acquiring black-market chicken from the neighboring province. The supply chain was completely broken. It felt as though we were living in a Petri dish, albeit one without a stream of nutrients to keep the organism alive. Or even worse, like we were being punished, taught a lesson, brought to heel. Banks were all closed. ATMs were out of cash. The roads were blocked by police. And we would not have been able to leave our homes even if there had been services. There was nothing anyone on the outside could do about getting us direct aid. The city was sealed from the outside world.

As I mentioned, Da Nang had been a happy city, and much of its verve and bonhomie was because of one man.

Not so long ago, Da Nang had a progressive and very popular chairman of its people's committee—the equivalent of a mayor. In a single-party Communist state such as ßVietnam, for a politician to attain this status is highly unusual. But Nguyen Ba Thanh, a native son of the city who served as the central city's top official from 2003 to early 2013, broke the mold in many ways.

A man whose physical build and blunt style inspired comparisons to Tony Soprano, Nguyen spoke out against corruption and pledged to prosecute public servants who were on the take. During his tenure, Da Nang was transformed. Even the normally ultra-conservative national press praised Da Nang, and Nguyen in particular for the city's undeniable prosperity. From the June 3, 2012 edition of the *Vietnamnet Bridge*, a state-supported media outlet:

> The city's success is so great, that the central government some-times considered Da Nang's breaking-the-rule moves as experimen-tal steps for the country. The city's success is closely attached to the talent and determination of its officials, including Party Secretary cum Chairman of the People's Council Nguyen Ba Thanh.

During the Nguyen years, laws were put in place to keep overly aggressive street vendors from hounding people while they ate at outdoor cafés. Locals joked that the city was the only place in Vietnam without any graffiti. He instituted a generous social welfare program.

Perhaps his most ambitious proposal came in 2008, when he spearhead-ed a proposal that would allow constituents to directly elect candidates for city leadership positions to represent their interests, including the people's committee and its chairman, giving citizens, again, in the words of *Vietnamnet Bridge*, "the right to directly choose the city's top official through an open election." The proposal was rejected on legal grounds in 2008, and when it was brought again to the national leadership in 2012, it was ruled unconstitutional.

Nguyen failed to make national reforms, but his influence on Da Nang remains visible to anyone spending time in the city. The construction of bridges crossing the Han River was Nguyen's apotheosis. At 1,850 meters, the Thuan Phuoc Bridge is the longest suspension bridge in the country. The Han River Bridge is the only swinging bridge in Vietnam. The Tran Thi Ly Bridge, the tallest of the lot, is built to look like a sail.

The Dragon Bridge is the most spectacular, a golden body that rises and falls from a sharp tail on the north side to a mouth that billowed fire and smoke for crowds of onlookers one night of every week during better times. There is the Nguyen Van Thoai Bridge, actually built by the Americans during the war and refurbished as a pedestrian walkway that has come to be known as "the lover's bridge," for the college students who bring dates to the bridge on the weekend to enjoy a free view of the Da Nang skyline and the rest of the bridges, each lit up with its own unique undulating pattern of color. These are monuments to the vision of Nguyen Ba Thanh. And in 2021, you will not find many in Da Nang who don't remember him fondly.

This is not to say he was perfect. His decision to relocate nearly one-third of the city's inhabitants for urban improvement was opposed by many and is still resented by some. Others saw his decision to fly to the U.S. to receive cancer treatment just before his death as a betrayal. If Vietnamese doctors were good enough for them, why were they unqualified to treat the dreamer from Da Nang? And where did the money for his treatment come from?

After his final term as chairman, he was appointed to a cabinet-level position created to fight corruption, where, after leveling charges of improper behavior at a political rival, Nguyen and others were accused of financial improprieties linked to the financing of the Han River Bridge. High-ranking officials went to prison. Not Nguyen Ba Thanh, but some close to him.

Despite his critics, in the end, as news of his deteriorating condition spread through the city, hundreds of people, even some of those whose own land had been reclaimed for one or another of his ambitious projects, packed his front lawn in a vigil, weeping publicly—not a common occurrence in Vietnam—over the former chairman's impending death.

The party line has always been that Nguyen died after an unsuccessful attempt at cancer treatment in the U.S. But the number of independent Vietnamese websites arguing that he had been poisoned by Polonium-210 or a similar compound and died from acute radiation syndrome—essentially assassinated—was so large that the Vietnamese government felt compelled to issue a statement denouncing these stories as baseless conspiracy theories.

From inside the country, it is impossible to connect to any URL that repeated these rumors so it's impossible to research. Still, if you happen to be sitting at some coffee shop in the city and strike up a conversation with a local and are able to get the person to let down their guard, when you ask about the death of Nguyen Ba Thanh, chances are he or she will look both ways before handing you a crooked smile and looking at the ground.

Whatever the truth may be, conspiracy or cancer, since his death, the chairmen selected to lead the people's committee of Da Nang have been far less flamboyant and certainly less dedicated to reform.

In better times, there was always a flurry of activity in the neighborhood surrounding Nui Thanh and Hoang Dieu Streets south of Nguyen Van Linh, a uniquely Vietnamese collection of open-air barber shops, air-conditioned hair salons, newspaper stands, and coffee shops where elegant old men smoke gracefully and nurse cups of coffee and glasses of traditional tea for hours, taking occasional breaks to answer smartphones given to them by grandchildren. Street vendors pushed colorful carts of toys or lounged on motorbikes in the shade next to pallets of whatever fruits happen to be in season with the price per kilo scribbled in marker on whatever loose cardboard happened to be nearby when they found a spot to park. Neighbors chatted at the counters of the same small pharmacies they'd used for decades, pharmacies that almost always closed for at least two hours at lunchtime so the owner could take a proper nap. Old women wearing conical hats rode by on old bicycles filled with fruit or flowers or bags of waste on its way to be recycled or reused.

A motorbike mechanic was stationed on every block, usually highly skilled, the blacker his hands the better. Locksmiths and milk tea stands and banh mi sellers filled the sidewalks in front of small home repair outlets, secondhand fan dealers, noodle shops run by ancient couples and computer repair stores run by upstart university students. The place was alive with energy. Pretty women in tight-fitting skirts, handsome men in tight-fitting business suits, old ladies with smiles so consistently wide as to leave permanent, ear-to-ear-creases on their faces popped in and out of banks. Even the alleys were alive with nail salons, banh xeo restaurants, and tap hoas—uniquely Vietnamese convenience stores run from living rooms where beer and baby formula could always be purchased by the can, and where the freezer in the corner may or may not be filled with ice cream bars.

I'd always found the place a photographer's dream. After the lockdown had finally ended, what I saw as I drove down Hoang Dieu toward its intersection with Trung Ngu Vuong left me too depressed to pull out my camera. It was barren. There were very few people outside. Those I saw were pale and destitute. They had those glazed blank looks in their eyes we are used to seeing on televised streams from war zones. As far as I could tell, the only difference between this part of the Hai Chau District and the footage I'd seen of conflicts around the world was the lack of bombed-out buildings. The people looked the same. Filled with despair. And tired. So tired. Too tired to be angry. Too tired to be sad. In the posture of the shirtless old men and the women in faded sundresses poking their heads out of half-open doors and slumped over plastic chairs beside alleys, lived an exhaustion I've never seen in this city. It looked as though they'd crawled out of caves after months underground, and this was not far from reality.

Homes and apartments in the densely populated city center, especially homes in the alleys, don't receive much sunlight on the brightest of days. Folks who call the nooks and crannies of these middle-class alleyways home—and to be clear, many homes there are large and ornate, not in any way those of impoverished people—get their daily dose of Vitamin D from trips to markets or cafés in the morning and walks around the neighborhood in the late afternoon. A 24/7 curfew meant no sunlight for nearly a month. A broken supply chain meant, at the very least, severe food insecurity for nearly a month. The barricades at the end of the alleys meant no way in, no way out, no way around, and certainly no way through for nearly a month. I knew one thing: This lockdown and its experiment with radical social distancing had inflicted untold collateral damage, physical and mental.

A neighbor confided in me he hadn't felt that way since he was a child during what he called "the time of rations," between the end of the war in 1975 and normalization of relations with the U.S. nearly 20 years later. I can only imagine how much worse it was in the heart of the city than for those of us in my neighborhood. For we had the sun. We had plants to water and views, sometimes even walks down sun-drenched streets to makeshift Covid testing sites. They had nothing.

∿

In Da Nang, during the darkest days of the lockdown, having somehow acquired the most precious form of currency in the city—the travel pass—real estate speculators began showing up at small shops in the prime real estate around An Thuong, the neighborhood in My An Ward affectionately referred to as "Crackertown," because of the large number of expats living in the quiet neighborhood near My Khe Beach.

Americans know this as China Beach, for which the television series of the 1980s was named. It is the place where Marines first came ashore in 1964 to be met by long-haired, slender Vietnamese women in ao dais, the traditional dresses that to many show just enough but not too much of the natural curves of the women wearing them. Much like other traditional feminine dresses, such as the Indian sari, for critics, the *ao dai* has become a symbol of the post-colonial male gaze, though if you were to ask any Vietnamese woman which of her possessions she prizes most, her *ao dai* collection would always be high on the list.

In case you're wondering if this is where you jump off, let me assure you this is not an essay about the enthusiasm of my comrades in the feminist movement. This is about something else. I love America-bashing. When it comes to criticizing the homeland, I'm on board. We fuck a lot of shit up. We invade a lot of perfectly good countries. We bomb the hell out of old men and women and children and teachers and people playing chess in coffee shops. We have done and continue to do horrible things. In fact, we do so much of this we often fail to realize that just as cultures in other countries are perfectly capable of sexualizing their own traditional clothing, leaders of other countries are perfectly capable of fucking their own people without our help.

It is no small irony that vulture capitalism is operating at full speed in one of the few remaining openly Communist countries left in the world. These well-dressed investors went door to door, the more desperate-looking the business the better, knocking, inviting themselves in, offering pennies on the dollar for what had been and will likely become again some of the most coveted places to set up shop in the city.

One owner I know had two sets of buyers come by in the span of a few weeks. He is fortunate, for he has a nest egg, enough money stashed away to get through the lockdown, no matter how long it lasted. Others, usually Vietnamese couples who had scrimped and saved and invested every last penny into a bakery or set of apartments when the city was booming and the kids were grown, had enough money set aside for a month, six months, maybe a year, but after two years of little to no income, were far more vulnerable to accepting a few small stacks of bills. And when they did succumb to the pressures of poverty and sell, it is safe to assume the deed to the property did not stay in Da Nang for long. It never does.

Since I've known the region, Central Vietnam—especially Da Nang—has had an independent streak. I have always noticed a subtle mistrust of outsiders, not foreigners, but fellow countrymen from other regions, particularly the north. Historical events dating back at least as far as the War with America would, in the eyes of some people, provide reason for resentment of those with the chains of power. As the location of a large American military base, allegiances were mixed. They had to be. In such an environment this would be a mechanism of survival. But even now there seems to be a considerable cultural divide between Central Vietnam and other parts of the country, at least in the minds of those from Da Nang. When I pressed a friend of mine about why people from Da Nang dislike Hanoi so much, his answer was straightforward..

"People from Hanoi are takers, not givers." When it comes to patterns of buying and selling land between Da Nang and the ancient, tourist-friendly city of Hoi An, one can sympathize with this point of view. Though the exact numbers are impossible to calculate, investors from outside the region, often from the north, have purchased large swaths of real estate over the past couple of decades. Much of it remains empty, presumably waiting for the post-Covid boom. Large French-style villas occupy other chunks of land, and often one or two families will own several, sometimes using them as vacation homes and other times renting them out. I know one of those investors very well. She happens to be my girlfriend. Her family owns several hectares.

Three months after the most restrictive social distancing decrees were rolled back, ads in *The New York Times* tell us Vietnam is open for business. Just today, a recent local newspaper reported that on December 15 regular international flights into the country will resume and gradually increase to pre-pandemic levels, though as we have learned the hard way, proclamations like this must be taken with a grain of salt. Hope can be a dangerous weapon.

As is the case in other countries, pockets of Covid-19 still wreak havoc in parts of Vietnam, including Ho Chi Minh City. And there is still a shortage of vaccines, but 95 percent of the country has had at least one shot. More than half have had two. High-quality therapeutic treatments are now available. While people continue to die from the virus, the numbers are falling. Here in Da Nang, there are almost no restrictions on daily activities.

And yet, a pall hangs over the city. Hundreds of thousands of people remain unemployed. Though numbers will not be officially published for years, if ever, an eye test of the city will reveal the majority of businesses shuttered, many with "For Sale" and a phone number spray-painted on walls or cardboard signs hung on chain link fences. Many have already been leveled, cleared to make way for whatever comes next, rubble hauled away or shoved to the side of the property. Owners of many small businesses that have successfully weathered four brutal lockdowns are unwilling to open, afraid another will shut them down for good. Hotels, coffee shops, and restaurants that have survived remain mostly empty. People simply can't afford to eat out.

Last weekend, my girlfriend and I made the 20-kilometer drive to Hoi An. The last time we had been there, it was packed with tourists, and I hadn't really appreciated the beauty of the place. It felt more like an amusement park than a cultural treasure. A Southeast Asian-themed Disneyland. This time, the streets were empty. The extraordinary beauty of the ornate architecture, the ancient wooden bridges connecting manicured banks of small rivers, the antique boats, and the shrines and temples spread out across the ground like a giant textured oil painting. Lotus ponds lay still enough to reflect every detail of the sky. Old-fashioned Vietnamese lanterns hung from nearly every ceramic awning. It seemed perfect. Idyllic. It was perfect.

For about an hour. I'm almost ashamed to say it took me so long to see them, but they were there, the same "For Sale" graffiti scribbled across Da Nang, less conspicuous, but just as prolific. Just as obscene. As obscene as the tourists prowling the streets, people wielding cameras, looking for the perfect picture in a town too decimated to put up a fight. Too beaten down to make them work for that shot.

∿

On an evening not too long ago, I rode my motorbike to the head of the Dragon Bridge, the golden arc of undulating yellow steel crossing the Han, I finally stopped, pulling out my ten-year-old Canon Rebel. The bridge, normally filled with motorbikes and automobiles, was empty. After several days of rain, the sky had cleared. The familiar soft blue of a Central Vietnamese afternoon covered the city and the highlands to the north collected layers of thick white clouds, beautiful and harmless. After all that time stuck at home, it was impossible not to smile.

Romantic. The view was so romantic. I thought of another city, much larger, rife with monuments and flags, traffic, slums and palaces, its cobblestone streets not unlike New Orleans, only with a past perhaps even more redolent of history.

"If your mother tongue is not Vietnamese, Hanoi is an incredibly romantic city," is another phrase I hear from time to time. I suppose it means exactly what it implies, that if you could understand the conversations being had by the cosmopolitan couple on bench next to you as you gaze across Hoan Kiem Lake in the Old Quarter of the city, you would be much less likely to enjoy the view.

What would that couple be discussing as they melted into each other's arms? Presumably the price per hectare in Da Nang or Quang Nam Province.

III:

COPING

You can get used to anything. Isn't that what they say? Those of us who could afford it got used to staying at home. The rest of us got used to being scared. We went to work, we bought masks, or sewed them ourselves, or refused to wear them.

What you never get used to is fear. Some of us lived with it. Some of us chose escape.

Under the Dog Star

BRIAN CULLMAN

SO, RIGHT NOW YOU CAN'T GO TO A BAR, A CAFÉ OR a barbershop; you can't shop in a bookstore, go to the movies or a yoga class; forget about going to a library, a museum or a bowling alley; you can't go to a club to hear music or work out at your gym.

What you can do is adopt a dog.

Bide-A-Wee, Animal Rescue and the ASPCA are suddenly overwhelmed with requests.

People sheltering on their own or with their family are suddenly looking for steady and non-judgmental companionship.

How likely is it that your wife or kids are going to happily sit through that second New Riders of the Purple Sage album again?

Your dog won't mind a bit!

Is your husband ready to curl up and watch eight consecutive episodes of *Top Chef,* including the one where Padma references five different U2 songs to explain her theories of exotic but homeopathic home cookery?

Your dog is ready!

Step outside for a moment.

See all those people with masks and gloves, not making eye contact, keeping a safe distance, hugging the sides of the buildings, and nervously assessing anyone coming their way for the cough or the sneeze that might topple their world.

Now look down.

The dogs they're walking are dancing down the street with nothing but joy in their step, tails wagging, like every day is Christmas.

A dog's idea of heaven is for nobody to leave their side. Ever!

Whoever came up with the idea of sheltering in place loved dogs.

And it seems like you're in very little danger of getting the virus from your pet, and very little danger of infecting them.

Yes, there was a story in the paper about two cats who appear to have come down with very mild cases of the coronavirus, but then again, these are cats, so how reliable is that information? You have to ask.

And how did they get tested when we can't?

Years ago, I was sent to Siberia on a story. I met with a digital shaman who could fax the dead, with sorcerers who could realign the breath of the world, with hustlers who could make money magically disappear. And almost every place I went, from Novosibirsk, a city of two million people where there are only three restaurants, to Irkutsk, all the way in the East, where the rain just hangs in the air, waiting for instructions, and almost every place I went, the second or third question people would ask me was did I have a pet? A dog? A cat? A monkey?

I mentioned this in passing to my translator. I thought it was funny. He didn't.

"Oh, maybe you haven't been here long enough to notice. People are fixated on their pets. They let their dogs and cats eat from their plate, they spend more time talking to their pets than to their lovers. Go into enough homes, you'll see."

He took off his black-rimmed glasses and put them down on the table, directly between our two cups of tea, and they glinted and shone for a moment with the wild, indecorous light of a passing strobe.

"You can't have 75 years of repression and not have it affect you at the deepest level. We lived in an atmosphere of absolute mistrust. You couldn't be sure of your family, your teachers, your neighbors, your lovers. Everyone was a potential enemy. So people learned to talk in code, to find ways of saying everything and exposing nothing. So who do you talk to? Your dog! Your parrot! Your hamster! Your monkey! They're the only ones who can't turn you in, who can never betray you. They are your safety, your refuge.

"When there is nothing, they are everything."

I Want to Leave,
I Have to Leave

TIM PAGE

August 31, 2020, New York City

I've arranged for my absentee ballot; I am unmated and have no dog; my children are grown and scattered; I am retired and nobody needs my physical presence anywhere. I'm tired of being alone in a New York apartment, and I am horrified by what I see going on in this summer of plague and Trump.

I want to leave. I have to leave.

In my mid-sixties I am still wavering from a traumatic brain injury that, by actuarial standards, "should" have carried me off a few years earlier. But I had not only survived but grown hungry again, only to find myself holding on in what has been too often described as the "epicenter" of the coronavirus. Several friends had already died and I watched televised images of the impromptu morgues cobbled together across New York City—tents, trucks, parking lots, Central Park.

Nobody knows what is happening, only that things were clearly getting worse. It was like the early months of AIDS, when you would run into a suddenly gaunt acquaintance on the street and then learn two weeks later that he had died from a strange sickness that didn't yet have a name.

Increasingly, I had stayed indoors. Counted-out pills began and ended my days, interrupted by food delivery, a phone call or two, and the droning of television shows I found myself unable to follow.

Two people in the building tested positive at the end of June. Warning signs went up in the elevators, and the doormen started wearing masks and handing us our mail in rubber gloves. We kept a distance from our neighbors and when we passed in the lobby, we would turn our faces away and attach ourselves to opposite walls, moving sideways, sometimes nodding but never speaking. For all we knew, a shared breath might kill us.

Earlier this month, Mort, a 91-year-old relative was admitted to a New York emergency room with pneumonia. That's all I was able to find out. His wife of 60 years had died in May. They were loving friends to me from earliest childhood, the sort of people who'd select presents that you'd actually *want* when they came for Christmas dinner. This morning, I thought of calling around to local hospitals to find out where he was but what could they say? and why should I add to their burden? I couldn't visit and Mort would be much too busy, fighting or dying, to interrupt with vain messages from a world he was already shaking off. And so, numbed, I made some tea and started the day. He died the next week: there was no service, of course, although maybe one will come later. By mid-August, depleted and half-mad, I hadn't left my building in weeks. Finally I made an arrangement with myself: if, as it seemed, we were all going to be extinguished, I wanted to spend one more winter in reasonable human dignity, during which I could read and think and listen to the music I loved. But every day it seemed as though another country had closed off to us and there were not yet even rumors of a vaccine.

And then one afternoon, when the anxiety grew too much to bear, I bought a one-way ticket to Belgrade, Serbia. Just like that—called up and booked it, as though ordering a pizza. Next Friday night I will be leaving for a place I've never been with plans to return sometime in 2021, although that, like everything these days, is subject to change.

Why Serbia? I could tell you many stories about the glories, tumult, beauty and sadness of the Balkans—all true and vividly present—but my choice finally came down to pragmatism and convenience. Belgrade is still open to Americans right now, and there is a flight that will effectively take me from passport control to passport control, with no changes of plane in the middle of the night, which I could no longer manage myself. It is presently the only nonstop flight to Europe where foreign passengers can leave the airport immediately after the formalities and settle in town.

I'm off.

September 4–5, 2020, in flight

The nights since I arranged for my travel have been clotted with terrifying dreams. In one, the plane was transformed into a bumpy emergency ward, with my reclining fellow passengers shrunken into bandaged, glass-eyed mummies, wheezing and coughing to the accompaniment of beeps that would not stop. Another dream was set in a Dr. Zhivago snowstorm, and I was marshalled into a line of frozen-footed, ragged asylum-seekers chasing a rumor of an admitting bureaucrat, thousands of people ahead of us and around a corner.

And yet every morning, as I shook off the night and banished my nightmares, this venture seemed at least plausible, potentially exciting, and maybe even renewing, no small matters at the age of 65.

I finished packing my carry-ons and took a last look around the apartment where I had lived on and off since my early twenties, wondering if I would ever be back. At a younger age, sentiment would likely have softened me and I might have stayed. But I'm more courageous now. More than that, I have nothing to lose. My car was waiting, the flight was due to take off in four hours, and I set out to JFK, leaning forward.

I hadn't been in an international terminal in almost a year. There were more guards than travelers and everybody was reduced to pairs of suspicious eyes above light-blue Covid masks. The airport looked like an abandoned shopping mall and it was almost impossible to believe that a branch of the Palm steakhouse—stuffed with vigorous, juicy young people spending too much money on meat and lobsters the size of small pets—had once operated somewhere in the dark, behind the dingy plexiglass.

I welcomed the release from gravity as the Air Serbia jet lifted off from New York. I ate a little, pushed my seat back, took an Ambien, curled up and tried to be comfortable. And then there was oblivion, followed by a waking amidst bustling flight attendants serving morning coffee over green German fields as we flew south from the Arctic. I was quietly pleased that hours have now gone by during which I have not understood a single phrase.

September 11, 2020, Belgrade

I made it through customs in ten minutes and was asleep in my Belgrade hotel an hour later. Within days, I'd taken a small but comfortable Communist-era flat in Dorćol, a hallowed neighborhood at the confluence of the Sava and Danube rivers. My rent was $550, including utilities and a little balcony. Here, I thought, I might burrow in and survive for a while, waiting for better times.

One of the first surprises was how easy it was to keep in touch, through email, Skype and WhatsApp. My East Coast people would call in the late afternoon and my West Coast friends, nine hours before me, would ring about the time I woke up. It was the first time since my early twenties that I had no idea what the next few months would bring, a situation both frightening and liberating.

September 20, 2020, Belgrade

It's the beginning of my third week in Belgrade and I like the city a lot. The people are fiercely friendly and eager to help. The mood is much less fearful than it is in the States. There are fewer than 500 cases in Serbia now—way down from July—and only some 700 deaths since the pandemic began.

My friends back home have asked me about masks, much slandered right now in the United States. Serbia has taken them very seriously, especially indoors where most stores won't let you in without one and lines are formed in five-feet intervals as we wait calmly. The fact that Serbia has been occupied by both Nazis and Communists well within the lifetime of many of my Facebook friends means that Belgraders know what "freedom" is and that it has absolutely nothing to do with refusing to wear a mask in a time of infection. (The frivolity of those militia macho men wearing their guns to "protect" them at the corner grocery!)

Outside, it is a different story: your waiter may be masked and will point out the hand sanitizer on the table, you will be seated as far from other customers as possible but no mask is required and you relax and hope that the breeze will carry away the virus. Everybody knows things will worsen as things grow colder and we are forced to move inside but we are playing for time, with a spirit of "If worse comes to worst, we will all die but for now let's enjoy this gentle evening."

I am determined to survive.

October 5, 2020

It has been a soft, brilliant autumn and the leaves are just starting to brighten. There is an agreeably grimy edge to my part of the city—think East Village or the Haight 30 years ago—and graffiti is everywhere, as so often in dynamic neighborhoods. The big difference is the minimal crime and a resultant lack of fear. With a population of eight million, Serbia had a grand total of 108 homicides in 2018, while my beloved city of Baltimore, with barely half a million residents left within its borders, buried 300 of them last year.

Belgrade delighted me from the start, particularly the warm, proud, serious people. I was welcome to work outside a café all day and greet new friends who passed by on Strahinjica Bana. The city is a carnivore's delight—I've not eaten so much meat in years and it is certainly the staple dish, to the point where one waiter, in halting English, asked me what meat I would like served as a side dish to my meat.

Fruit dishes were presented with a little pitcher of purified honey, and the combination was delicious overkill. The red wine was hearty and succulent, tasting of dark soil. Young people rode scooters through the stalled traffic and said "Ciao" without self-consciousness. At times, I felt as though I was in *La Dolce Vita*: in other sections of town, more recently bombed, I was reminded of the battered Vienna of *The Third Man*.

This fall, it has been fun to write outside a Belgrade café and greet new friends who would pass by. Yes, the city was dirty and the postal system impossible: FedEx and DHL your best bet and your package might still take weeks to arrive. And yet it was also a city where many surprising things were easy—a painless emergency root canal and an immaculately polished crown accomplished in four days for $270!

I do wish there weren't so much smoking. I'm told that everybody who isn't a smoker feels as I do, but there aren't that many of us. You can read medical history on the faces of older Serbs, people hollowed and sick before their time, due largely to cigarettes. It is virtually a national pastime. The addiction is less common among young people although you'll find no shortage of it there either. Some restaurants have begun to set aside sections for non-smokers, but many more people want to smoke than not smoke and so the air is fogged and this is the thing I like least about the city.

Today it is a month since I arrived—already the second-longest unbroken stay in another country I've ever experienced. At my age, I no longer have much interest in playing the tourist game of adding to a private checklist of sights seen. A proper understanding will demand study and reflection, and right now I am more interested in the passing show.

So for the present I'm just getting lost, walking around Belgrade until I'm exhausted, past butcher shop and green grocer and a pasta store that has been in operation since 1921, and the woman who sells flowers on the next corner every day with a serene golden retriever at her feet. How many children drop to the pavement every day to commune with the dog, who not only tolerates but seems to welcome them all, thumping her big tail or rolling over on her back?

Those who speak English can make sense of things by signing on to the Belgrade Foreign Visitors Club on Facebook, a group of more than 9,000 people who answer questions on everything from finding a neighborhood to a course in Chinese cooking to the purchase of a pet chinchilla. I'm learning where the roads go, and I can occasionally pronounce their names. Today I was greeted on the street by a waiter who had served me a few days before and the recognition made me happy and content, as though I'd fallen into a new home.

The history of Belgrade is long and bloody—the city has been razed more than 30 times, all the way back to Attila the Hun—and many of the streets are named for ancient heroes unknown in most other places and often mislaid here. The legends are resonant and deeply felt with a complicated history unknown to most Americans. One can imagine a great national epic—a "Ring" Cycle or "Kalevala"—emanating from Serbia, and an evening-length bar conversation can be built on the events of 1389 alone. (For fear of any misstep, I'm not even going to try to summarize this!)

Because it has not been wealthy in many years, Belgrade seeks out more primal pleasures—and finds them. I've not been so simply happy in a long time as I was on a cold, sunny afternoon watching Belgraders play fetch with their delighted dogs on the hilly grounds of the Kalemegdan fortress. Similar games have been played here since the Roman Empire, and some of the bricks were laid then.

I'll be in Serbia for a while and I am glad to be here. I've never felt less than welcomed and we certainly do not walk around in a state of dread I had gotten used to in the States. And how strangely satisfying to awaken to a drunken quarrel down the block without the slightest worry that it will end with gunfire.

October 20, 2020

"We all have two lives, and the second begins when we realize we only have one."

These lines have been attributed to Confucius. So have a thousand others, many sounding as though they were actually fashioned by a renegade hippie trying to drag Hallmark cards into the 1970s. Still, tracking down this quotation, it does seem to be from Confucius himself, and I like it even more now that I know that its pedigree.

I've been watching the American election closely (probably too closely) and I miss many people and places in the United States. God knows I'm rooting for my homeland to recover. But my writing has been my life's essence, and I felt that I could no longer do anything at all in New York. Here I can at least hope to create something that can be held in the hands of strangers someday and let them all know What It Was Like in the cataclysmic 2020s.

I am reading *Black Lamb and Grey Falcon,* a gigantic book by the British author Rebecca West written after some months in Yugoslavia just before World War II. I am astonished by how fine it is, with masterly storytelling and eternally inquisitive travel writing that remind me of Herodotus. I do not know the history and politics of the area well enough to vouch for its veracity, but as pure writing it seems to me a permanent book, something that will always offer something new, that can be picked up anytime.

I wish I could talk to my parents, who were kind enough to bring three kids along for a two-week bus tour of Europe in the summer of 1967. It was the sort of rush job that has been teased in articles and films; we went to Milan and Venice on the same day and "did" Florence for lunch as part of a long drive down to Rome. The children wondered about the bidets, no explanation readily offered, just something mysterious in the bathroom that could spray the ceiling if we turned it on full. We were horrified by the fish served with their heads in Paris. You know the rest. *Mona Lisa*? Check. Gondoliers? Check. And so on.

Most days we were squeezed into a crowded bus that we boarded around 7 a.m. Kodak had given me a new Super 8mm camera to try out for a commercial they were making about my backyard movies. (It is now sobering to watch the sharp annoyance apparent on the faces of fondly remembered, long-dead fellow passengers as I ambushed them on film.) Not yet teenagers, we found the rides mostly tedious, especially the day that somebody vomited in the aisle as the bus lurched its way around some Alp. But the experience was planted.

December 1, 2020

Oddly enough, in the year of pandemic, I've scarcely been sick at all. When I stopped shaking hands and riding subways, isolating myself most of the time, germs just didn't pierce my shield and haven't since 2019. And so it was weird to wake up today with a genuine old-fashioned cold. I'm feeling lousy but I can taste and smell, and it doesn't seem a harbinger of anything worse. I'm relieved, if still a little annoyed.

I'm thinking of all the bacteria we used to absorb in any given day back in New York. Shaking hands, social kissing, riding trains, hitting a bar, taking a couple of plane trips a year, love affairs for the young or lucky—all carried out without thinking. I'm wondering what percentage of those germs still reach us now (one in a hundred? one in 10,000?). Yet the deaths keep coming, although there are now, finally, rumors of a vaccine.

If a vaccine is coming, it looks as though I will have to get it outside Serbia, for I have now outstayed my legal welcome. Most of my readers who have crossed the Atlantic have spent their time within what is now the European Union, which encompasses most of the popular tourist destinations (including, until recently, Great Britain). But the whole area has been off-limits to Americans since the spring. Serbia is not a part of the EU, which meant that it could admit me, but only for 90 days at a time. After that, I would need to find a new hideout.

Balkan old-timers tell of the days when visitors were able to drive into a neighboring country, have a drink, and then cross back to claim another 90 days in Belgrade. These were commonly known as "border runs." Everything is more complicated now and I must leave by December 5. I'm too old and too confused to risk some sort of deportation, although I have friends here who have been staying on for years without any trouble.

I'm also in search of better air. The buses and old cars, running on diesel fuel, puff black smoke. A cloud settles on Belgrade in mid-November, as heaters switch on, and the pollution becomes uncomfortable. An average salary in Serbia is about $1,000 a month and many citizens live on far less. Electric heating can cost $400 a winter: the same place can be warmed for about $75 if you use wood and bituminous coal. The practice is illegal but the rules are widely ignored and the effect on the air is calamitous.

With the onset of winter and the general disappearance of the sun, the city is suddenly iron-gray. We've had a surge in cases and it is time to take things more seriously. The trees are either brown or bare and it will grow much colder in December. I'll be permitted to return to Serbia in three months. Much will have happened and maybe I'll have a clearer path ahead of me.

I decided to move to Croatia, which is in the European Union but not yet in the Schengen Zone, the alliance of European nations that offers a common visa, and therefore a stray American is still welcomed. I arrived in Zagreb only a few days before Croatia was closed to us too but, having crossed the border, I was allowed to stay on and made it through both holidays and a month of earthquakes in relative calm.

Zagreb is hibernating this year. Some stores are open but admission is strictly controlled so there is usually a wait. Then we come and go quickly. Restaurants are limited to delivery only. Looking out my window the morning after my arrival, I see hardly anybody without a mask. It is clearly a wealthier city than Belgrade, more formal and at least half again as expensive, but not so costly as the States or Western Europe. The roads are wide and stately. Libraries and theaters are plentiful, and some of them are still open even in this calamitous December. The museums range from the traditional to the decidedly quirky—a hangover museum, a Museum of Broken Relationships and even a torture museum, which I would probably have thought very cool as a teenager and will not now enter for any reason. There is a Museum of Naïve Art (meaning untutored, folk or outsider) that will demand a visit. And then there is the street life, although all restaurants are closed through December 21 and everybody is carefully masked.

Large parts of the city are most easily reached by those willing to walk, and I found myself inspired by everything around me and managed to climb eagerly and happily. I walked through a fine open market, and I am reliably informed that if you adopt a fruit or cheese or bread vendor (or they adopt you) soon you will be the recipient of their finest items. The oldest pharmacy in Zagreb is said to have been opened in 1355 by Nicolò Alighieri, a great-grandson of Dante Alighieri, and it is in business still. Zagreb prides itself on inventing the solid-ink fountain pen, the mechanical pencil and the necktie (*kravata*), and there is always a continuing argument about exactly which part of the former Yugoslavia "owns" Nikola Tesla.

News of a vaccine was announced in November, and by March, Serbia was offering treatment to anybody who was in residence and—for a time—to all the countries in the Balkans. I was struck by how well-ordered the process was—brief interviews with several people about my past and present health, a kind nurse who recognized my age and fear and then escorted me through the gigantic Belgrade Fair conference hall, a doctor who greeted a stranger tenderly, then jabbed me precisely just below my shoulder. There was the uncomplaining efficiency common to a disaster site: you behave because you must behave and there is no time for foolishness.

Buffered from the virus, I kept traveling. It had become obvious that we were all in a new and unrecognizable world that required constant adaptation. Sometimes, reading the infection rates around the world, I felt like a cartoon stockbroker following the ticker tape trying to decide where I would go next.

During my 300 days away from the United States, the only countries I visited were places I had never been. In addition to Serbia and Croatia, I went to Montenegro, North Macedonia, Slovenia, Bosnia-Herzegovina, Albania and Hungary—all once closed to me for political reasons, and ironically, now the only places that were open. But by early June 2021, it was once again possible to go back to the traditional parts of Europe I had visited so long before.

My first stop was Vienna, just beginning to stretch open once more, with vaccination records required to enter any restaurant. My form is unusual, presented in Cyrillic, Latin, Serbian and English. But when our young server saw it, the coolly formal Viennese professionalism that borders on hauteur softened immediately and I could read her happiness above her mask. It turned out that she was Serbian, from a village outside of Belgrade, another young person off to the Big City but glad to find a compatriot who knew where she came from. Which, I guess, I do.

With gratitude to Brian Henry Cullman, who helped me begin to organize a massive amount of memories.

Modesty Blaise

SUSAN ZAKIN

WHEN THE LOCKDOWN STARTED—THE FIRST ONE—there was an odd pause. I remember glancing around my house, noticing things that I'd walked past for months in a rush, not actually seeing them. On the entryway table I'd stashed a few books I hadn't gotten around to reading. One was a Modesty Blaise novel. I think it was (don't laugh) *The Impossible Virgin.*

I'd ordered it because I had a vague memory of Modesty Blaise from my childhood. I must have seen the dreadful '60s movie with Monica Vitti and Terence Stamp. Modesty Blaise was billed as the female James Bond and my entire family was fanatical about Bond, James Bond. I have a friend from Kenya whose name is Catherine Bond. Every time I write her an email I chortle silently, thinking, *Bond, Catherine Bond.* She's British so the accent is right.

I have a weakness for pulp novels some decry as colonial: James Hilton's *Lost Horizon,* H. Ryder Haggard's *She. Tarzan,* of course. These are archetypal stories and my African stepsons love them, too. I've always suspected that there's an adolescent boy lurking inside me, refusing to grow up.

These novels are, of course, "boy" books, but Modesty Blaise reminded me that girls could have adventures, too. The books were a revelation; more than that, an escape. For the next two months I lived in Modesty's world, in post-World War II stories that felt resonant in our own time of mass migration and fractured nation-states.

Modesty Blaise had the backstory to end all backstories. In 1945, a young war orphan escapes from a displaced persons camp in Greece. Remembering nothing of her past, she wanders through the devastated postwar landscape: the Mediterranean, the Middle East, North Africa. An older man, a Jewish-Hungarian refugee, befriends the feral child and educates her.

By the time she's 19, Modesty Blaise is heading a criminal gang in Tangier. She meets a Cockney named Willie Garvin and gives him the recognition for his character and talents denied him by his upbringing. Fast forward: The two grow rich and retire from crime.

The series begins when a British secret service officer recruits them for a special mission. And then another. I roared through the books. When I'd finished all of them, I ordered the comic strip collections. I didn't want to leave Modesty's world. Not until the pandemic was over, at least.

Spies, international intrigue, exotic locales. What's not to love? But what truly seduced me into these stories was the template for female strength assembled by the author, a British writer named Peter O'Donnell. A man, in fact, but after I'd read enough of the books, I did wonder about his proclivities.

Modesty's loyal lieutenant, Willie Garvin, is a tactician, action over thought, a simple bloke, really, but deadly. He can throw a knife with uncanny accuracy but doesn't always anticipate problems. Modesty is strategy personified, superb at sussing out her opponent's next move, whether she's practicing martial arts with Willie or fighting a succession of Bond-like supervillains. Or, at times, dealing with an ill-chosen lover.

Hey, it happens. In every one of these pulp novels, Modesty and Willie find themselves in impossible situations—part of the fun is not seeing how O'Donnell can steer them out of trouble—and it's always Modesty who thinks their way out.

Not that there isn't damage. On at least one occasion, Modesty lets herself be raped because it's the only way to get out of a bad situation. One of her many talents is using an obscure Eastern meditation technique to leave her body (also handy when one has been shot) while remaining aware of everything that's happening. Have no fear: justice will eventually be served. Modesty Blaise persists.

These days, we call this quality resilience. No matter how much we fight for equality, violence against women will always be with us. Without downplaying the damage, author Peter O'Donnell gives the reader a template for reassembling one's sense of self and, at best, coming out stronger for it.

It's not that Modesty hasn't got some pretty serious mileage. She's that rare woman who accepts the truth about the men in her life. Seeing them so clearly, she understands that none are quite a fit. Perhaps that's the damage: Modesty's unwillingness to, er, commit. Or it's that damn clear-sightedness.

Modesty's only long-term relationship is with Willie Garvin. Modesty and Willie aren't lovers. They're closer than that. Perhaps this is the best a strong, intelligent woman who's used herself hard can hope for: a comrade-in-arms who's seen her wounded and weak but still calls her Princess.

Covid, I realized, felt like a throwback to the days of world wars, times of violence and scarcity that annealed the spirits of men, and lest we forget, women. The plague created a real crisis, rather than the self-inflicted ones to which I'd become accustomed as a young woman in a time of relative ease and affluence. Modesty Blaise invoked the toughness of the Greatest Generation. I'd spent the first half of my life excoriating my parents' refusal to acknowledge pain. But acknowledgement is only the first half. It's a matter of healing the wounds, maybe not completely, but as best you can.

And driving a Jaguar, if you can manage it.

When I read these books, I felt invincible, like Modesty, if not quite as deft at martial arts. When death intruded into every thought, every movement, every decision, forcing an intimacy with mortality shocking to Americans who had spent their lives protected from smallpox and tuberculosis, war and insurrection, I needed Modesty Blaise.

Donald Trump Stole the World From Us

MIKAL GILMORE

IN THE LAST SEVERAL DAYS I'VE SEEN the strain the pandemic puts my wife, Elaine Schock, under. She has lost some of her routine—regular office hours, Pilates training, boxing sessions, the occasional restaurant visit and, of course, travel. There may be much about that last one she doesn't miss, since it can be exhausting, but at the same time it means she doesn't get to see and visit with the people she really loves in her work as a music publicist—Willie Nelson, Toby Keith, Mickey Raphael, Willie's wife and sister Annie and Bobbie, all their extended family and network of friends. Life has changed.

I was telling Elaine a while back that the nicest trip I ever had with anybody was accompanying her to Nashville at the end of 2018. We went to the Grand Ole Opry; the Country Music Hall of Fame Museum; a formal dinner and concert where I wore tails (and looked swell); we had dinner and drinks at the best restaurant I've ever been to; I bought myself some new boots and I think I got Elaine something at the same store; then one night—before sleep in the hotel room—we made the only big impulse decision we've ever made: We picked out Ruby, our Goldendoodle.

As I was saying all this to Elaine I realized something like that couldn't happen now—it would risk our lives—and maybe it never can happen again. Maybe we'll never sit in a restaurant again, late at night in a low light, me wondering if I should get a chocolate soufflé. Maybe we'll never sit in a theater again or a nightclub or music hall. I suspect things might improve enough that such times could be possible again—especially when and if a vaccine arrives—but will we trust the world the same way again? Maybe Elaine will but maybe I won't.

I've thought a lot lately about my mother, Bessie Gilmore (born in 1913), and my oldest brother, Frank (1940). My mother began withdrawing from the world after I graduated from high school in 1969. She still went out, met me for lunch from time to time, but it became less and less often. After my brother Gary was executed for murder in Utah, in January 1977, my mother shut herself into her trailer and never walked outside again. She'd had enough of the world. It had hurt her too much. She didn't trust her friends. She didn't want them. She stopped talking to them and only spoke with and saw my brother Frank, who lived with and cared for her in their trailer. Her health failed as if she willed it to. Her hands could barely hold her coffee cup. She watched TV, she still kept up on events, she'd still call me. The day after John Lennon's death in 1980 she rang and said: "I know you liked this man and you must be hurting right now." Other calls she'd ask what I thought about so-and-so winning or losing an election, in the U.S. or abroad. She'd ask if I was still a Communist. I said, No I'm a Democrat, just like you. She'd say, For all the good it does us.

One day she was sitting at the trailer's kitchen table talking to Frank when her mouth erupted in blood. Frank rushed to help her then called an ambulance. It turned out she had a perforation in her stomach and was in and out of consciousness. She didn't live long after that. I hadn't known she'd died until a friend visited me at Rhino Records in Westwood, where I was working, and took me out back to the small parking lot and gave me the news. I felt like I'd been punched unconscious.

My brother Frank had, in some ways, started pulling out of the world at a much younger age, in his twenties, after he'd been drafted but refused to carry a gun and ended up in Fort Leavenworth, until Senator Wayne Morse won his release. My brother was never the same after that. He told me the night he got back that he didn't trust the world anymore. I learned only recently that he'd been beaten while at Leavenworth for refusing to align with white prisoners against black inmates. As a result, he was already fairly withdrawn before my mother died. After that he became totally reclusive. I lost him twice in my life for years-long stretches and only reconnected with him in recent years, when he learned I had cancer. Now he lives in a senior care center in Canby, Oregon, that has been overrun with Covid-19, though it has stayed out of the hallways of his part of the building. I don't know if I'll ever see him again. I don't know if I'll ever fly again.

The point of all this is that many of us have been forced of late to leave the world, withdraw into our homes, and right now that's for the better. Those who can't handle it are understandably manifesting a kind of normality—they miss the social world—but too many of them also manifest an abnormality in their hostile reactions to why this change is necessary. Some say the caution is unnecessary, that there really isn't a deadly pandemic at work in the land, that this is a conspiracy meant to turn America against Trump and win Joe Biden's election in November. Yeah, they really believe that fucked-up shit. This is what Trump has done to us. He has abandoned and pressured us into wards and homes of sickness, he has gassed and chased our friends and families and children and brothers and sisters in the streets, and he has severely and dangerously divided us—all for one reason: The affirmation of his self.

I want to note a passage from Mary Trump's book, *Too Much and Never Enough*, which I finished reading the other night:

> Donald's need for affirmation is so great that he doesn't seem to notice that the largest group of his supporters are people he wouldn't condescend to be seen with outside of a rally. His deep-seated insecurities have created in him a black hole of need that constantly requires the light of compliments that disappears as soon as he's soaked it in.
>
> Nothing is ever enough. This is far beyond garden-variety narcissism; Donald is not simply weak, his ego is a fragile thing that must be bolstered every moment because he knows deep down that he is nothing of what he claims to be. He knows he has never been loved. So he must draw you in if he can by getting you to assent to even the most seemingly insignificant thing: 'Isn't this plane great?' 'Yes, Donald, this plane is great.' It would be rude to begrudge him that small concession. Then he makes his vulnerabilities and insecurities your responsibility: you must assuage them, you must take care of him. Failing to do so leaves a vacuum that is unbearable for him to withstand for long. If you're someone who cares about his approval, you'll say anything to retain it. He has suffered mightily, and if you aren't doing all you can to alleviate that suffering, you should suffer, too...Over Donald's lifetime, as his failures mounted despite my grandfather's repeated—and extravagant—interventions, his struggle for legitimacy, which could never be won, turned into a scheme to make sure nobody found out that he's never been legitimate at all. This has never been more true than it is now, and it is exactly the conundrum our country finds itself in: the government as it is currently constituted, including the executive branch, half of Congress, and the majority of the Supreme Court, is entirely in the service of protecting Donald's ego; that has become almost its entire purpose.

Donald Trump has taken the world away from us, maybe even the prospect that the world will ever again resemble what it once was. It is an almost unthinkable development: The man elected to be president of the United States has taken the world—the streets, the bars, cafés, shops, music shows, travel (he'd even like to take postal delivery), even health, life, and family—away from Americans. We are on our own, in our homes, waiting for that specter above us, the angel of death, finally to pass over.

It occurs to me that I might handle this better than some because I've had an internal self that lives in connection with books and movies and music. Those things have always been an essential part of the world to me. The lockdown has only driven me deeper into those resources. That, plus I've already died and come back a couple times—once from cancer, another time from a fall and head injury. Perhaps even more than a couple times.

Maybe each time I come back I'm less present in the world. Back in the mid-1970s, before Gary committed his murders and was subsequently shot to death, my mother had to go to the hospital for emergency surgery—an earlier version of the stomach perforation that eventually killed her. I remember feeling that it was as if in some way she'd already left the world. Later, when she suffered so much more, I had to wonder if surviving that had been the better for her. Sometimes I wonder the same for myself. I don't want to end up like her and my brother Frank: shut off from the world, mistrusting it so much that I won't reemerge into it.

Right now, though, there's no other option, unless I want to defy safeguards and potentially endanger others.

But I won't do that. I have a family that certainly wants to reemerge into that world again, and we have a baby in the house who will, one way or another, be growing up in a world brought lower by a terrible man. He is only a baby now, but Aiden will be one of the rebuilders. That much I'm sure of.

Auden at Easter: With Best Wishes From Your Headmaster

STEPHEN DERWENT PARTINGTON

THE PRINCIPAL'S 4TH SUNDAY CHAT TO PUPILS – AS ALWAYS WITH THESE SUNDAY CHATS, YOU MAY READ THIS OR IGNORE IT!

FROM: Mr Steve, Principal, Lukenya British Curriculum, Athi River, Kenya, April 2020.

This is Easter Sunday, near the start of the regular school holiday. [A long-ish, 20-minute read, addressed especially to our seniors; you'll forgive the length, remembering that I'm also an author!]

TOPICS: Love as Respect for Each Other; Sacrifice, the Wider Meaning of 'Friendship,' and Charity; Justice and Goodness in the Face of Difficulties; Easter.

ON THE DAY on which the Second World War was declared, one of my favourite British poets, W.H. Auden, sat in a seedy American café and wrote 'September 1, 1939,' a poem hoping that the war would swiftly end. It contains the line, 'We must love one another or die.'

The war did NOT swiftly end.

Auden later claimed not to like this poem, but literature has a habit of living on regardless of what its author wants, and that line remains as one of the most simple and urgent in twentieth-century poetry: 'We must love one another or die.' It is a straightforward and possibly even naïve cry of the poet at a time of great danger, at the outset of great death across the world from Europe to Asia to America to, almost inexplicably, our East Africa. Auden was a poet of real conscience. Year 10 and 11 Literature students: Auden was a contemporary of George Orwell, whose novel *1984* we're studying, and the two writers shared many social views, even if they didn't ALWAYS get along.

'We must love another or die.' Although Auden strongly believed that by the 20th century poetry had lost its old power to influence the world, he still believed, as he ALSO writes in this poem, that those he called 'The Just' had an obligation to continuously communicate with each other about their HOPES for the possibility of peace and justice in the world. Regardless of all the difficulties, violence, cruelties and injustices of his troubled age, Auden told us that we each of us, even in our SMALL WAYS, have the duty and the ability to say and do the right thing while wars rage and hatred seems to triumph.

Auden's 'We must love one another or die' is a simple and wise message, but it's NOT an easy thing to do. For example, during a time of conflict, who amongst us is strong enough to really argue for peace, when armed men in uniform are patrolling the streets? Or when the perfectly innocent are being discriminated against just because of their religious beliefs, skin colour, gender or politics, who amongst us is really strong enough to even QUIETLY raise our voice in support of those people, when everyone else is shouting abuse or throwing punches? It's easier to reach for the stone, to join in with the wrongdoing. In schools we call that pressure 'Peer Pressure,' and we always hope you can resist it.

Stop, and take a deep breath... Take a minute, and ask yourself: 'Am I strong enough? Am I, when wrong is happening, able to stand up to say and do the right thing, to be counted amongst the wise, just, kind and good?' It's not easy.

Easter is now upon us, and I hope that you all have an excellent time with your parents and other family members, whether you're gathering together or whether Easter this year is a little stranger, a little more restricted and solitary. As excellent young people, you deserve to have fun, and to spend time with those who matter to you. I wish you fun, I wish you laughter, I wish you HUGE amounts of chocolate!

Now, in the Christian tradition Easter is a time when Jesus voluntarily gave up his life on behalf of others, in order that THEY might not die.

At Easter, I'm often reminded of John 15: 9–17—yes, I know you think I don't know my Bible very well, pupils, but you can't be a student of the history of English Literature without knowing that book very well indeed! In this section of John, Jesus is reported as saying, 'Love each other as I have loved you. Greater love has no one than this: to lay down one's life for one's friends... Love each other.' And the type of 'Love' that he means here isn't 'romantic love' or anything like that; rather, it is what the Greeks called 'Agape,' or the unconditional mutual 'embracing' that people might have for each other even if they personally don't know each other. It is a brotherly and sisterly love of the sort that transcends superficial differences of class, gender, race, creed, and so on. It is exactly what Auden meant with HIS use of the word 'Love.'

But Jesus goes further than Auden; to be fair, prophets USUALLY go further than poets! Auden gives us a pragmatic, 'We must love one another or die,' almost as a warning, as a way to avoid future war. It's an important message, yes; but Jesus goes further and tells us that sometimes the very greatest love MIGHT BE to offer yourself to save somebody else. I don't think he's expecting us to do this every moment of every day, or that we should all go around offering our very LIVES, but he IS suggesting it as the IDEAL when necessary, as the ultimate form of Love, and it's worth reminding ourselves this Easter that this is exactly what Jesus DID later do, according to the Bible: by his own example, he lived that ideal and he laid down his life for his friends. And by 'friends' he didn't just mean his listening disciples; rather, he meant EVERYONE, and indeed the New Testament is full of examples of people acting altruistically and lovingly towards people other than 'their own.' The Good Samaritan is a classic example. In the Christian tradition, everyone is capable of being a 'friend' in the sense that Jesus meant: an equal, a brother, a sister, a fellow. In John, Jesus extended the idea of friendship to include EVERYONE, even those who according to the societal structure of his age would have seemed to be 'lesser' than him.

According to the Christian tradition, Jesus laid down his own life for EVERYONE, then, on behalf of all of us, his 'friends.' And he did this so that we might not have to always make quite such a grand self-sacrifice ourselves. He bore the burden himself. He achieved the ideal that he spoke of: according to the story, he laid down his life for his 'friends,' for US.

But most readings of John 15 don't leave things there, with Jesus' later death. Most interpreters of John still remind us that the ideal, that which we should always aim for, is the desire and the practice of doing the very best for OTHERS, even if we don't personally know them, and even if this means some sort of sacrifice from us. Jesus' death wasn't the end point of his lesson; rather, it was the start of what we ALL have to do. We MUST 'Love each other,' as Jesus stated, and we MUST be willing to demonstrate that love, even in the hardest of times, even when the world would have us do the WRONG thing. This is the message in John, and it's the wider message of Easter, Christianity's most important festival. Maybe this is what the 'resurrection' means, in a sense: the living on, after his death, of Jesus' love for humankind...

TODAY, and throughout this Easter period, we are probably with a small group of people we know, who are our relatives and friends, and who are therefore 'us' in some sense. Now, sharing with 'our own' is always easy. And at different times, we ALL occasionally retreat into cocoons of 'our own': our own family, our own close friends, our own ethnic group, our own estate, our own language group, our own countryfolk, and so on...

That's not the end of the world, and there's no fundamental problem with that; after all, your family matters. HOWEVER, there IS a problem if we ONLY respect, accept and love 'our own,' because that's lazy—that's such a lazy and 'small' type of love that it's almost not love at all. NO, as I mentioned in my first Sunday chat, the challenge and the joy and the triumph is to love in the sense of 'agape' ALL people, regardless of how distant, different or 'other' they might seem to be. The willingness to speak up or act with and on behalf of people we don't know, and who are suffering, is the greatest thing a person can do, because it is to treat other people, even apparent 'enemies,' as friends, in the way that Jesus advised and that Auden suggested The Just always should.

Perhaps, then, Easter is the perfect time to reflect upon CHARITY, especially at a strange time like this, when Covid-19 is seeing many people, especially the poor and disadvantaged, struggle. Numerous people have lost their jobs, or have had to endure pay cuts; the poor when urged to stay at home in 'lockdown' or under curfew, suffer much more than we do in their densely populated slums and shanties around the world; and, generally speaking, the poor if they have jobs are laborers, meaning that they can't safely 'work from home' in their multi-roomed houses when you and I as the more privileged sometimes CAN; plus, the increase in food prices and the costs of other essentials at a time like this always affects the already poor more than it affects the rest of us, those few of us who can temporarily cushion ourselves.

It is important at a time like this (and indeed ALWAYS) to treat the poor and otherwise disadvantaged not only as 'others,' as separate, but rather as 'friends;' to treat domestic staff, also, not as servants but as friends. Indeed, this is EXACTLY what Jesus said, word for word, in that same extract from John's Gospel: 'I no longer call you servants...Instead, I have called you friends.' And so, we must ask ourselves: 'WHAT CAN I DO IN TERMS OF CHARITY FOR THOSE WHO SEEM DIFFERENT BUT WHO ARE, LIKE ALL PEOPLE, MY

'FRIENDS' IN THE BIBLICAL SENSE?' 'Charity' is a funny word, because we think we know what it means. It seems so easy, doesn't it? We think it means throwing a bag of maize meal into a supermarket box whenever there's famine, or putting ten shillings into a tin at the supermarket checkout, or donating a few books to a local school, or passing our old hand-me-down clothes to the maid...

Well, these ARE kindly acts, well-intentioned and presently necessary, and so keep doing it; but that's not ALL that charity is or should be. True charity means working to improve the world sufficiently so that those poor aren't quite so poor in relation to us as they ARE, that the inequalities and injustices of the world are solved and sorted to the best of our collective ability. At a time like this, for instance, when across the world we're seeing the bravery of medical personnel and other essential workers and the importance of functioning National Health Systems, it probably means reflecting upon how, once things return to normal, EVERYONE can better access quality health care, and not just the rich.

Because we're students, we might reflect upon Education as well. I always feel privileged to be your school Principal, and every day you're not here I and your teachers all regret your absence, because we entered education to teach and support young people—young people who are not 'our own' in the narrow sense of that term. But if schools don't reopen next term, you'll at least have much more chance of accessing a continuing quality education over the Internet than, say, a child in one of our neighboring PUBLIC schools. Every minute that the closure of schools continues, children in poorer public schools and poorer private schools in impoverished areas have less of a chance of catching up with their age-mates from richer schools. This is also an injustice of sorts, which a few charitably donated, secondhand textbooks can't successfully solve. But how could we, once all this is over, work to create a fairer society in which we all contribute towards a more accessible quality education system for all?

These are not easy things to answer, and it's not for me to TELL YOU the solution to the question, 'How, after all this, can we have a fairer society for all in which everyone has decent access to quality health, education and other services?' It's for YOU to think, and for you to talk to your parents, who probably have their own ideas. But it IS our job, ALL OF OUR JOBS, to at least ask the question, and to suggest answers of some sort, because in our heart of hearts we all know that buying a tub of Blue Band for our gardener ISN'T the answer to the world's injustices.

And so, seniors: this Easter, let's at least ask ourselves the difficult questions raised in this chat of mine, questions that it's clear poets such as Auden and world religions from Christianity, Islam, Buddhism, Hinduism, Judaism to others would want us to ask, and that people of no faith often ask. They include...

'How can I better respect others beyond those of my own age, faith, fashion interests, gender and so on?'

'How can I treat distant folk as friends?'

'How can I become one of Auden's "'Just,'" one of Jesus' Loving?'

'How, in my own small way, can I lay down my life for those "friends?"'

'How can I change the world for the better, in smaller or larger ways?'

'How can I, curfewed and cocooned for now in the chrysalis of my home, emerge after all this as a better person, willing to help and to serve?'

These are BIG questions. But Easter is a BIG moment in the Christian calendar every year, and this period of Covid-19 is a BIG issue that spans the world, as an embrace might also spread around the world—it's a strange BIG time for you as young people. At BIG times like these, we might as well think what it means to be BIG-HEARTED, what it means to grow up into adulthood. Maybe just a smile and a kindly word; maybe more—maybe, for some of us who want to serve, it will be MUCH more.

But how, in our own smaller or larger ways, can we be BIG enough to live the truth of these two statements?: 'We must love one another or die'; 'Greater love has no one than this: to lay down one's life for one's friends.' You don't have to be a 'savior' or a great poet, or even a great thinker: but you DO need to think, and we ALL need to be better, to be GOOD, or as good and as kind as we can possibly manage.

Have a wonderful few days, students; be well, and know that your teachers admire you.

With all best wishes from Lukenya British Curriculum,
'Mr. Steve,' Principal, and all of your teachers.

Still Swimming

ROSEMERRY WAHTOLA TROMMER

And so I pull the purple comb
through my son's thick hair,
the same way I've seen
the stylists do at Great Clips.
Wet the hair. Comb it through.
Part it. Hold it between
two fingers. Cut vertically. Snip,
and his hair falls to the floor.
Comb it through. Snip. Snip.

We both know that I
have no clue what I'm doing.
So we laugh as the hair
piles up on the floor.
We chatter, the way
a stylist and customer would,
talking of school and his friends
and his unruly cowlicks. Snip.

I remember that time
I was trapped underwater
by the river's hydraulics,
how I stared up at the light
shining through the surface
and thought, I don't think
it's my time yet to die.
And the river spit me out
and I swam hard as I could
through the rapid toward shore.

I don't think it's my time yet
to die. Nor my son's. Though

all around us the news of dying—
the numbers increasing every day,
stories of beloveds who are gone.

We ask ourselves, how do we
go on? And meanwhile, we do.
We go on. And because my son's hair
is too long for his taste,
I learn how to cut it by cutting it.
How much more will we learn
as this goes on? How to share?
How to grieve? How to let go? How to live?

And meanwhile, life spits us out
into sunlight, and we come up into another day
spluttering, gasping, surprised
we're alive, and we swim, what a gift
to find we're still swimming.

IV:

THE PLAGUE
OF POLITICS

Since humans have lived on Earth, plagues have changed the outcome of our political machinations. So writes Yale professor Frank M. Snowden in *Epidemics and Society: From the Black Death to the Present*.

Snowden is an historian, not an epidemiologist, and his book is a readable accounting of how plagues elicit similar behavior across the centuries, including, in his words, "scapegoating, mass hysteria, and outbursts of religiosity." Plagues have changed the course of history, including Napoleon's defeat in Russia, now attributed to diphtheria, typhoid, and that perennial favorite, dysentery, rather than the snow of legend.

Plague even provided a plot point in *Romeo and Juliet*. When Friar John was on his way to deliver a letter to Romeo with the news that Juliet was alive, he was stopped by officials who suspected that he came from a house "where the infectious pestilence did reign." They prevented him from reaching Romeo with that crucial message and the rest is *liebestod*.

Many countries were already in crisis, with authoritarianism on the rise, and free-floating rage searching for targets. Donald Trump capitalized on every fear, every resentment, every suspicion that we had somehow been cheated. Americans *had* been cheated, of course, for decades, not by their government but by the greed and corruption unleashed by Reagan-era deregulation.

On May 25, 2020, these forces converged in Minneapolis. Police officers arrested George Floyd, a 46-year-old black man, after a convenience store employee called 911 and told police that Floyd had bought cigarettes with a counterfeit $20 bill. Seventeen minutes after the first squad car arrived at the scene, George Floyd was dead, killed after police officer Derek Chauvin pressed his knee on Floyd's neck for eight minutes and 15 seconds. Video records show that Chauvin kept his knee on Floyd's neck for a full minute and 20 seconds after paramedics arrived.

From all reports, George Floyd had been a gentle soul. He had his own troubles, including drug addiction. But it may have been the pandemic that took his life. As Americans were locked down, restaurants lost business. Many closed. Floyd had lost his restaurant job and was struggling financially. Perhaps the bill was counterfeit, a signal of desperation. Surely not a capital offense.

In a country where driving while black could be fatal, Floyd's murder was one too many. By June 6, half a million protesters turned out in more than 500 U.S. cities. The protests began a wider examination of police violence and the nature of policing itself. More than that, they gave a new generation of activists a sense of power and purpose. Counterprotesters appeared. One of these, a 17-year-old named Kyle Rittenhouse, would kill two protesters, Anthony Huber, 29, and Joseph Rosenbaum, 36.

Would the protests have been so well-attended or had the same edge if Americans hadn't been locked down and stressed?

Left unresolved was the country's treatment of immigrants. For roughly two years after Joe Biden became president, Covid-19 continued to be used as a pretext for turning away refugees and asylum-seekers.

And when the election came and Biden was elected, Donald J. Trump did everything he could to stage a coup d'état, egging on demonstrators who came to Washington, D.C. on January 6, driven by the mistaken belief that Joe Biden was not the genuine winner of the 2020 election.

Fear of death was constant. Was the insurrection a veiled, hysterical attempt to fend off mortality? Historians will debate this in coming decades. All we know now is that the plagues are still with us.

Fear and Loathing in Portlandia

TOM HENDERSON

Tim Snyder ("On Tyranny") made the point that BORTAC and DHS troops in Portland are the most recent example of an authoritarian strategy that has been used successfully for thousands of years. The leader spends lots of energy and money on border-protection troops, because these soldiers operate in a twilight zone of lawlessness, where the job is to keep alien people out of the country at any cost. Once they understand their job, the leader brings them into the interior to quash dissent, because no other troops will have comparable experience with dehumanizing the enemy. Historians have long regarded this last move as the signal that the final transition to authoritarianism has begun. There's no reason to believe that this moment, as unfolding right now in Portland, Seattle, Chicago, is any different. Consider well. We will have to act.

— Ted Mooney, novelist

Congress and the courts must step in. Otherwise, having found his army, Trump is sure to use it again in coming months. Bullying Democratic mayors and governors plays well with his base, whose support was beginning to waver due to Trump's disastrous mishandling of Covid-19.

More chilling, he could deploy his paramilitary forces in Democratic strongholds on Election Day as a means of suppressing voter turnout.

— Elizabeth Goitein, Brennan Center for
Justice's Liberty & National Security Program

BACK IN THE 1990s, MEMBERS OF President George H.W. Bush's administration gave Portland, Oregon, the nickname "Little Beirut" because of the protesters who showed up whenever he hit town. In those days, we joked about the ubiquity of these skateboard anarchists in progressive bastions like Portland and San Francisco, calling them Rent-a-Riot.

Nobody's laughing now.

Portland is ground zero for a sometimes absurd, often frightening face-off between free speech and authoritarianism. In the last several weeks, federal police without badges or insignia have been snatching protesters from the streets and forcing them into unmarked vehicles. So far, as far as anyone knows, all of them have been released without any charges.

Whether the administration is ginning up an American version of secret police, looking for B-roll for Trump campaign ads, or hedging their bets and waiting to see how far they can take this unmarked cop car business simply isn't clear yet.

What does seem clear is that the city that inspired the TV satire *Portlandia*, home of vintage cassette tapes, DIY, organic everything, and stratospheric real estate prices, is a dry run for *something*.

Trying to figure out what's really happening usually lands you with a whole lot of cognitive dissonance. Most days, you could be forgiven for thinking there's a summer festival going on across from the Mark O. Hatfield United States Courthouse in downtown Portland. Visitors can buy "Black Lives Matter" T-shirts and other merch from a tent on the plaza or sample a plate of Portland's increasingly famous Riot Ribs.

If you had been in Portland in 2019 instead of 2020, you might not notice much of a difference at first. A third or so of the people are wearing masks, but that could be chalked up to a particularly vicious allergy season. The courthouse is boarded up and sprayed with graffiti, but there are strip malls in the suburbs that owe the same debt to Jean-Michel Basquiat's rough drafts of history.

At night, though, it's different. This is the arson, vandalism, and violence that America is seeing on social media and the news. The streets around the courthouse are swarming with protesters. Some are sedately middle-aged and middle-class. Others are young and edgy. Some are likely to be *agents provocateurs*.

At night downtown Portland becomes a dark landscape of tear gas, rubber bullets and stun grenades. But what is truly frightening about these protests is the presence of armed men trolling the streets in unmarked rental vans. Some are federal officers: U.S. Border Patrol Special Forces deployed by the Trump administration to quash protests. Others may not be federal officers at all, but mercenary soldiers under contract to the U.S. Department of Homeland Security.

Some are calling them Trump's private army.

The protests started in late May. They weren't particularly violent but there was the odd incident of vandalism, a window broken, garbage bags set on fire. Nothing Portland hadn't seen before, although these actions might have been on a larger scale. In court files, officials charge that protesters caused $50,000 in damage to federal buildings, including tearing down security cameras and breaking glass doors.

The tactics were familiar. But this time, the cause drawing residents to the streets was different. Portland protests have usually been about war or environmental issues, rather than race. Oregon is three-quarters white, a dramatic contrast to neighboring California, where whites make up only 37 percent of the population. And Portland is the whitest of the white: of the 35 U.S. cities with populations over 500,000, Portland has the highest proportion of non-Latino whites; 71 percent, according to census data. The city's affluent progressive vibe and its penchant for eccentricity are known; the history of racial division less so. But that history is the city's invisible undercarriage. As one protester cracked wise to a reporter: "There are more Black Lives Matter signs in Portland than black people." Portland's racial makeup isn't a fluke.

Oregon once had some of the nation's harshest white supremacy laws. As the *New York Times* recently reported, a 19th-century lash law called for whipping any black person found in the state. In the early 20th century, the Oregon legislature was dominated by the Ku Klux Klan.

While Portland has changed, the legacy of racism remains. The average black family's income is half that of white residents. Police shootings are disproportionate to the population. While the city's current liberalism is genuine, structural inequality persists, exacerbated by gentrification.

That divide caused divisions among the protesters themselves. E.D. Mondainé, the president of the Portland NAACP, worries that the predominantly white protests turn outrage to theatrics. The protesters who have garnered the most press coverage are Christopher David, a 53-year-old white Navy veteran dubbed "Captain Portland" after being roughed up by police, and an anonymous white woman known as "Naked Athena" who confronted lines of police wearing nothing but a Covid-19 mask. In a July 23 op-ed in the *Washington Post*, Mondainé said he didn't necessarily see an ally in Naked Athena.

"I see something else, a beneficiary of white privilege dancing vainly on a stage that was originally created to raise up the voices of my oppressed brothers and sisters," he wrote. "In this, she is not alone. As the demonstrations continue every night in Portland, many people with their own agendas are co-opting and distracting attention from what should be our central concern: the Black Lives Matter movement."

Mondainé was equally disparaging about the Wall of Moms, women who nightly lock arms to protect protesters from police and federal agents. "The Wall of Moms...might ease the consciences of white, affluent women who have previously been silent in the face of black oppression, but it's fair to ask: Are they really furthering the cause of justice, or is this another example of white co-optation?"

Other black protesters viewed the white activists as essential to their safety and to the eventual success of the Black Lives Matter movement. Julianne Jackson, a black activist from Salem, Oregon, works with a group of young activists who are bringing the Moms food and other provisions.

"I really didn't even know I had allies," she said. "Speaking out on these issues would have made my life really uncomfortable. People of color are really seeing some hope in their communities. It's also great that racists are being outed left and right."

∿

Despite these divisions, the protests chugged along, becoming the country's longest continuous Black Lives Matter demonstrations. Outside the three or four blocks around the courthouse, the rest of the city went about its business, as much as anyone is doing in these Covid days.

Then, in late June, the unmarked police vehicles arrived. So did the tear gas. And the tough special forces guys, grabbing protesters, pushing them into their vehicles, and holding them without charges. *Politico* reported that 114 federal officers had arrived to protect U.S. government buildings, as part of a mission called "Operation Diligent Valor." Whether valor was required to arrest anarchists, suburban moms, and dads armed with leaf blowers to disperse tear gas and using pool noodles as shields may be questionable, but the officers were undoubtedly diligent.

Over the past few days, there have been 42 arrests. Protesters, and even some bystanders, reported being shoved into unmarked vans by agents who were not wearing badges and who refused to identify which law enforcement agency they worked for. One of them was 29-year-old Mark Pettibone of Portland, who told the *Washington Post* he was pushed into a van on July 22.

"I was terrified," Pettibone told the *Post*. "It seemed like it was out of a horror/sci-fi, like a Philip K. Dick novel. It was like being preyed upon."

Pettibone said he was taken to a holding cell in the federal courthouse and asked if he wanted to waive his Miranda rights. He refused, he told the *Post*, and eventually he was released.

Pettibone's experience is echoed by others, but it's next to impossible to know in such a chaotic environment if everyone has been released.

"People are being literally scooped off the street into unmarked vans, rental cars," Portland mayor Ted Wheeler told CNN on Sunday. "Apparently, they are being denied probable cause, and they're denied due process. They don't even know who's pulling them into the vans."

There are "dozens if not hundreds of federal troops descending upon our city, and what they're doing is they are sharply escalating the situation," the mayor added. "Their presence here is actually leading to more violence and more vandalism."

U.S. Attorney Billy J. Williams of the District of Oregon requested a federal investigation, and Oregon Attorney General Ellen Rosenblum filed a lawsuit in federal court against the U.S. Department of Homeland Security (DHS), U.S. Customs and Border Protection (CBP), U.S. Marshals Service (USMS), and Federal Protective Service, as well as ten law enforcement officers. In the meantime, the administration is reportedly planning to send special forces to more American cities.

∿

Nation magazine correspondent Ken Klippenstein tried to find out exactly who the federal officers are, and how they get the authority to crack down on protesters. An internal memo Klippenstein obtained describes a special task force created by the Department of Homeland Security to implement President Trump's Executive Order on Protecting American Monuments, Memorials, and Statues and Combating Recent Criminal Violence.

Dated July 1, the memo is titled "Public Affairs Guidance: CBP Support to

Protect Federal Facilities and Property" and marked "For Official Use Only." It creates the Protecting American Communities Task Force (PACT), tasked not only to assess civil unrest but also to "surge" resources to protect against it. Overseen by the U.S. Department of Homeland Security, the task force includes the Federal Protective Service, the U.S. Marshal's Special Operations Group, and the Border Patrol Tactical Unit (BORTAC).

It is worth pausing to look at BORTAC, which is unfamiliar to most Americans. The Border Patrol's equivalent to Special Forces, BORTAC operating largely in secret, BORTAC agents are trained for SWAT-style raids on organized gangs smuggling immigrants or drugs across the U.S. border. They have been deployed in Iraq and Afghanistan, as well as Latin American countries, where the U.S. has historically propped up right-wing regimes.

Jenn Budd spent six years working as a senior border patrol agent until 2001 when she became a whistleblower. She calls BORTAC officers the "biggest guys, like the jocks in a football team. They live in tight groups like the Navy Seals, spending their time in military-style training.

"They don't exist within the realm of civilian law enforcement," Budd told *The Guardian* newspaper. "They view people they encounter in the military sense as enemy combatants, meaning they have virtually no rights."

In the *Nation*, Klippenstein reported that a spokesman confirmed that Customs and Border Patrol agents were responsible for Pettibone's arrest, pointing to authority under the Protecting American Communities Task Force memo. He noted that while other federal officers are required to wear insignia identifying their agency, this is not required of agents from the Department of Homeland Security.

But BORTAC officers were not the only special forces on the scene. Investigative reporter Bill Conroy uncovered documents revealing that some of the men in SWAT gear are likely to have been mercenary soldiers. The Department of Homeland Security employs more than 13,000 private military contractors from companies that include Blackwater corporate descendant Triple Canopy. Private contractors are supposed to guard federal buildings, but in Portland, reports surfaced that they were straying beyond their territory.

Portland local Chad Lingley made the connection to authoritarian crackdowns by right-wing regimes in Argentina and Chile, where in the 1980s, thousands of people simply vanished in an act of fascist prestidigitation. With the help of some friends, Lingley mounted billboards on a truck that he's driving around Portland.

"Dear Department of Homeland Security, great job protecting buildings instead of the Constitution," reads one of them. "Enjoy your new life in Argentina."

Lingley wasn't the only one noting the similarity of Trump's crackdown to the tactics used by Latin American dictators. The hundreds of Portland women demonstrating by linking arms to defy law enforcement called themselves The Wall of Moms as a direct tribute to the Mothers of the Plaza del Mayo, silent witnesses who gathered for 29 years in front of Argentina's presidential palace to demand that the government account for their sons and daughters who had been "disappeared" by the Argentine government during the U.S.-backed "Dirty War" of the 1970s.

State-sponsored terrorism by Argentina's military junta was thought to be responsible for 30,000 deaths and decades later, many of its leaders are in prison for crimes against humanity and genocide. Certainly a few unmarked cars and riot cops aren't equivalent. Are they?

∿

If you listen to Donald Trump, you might think that the entire city of Portland was a war zone. On July 20, reaching for a rationale for his administration's unprecedented use of special forces, Trump said that Black Lives Matter protests in Portland have made it "worse than Afghanistan."

In reality, day-to-day life in Portland remains largely unchanged. "Portland looks and feels like any other American city in July 2020, right down to the crowds of unmasked idiots stuffing into downtown bars every night," wrote Daniel Pickens-Jones, who has been posting dispatches on Facebook. "Until Friday, July 17, the protests drew about 100 nightly die-hards to the Justice Center, with occasional marches and rallies on or from the east side. People are now back out on the streets because of the escalation of violence from the state: the secret police kidnappings, the introduction of new battlefield weapons."

As Pickens-Jones noted, until Trump sent his tactical units to Portland, concerns over coronavirus—Oregon averages at least 250 new cases per day—had led to many protesters forsaking downtown for lockdown. Now there are between one and two thousand people on the streets every night. Increasingly, there is a sense that they are protesting more than the loss of black lives.

The real question is whether the Trump administration can send in armed police to more cities over the protest of Democratic mayors and governors.

The president already has announced plans for similar actions in Chicago and Albuquerque ("Operation Legend") using ATF, DEA, and FBI agents, and is sending Border Patrol agents to Seattle. Governor Andrew Cuomo blasted Trump for threatening to send his tactical forces to New York.

What do these places have in common? They vote blue. The fear among elected officials is the prospect of federal strike forces interfering with the November election.

"This is a democracy, not a dictatorship," said Oregon governor Kate Brown. "We cannot have secret police abducting people in unmarked vehicles. I can't believe I have to say that to the president of the United States."

"Here in America, you don't send secret forces into the street," said Sen. Jeff Merkley, an Oregon Democrat.

But apparently in Donald Trump's America, you do.

"It doesn't take a legal expert to know that what's happening in Portland, Oregon is an abuse of power," wrote Elizabeth Goitein, senior director at the nonpartisan Brennan Center in *Just Security*. "When unidentified federal forces dressed as soldiers pull people off the streets into unmarked vans, something is gravely wrong...this abuse is part of an ongoing effort by the administration to get around 'posse comitatus': the principle that the president cannot use the military as a domestic police force. The implications for the rule of law—and potentially for the 2020 election—are staggering.

While the Department of Homeland Security personnel deployed in Portland are not members of the armed forces, Goitein wrote, "the evidence is mounting that they are not there to enforce the law. Instead, they are acting as a paramilitary wing to assist the president in his longstanding goal to (in his words) 'take over' U.S. cities run by Democrats."

"More than racial equality hangs in the balance now," said retired journalist Anne Abercrombie. "This has become a fight over the future over the United States itself."

On the Rachel Maddow show, Yale historian Timothy Snyder counseled that peaceful protests are essential to fending off America's slide into authoritarianism. "If you're not protesting now, this would be a good time to start," said Snyder, author of *On Tyranny*.

But in a country where everyone is getting angrier all the time, can any protest remain nonviolent? While sober folks like 52-year-old history professor Maureen Healy have been among those injured by rubber bullets, the Youth

Liberation Front are doing their bit to raise the stakes on the protest side. The Youth Liberation Front is the most recent incarnation of a harder-edged activism that's popped up in the Northwest before. About ten years ago, the radical environmentalists of the Earth Liberation Front were thought to be responsible for blowing up mink farms and a resort in endangered species habitat. The 1999 World Trade Organization meeting in Seattle was disrupted by "black bloc" vandalism. Taking these protests into account, Portland's Black Lives Matter protests are relatively tame. The self-styled radicals don't seem all that different from the Wall of Moms and the pool-noodle-toting dads, just a little rowdier.

"We are a bunch of teenagers armed with ADHD (attention deficit hyper-activity disorder) and yerba mate — we can take a 5 a.m. raid and be back on our feet a few hours later ... we'll be back again and again until every prison is reduced to ashes and every wall to rubble," read one of the Youth Liberation tweets.

Yet in a city where a deep history of racism has been supplanted by an equally fierce commitment to making a better world, Mayor Ted Wheeler knows that protesters, whether moms and dads or yerba maté-fueled teenagers, are unlikely to blink first.

"President Trump needs to focus on coronavirus and get his troops out of the city," Wheeler said. "My biggest fear is that somebody's going to die. I want them to leave. This is going to come to a city near you if we don't stop it."

CHAIRMAN OF THE JOINT CHIEFS OF STAFF

WASHINGTON, DC 20318-9999

2 June 2020

MEMORANDUM FOR CHIEF OF STAFF OF THE ARMY
COMMANDANT OF THE MARINE CORPS
CHIEF OF NAVAL OPERATIONS
CHIEF OF STAFF OF THE AIR FORCE
CHIEF OF THE NATIONAL GUARD BUREAU
COMMANDANT OF THE COAST GUARD
CHIEF OF SPACE OPERATIONS
COMMANDERS OF THE COMBATANT COMMANDS

SUBJECT: Message to the Joint Force

1. Every member of the U.S. military swears an oath to support and defend the Constitution and the values embedded within it. This document is founded on the essential principle that all men and women are born free and equal, and should be treated with respect and dignity. It also gives Americans the right to freedom of speech and peaceful assembly. We in uniform – all branches, all components, and all ranks – remain committed to our national values and principles embedded in the Constitution.

2. During this current crisis, the National Guard is operating under the authority of state governors to protect lives and property, preserve peace, and ensure public safety.

3. As members of the Joint Force – comprised of all races, colors, and creeds – you embody the ideals of our Constitution. Please remind all of our troops and leaders that we will uphold the values of our nation, and operate consistent with national laws and our own high standards of conduct at all times.

We all committed our lives to the idea that is America — we will stay true to that oath and the American People.

MARK A. MILLEY
General, U.S. Army

cc:
Secretary of Defense
Deputy Secretary of Defense
Vice Chairman of the Joint Chiefs of Staff
Director, Joint Staff

Mayday, Mayday!

GREGORY MCNAMEE

ON MAY 1, 1971, I EXCUSED MYSELF—without official leave—from my parents' home in a Northern Virginia suburb 15 miles southwest of Washington, D.C., hopped on my bicycle, and got myself downtown to Lafayette Park. Behind the White House, the park was the epicenter, on that day, of a demonstration against the war in Vietnam and, more broadly, the Nixon administration.

I was barely 14: pimply, hormonal, and excited to be there, knowing that it could bring on trouble at home. My father was a colonel stationed at the Pentagon and this was the height of a movement against a war in which he had fought and been wounded as an Army Ranger in 1963, two years before the war became an American war.

Getting my bike through the crowd was harder than I expected: roughly half a million people were attempting to occupy the same space at the same time, their bodies definitely in motion and not at rest. Laid-back Woodstock vibes were not the order of that day: Mayday 1971, with its echo of distress calls for airplanes about to crash, was more like it.

The mood was serious, and seriously pissed-off. The crowd brandished militant signs and placards: the blue, red, and yellow banners of the National Liberation Front; the red flags of the Maoists; and the black flags of the anarchists. Many of the demonstrators wore steel combat helmets and fatigues bearing campaign ribbons and medals, designating them as members of Vietnam Veterans Against the War. Some had clamped on football helmets to protect themselves from police batons. After the assassinations of Martin Luther King Jr. and Bobby Kennedy in the spring and summer of 1968, there had been demonstrations in more than 100 U.S. cities. More than a few turned into riots. Nobody had forgotten the culmination of that summer of protest: the Democratic National Convention in Chicago.

Then as now, the Democratic Party was bitterly divided between moderates and progressives. The establishment candidate was Hubert Humphrey, a Minnesota liberal tainted by serving as Lyndon Johnson's vice president as the Vietnam War dragged on, vying with progressive antiwar candidate, poet and college professor Eugene McCarthy. These two had become front-runners for the party's presidential nomination only by default. Bobby Kennedy had been a unifying figure, profoundly so, but after he was assassinated, party divisions became irreconcilable.

Inside the Chicago convention hall, the party delegates chose Hubert Humphrey, flouting the majority of rank-and-file Democrats, 80 percent of whom supported antiwar candidates. Out on the streets, Mayor Richard Daley of Chicago, the ultimate machine politician, was doing exactly what Donald Trump is telling mayors and governors to do now: Daley's cops were out to "dominate" protesters.

With Chicago cops wielding nightsticks and tear gas, the city streets turned into a melee: four days and nights of violence, 668 people arrested, hundreds of demonstrators and police officers injured. Great books were written about those violent days, including novelist Norman Mailer's *Miami and the Siege of Chicago,* which, arguably, reinvented journalism into a hybrid of fiction and fact. Tom Hayden, a cofounder of Students for a Democratic Society and one of the protest organizers, would later become an influential state legislator in California and marry Jane Fonda. The charismatic Abbie Hoffman of the Yippies, an anarchist guerrilla theater group, became a culture hero for shocking the bourgeoisie with a combination of hippie freedom, Dada aesthetics, and Borscht Belt schtick.

And Richard Nixon was elected president. While most Americans wanted to stop the war, it turned out that they didn't want violence on the streets. Historians later said that Richard Nixon won the election in Chicago.

And we all know how that went.

So now it's July 4, 2020. Everything we thought we knew turns out to be wrong. Up is down, and down is up, to quote George Orwell. Instead of crushing us, it turns out that the military might save us. But we're not sure about that, just as we can't be sure of anything, in this new era of United States history.

As the son and grandson of West Point graduates, I look to the military for signs and portents of what is happening and what is to come.

∿

The high-stakes conflict began on June 1. Black Lives Matter protesters had been thronging the streets outside the White House, just south of Lafayette Square, the destination of my illicit bike ride 49 years earlier. Although the demonstrations were nonviolent, Trump had retreated to the White House bunker on May 29. But when reports of his descent surfaced he became irate at the idea that his courage was being questioned. To seize control of the narrative, Trump and his staff planned a photo op on the steps of the historic St. John's Episcopal Church, called "the president's church" across the street from the White House. But first, the protesters had to be cleared from the area surrounding the church.

U.S. Attorney General Bill Barr called in reinforcements: the Secret Service; the U.S. Park Police; the National Guard; the Capitol Police; the Bureau of Alcohol, Tobacco, Firearms, and Explosives; the Marshals Service; the Bureau of Prisons, Customs and Border Protection; and Immigration and Customs Enforcement (ICE)—along with paramilitary forces whose members refused to wear unit badges or show identification, in violation of international law. The 82nd Airborne was "in readiness," awaiting deployment against protesters.

Following what were reportedly heated conversations with the president, Governors Andrew Cuomo of New York and Jeremy Northam of Virginia refused to send their states' national guards, alarmed at the military force being massed. Republican governors in Tennessee, South Carolina, Utah, and West Virginia were more amenable, according to the *New York Times*. Reporters took note of the event as a constitutional crisis:

"Along with the troops, National Guard units from other states brought weapons and ammunition. Tens of thousands of rifle and pistol rounds were stored in the D.C. Armory and partitioned in pallets, labeled by their state of origin, to be used on American citizens in case of emergency."

The governors weren't the only people alarmed by the administration's attempt to use the military to tamp down dissent among American citizens. The *Times* reported that General Mark Milley, chair of the Joint Chiefs of Staff, was activating the National Guard in numbers because he didn't want the 82nd Airborne called in to quell the demonstrations. Milley knew that when a government turns soldiers on its own people, a line has been crossed toward tyranny.

Concerns filtered down the chain of command. Ryan McCarthy, who had served in the Army's elite 75th Ranger Regiment during the war in Afghanistan, pored over maps and strategized with National Guard and federal officials at a command post set up at the FBI's Washington field office in the city's Chinatown district. As the *Times* reported: "This micromanagement was a last-ditch attempt to keep active-duty troops outside the city."

The National Guard units and federal police dispersed demonstrators outside St. John's Episcopal Church. They fired flash bang grenades and tear gas at protesters, police shoving the demonstrators off the patio of the church and onto the ground.

The National Guardsmen later said that they were uncomfortable with what they were ordered to do that day. They were accustomed to being called in to help citizens after natural disasters. This was different, First Lt. Malik Jenkins-Bey, 42, acting commander of the 273rd Military Police Company, told the *Times*. "Typically, as the D.C. National Guard, we are viewed as the heroes. It's a very tough conversation to have when a soldier turns to me and they're saying, 'Hey sir, you know my cousin was up there yelling at me, that was my neighbor, my best friend from high school.'"

Attorney General Bill Barr, among others, continued to maneuver to keep the 82nd Airborne at a distance from the city, and in the end, they were not deployed. But Trump got his photo opportunity. Followed by TV cameras, he brandished a Bible in front of St. John's, accompanied by General Mark Milley, Chairman of the Joint Chiefs of Staff, who was dressed in combat fatigues.

The following day, Milley took the unprecedented step of circulating a memo to the military leadership—the Joint Chiefs and senior officers—that apparently was leaked to conservative commentator and never-Trumper Bill Kristol. The message was clear, if coded: he reminded the recipients that their duty was to uphold the U.S. Constitution, and that duty categorically extended to the First Amendment: the right to free speech. He added that members of the armed services were to obey only lawful orders—the clear implication being that unlawful orders might soon be issued by the White House.

That same day, June 2, retired Admiral Mike Mullen, chairman of the Joint Chiefs before Milley, published a scathing essay in *The Atlantic*, saying that he had been "sickened" by the events in Lafayette Square.

On June 3, Kristol tweeted the leaked memo with this understated comment: "This memo from Gen. Milley is pretty interesting—I'd even say startling." Echoing Mullen's words, General Jim Mattis, who had served as Trump's Secretary of Defense, issued a written statement to the *Atlantic* accusing Trump and his staff of violating the Constitution. Most outlets ran a quote that talked about unity and division, but this one was the truly significant statement:

"When I joined the military, some 50 years ago," Mattis wrote, "I swore an oath to support and defend the Constitution. Never did I dream that troops taking that same oath would be ordered under any circumstance to violate the Constitutional rights of their fellow citizens—much less to provide a bizarre photo op for the elected commander-in-chief, with military leadership standing alongside."

Defense Secretary Mike Esper quickly held a press conference to announce he would not invoke the Insurrection Act, the one lever through which Trump could turn the nation's military against the people.

The most significant move came a week later. On June 11, in a commencement address to the West Point graduating class, General Milley apologized for his role in the Trump photo op. He did it on video, soberly, and, reportedly, after much soul-searching, calling it "a mistake."

As I recalled my youthful bike ride, and the events of those days, I thought about a line in Milley's memo: "During this current crisis, the National Guard is operating under the authority of state governors to protect lives and property, preserve peace, and ensure public safety."

This reminder of the National Guard's limited mission was no afterthought. Even if the military refuses to obey an order from the Commander in Chief, the country has 450,000 National Guard soldiers. These could be in play, particularly in states with Republican governors, as they were on June 1.

Mark Milley is about my age, and like every adolescent who came to consciousness in the 1970s, I've no doubt he remembers the Crosby, Stills, Nash & Young song "Ohio" and its refrain: *Four dead in Ohio.* One of David Crosby's last appearances before his death was playing a blistering rendition of that song with Jason Isbell and the 400 Unit in 2022. Crosby and Isbell clearly believed it was time we were reminded of that song, or learned about it, along with the iconic photo of Mary Ann Vecchio screaming over the corpse of one of 13 unarmed student antiwar demonstrators wounded or killed by National Guard shooters.

It can happen here. It almost did on June 1, 2020.

While Milley and others averted a constitutional crisis, their actions may only have gained a reprieve. "I don't think we have to worry about the military following illegal orders from Trump," wrote Lucian Truscott IV, like me, the son and grandson of West Point graduates, in *Salon.* "At least for now," Truscott added, "they're on our side."

Note the phrase "at least for now." As the brass well knows, Trump tried to extend his political hold over the military, which has traditionally tried to stay well apart from the partisan fray. Trump's chief lieutenant in this effort was a 30-year-old former college quarterback with no previous political experience, John McEntee, who demanded loyalty to the administration as a condition of federal employment—and who tried to exert authority over staffing decisions at the Department of Defense.

There is a parallel, again, to May Day 1971. As protests mounted, Richard Nixon stopped short of invoking the Insurrection Act. But not before floating the idea to staffers, who discouraged him from crossing that threshold.

∿

On May Day 1971, there were helicopters in the air and armored personnel carriers—and, over by the Pentagon, where my father was at work, tanks—on the streets. I had to maneuver my bike through what looked like a battlefield on my way to Lafayette Park.

Just as I arrived, the tear gas began to fly. Columns of National Guard troops and flak-jacketed federal marshals marched against the crowd. Some demonstrators stood their ground. Some scattered. Some started to run, then turned back bravely and threw the tear gas canisters back at the troops.

Within moments I was leaning up against a building on Sixteenth Street, wheezing and puking. The gas cloud lifted, and a trio of Guardsmen came through the chemical mist. Their sergeant took a look at my face, pointed to an alley across the way, and said, "Ride your bike over there, get off the street, and get out of here. Just go home, kid."

It was sound advice, for it could have been an awful scene.

By the next year, as Lawrence Roberts writes in his book *Mayday 1971*, the police and National Guard were ready for war. So were the more radical elements of the New Left, who by that time outnumbered the moderates. The Weather Underground, committed to overthrowing the government, came very close to bombing the Capitol building.

In a scene that was uncharacteristically intimate, yet emblematic of that strange time, Richard Nixon, never comfortable around people to whom he couldn't issue orders, ventured out of the White House in the predawn hours a few days after Kent State. He wandered over to the Lincoln Memorial, where he encountered a surprised group of antiwar protesters. Nixon told them that he wanted the war to end just as much as they did.

He added that he hoped their opposition to the war would not turn them against their country, adding, "I know that probably most of you think I'm an SOB. But I want you to know that I understand just how you feel." He then switched the topic to college football before being swept away by Secret Service agents.

A few weeks later Nixon, continuing his oddly human turn, ordered a commission to investigate the violence at Kent State. But when the commissioners issued a report laying blame on the Guard for badly handling a peaceful protest, Nixon snapped back to form and responded with a 3,600-word rebuttal calling the student demonstrators "anarchists and bums."

Meanwhile, Henry Kissinger, the chief architect of Nixon's foreign policy, was musing aloud in the White House that maybe the thing to do was leave Vietnam, signing an agreement that would require the North Vietnamese to wait for "a decent interval," as he put it, before taking control of South Vietnam, whose government was certain to collapse. Kissinger was not primarily concerned with the rightness or wrongness of the war: instead he was worried about Nixon's reelection chances in 1972. In retrospect, Kissinger's *realpolitik* seems quaint compared to Donald Trump's blatant shakedowns. Kissinger, at least, had read the Constitution. Yet, for reasons that remain obscure, Nixon brushed Kissinger's suggestion aside. The war went on, and so did the demonstrations.

The largest protest in American history was the one that took place on that first day of May in 1971. It could have been terrible, as I say. That it did not turn out that way arose from a certain restraint on the part of the National Guard, whose soldiers fired tear gas but held back on cracking heads, unlike Richard Daley's cops in Chicago.

Of the infamous cop riot in Mayor Daley's fiefdom, Norman Mailer wrote in *Miami and the Siege of Chicago,* "The police attacked with tear gas, with mace, and with clubs, they attacked like a chain saw cutting into wood, the teeth of the saw the edge of their clubs, they attacked like a scythe through grass, lines of twenty and thirty policemen striking out in an arc, their clubs beating, demonstrators fleeing."

Doubtless the D.C. police would not have minded a shot at emulating their Chicago counterparts on May Day 1971, but they were kept from doing so by a chief of police, Jerry Wilson, who counseled restraint instead of violence.

He heroically resisted Attorney General John Mitchell's attempt to federalize the force after Nixon ordered, "Arrest the whole damn lot."

The police strategy was mass arrests. They commandeered a practice field alongside Robert F. Kennedy Stadium a couple of miles east of the Capitol (which didn't blow up, the Weather Underground having abandoned that project). When advised of the heavy legal caseload that would follow, the chief judge of the District's Superior Court warned Wilson that those mass arrests would be "a test of our commitment to the rule of law." Added Judge Harold H. Greene, with Solomonic wisdom, "Whenever American institutions have provided a hysterical response to an emergency situation, we have come later to regret it."

The police and, even more vigorously, the National Guard proceeded to arrest more than 12,600 demonstrators. It was the largest mass arrest in U.S. history, a record that has yet to be broken. The legal basis for the arrests was shaky: the next day, May 2, the Nixon administration revoked the demonstrators' permit—yes, someone had applied for a permit—to be on the National Mall, allowing charges of trespassing to be filed.

In all but about 80 cases, however, demonstrators were held—either behind the chain link fence at RFK, or in the courtyard of the city jail—for a few hours and then released. Like Donald Trump last month, Richard Nixon had wanted to call out the regular Army against the demonstrators. He ordered Richard Kleindienst, the assistant attorney general, to make it happen. Kleindienst summoned a general and conveyed the president's order.

The general balked, citing the Posse Comitatus Act. Passed in 1878, as white supremacists gained power after the Civil War, the laws were intended to ensure the federal military would not be deployed against U.S. citizens.

This June, the military once again staved off a constitutional crisis, one that threatens to be revisited so long as Trump is in office.

∿

The 1971 May Day demonstrations wound down on Monday, May 3. In later years, I regretted following the sergeant's orders and going home instead of spending a few hours in custody. The American Civil Liberties Union filed a class-action lawsuit for wrongful arrest and violation of the due process clause, resulting in payouts of as much as $12,000 to detainees.

I certainly could have used the money when the checks were written a dozen or so years after the fact. On the other hand, I had already been spending the bulk of my adolescence to date on restriction, and if I'd gotten busted that day, my father being a fair but disciplined man, I'd probably still be grounded today.

Where the antiwar movement had a single focus, the struggle today is carried out on many fronts: antifascist, antiracist, anticapitalist, pro-civil rights for one and all, the list goes on, all carried out by a broad constituency that incorporates every age bracket, every ethnicity, and every social class.

There is transformative, even revolutionary power in what we're seeing on the streets. And while there are many lessons to be taken from the past, our eyes need to be resolutely fixed on the future. Because it is not, in any way, assured.

Trump's Hidden Nation

MIKAL GILMORE

I'VE BEEN READING KARL OVE KNAUSGAARD'S six-volume, 3,600-page autobiographical novel, *My Struggle*. I recently finished the middle portion of *Book 6: The End*, a rambling 400-page essay about Adolf Hitler and *Mein Kampf* that is unlike any other part of Knausgaard's massive endeavor.

This excerpt is longer than any other passages I've quoted by any other writer (except Ross Macdonald, arguably more entertaining). I feel a little bad about that, but the points Knausgaard makes here shouldn't be missed—especially right now.

> Hitler expressed what the average German thought but declined to say, and he did so compellingly and with such conviction as to make it legitimate, and the more people who followed him in that direction, realizing that what one thought in one's own mind yet was perhaps wary of expressing could indeed be expressed, the more legitimate it became. The opinions Hitler expressed were clear and unambiguous, he concealed nothing, and they could easily have been repudiated, he and his party having no power on their own, such power being granted by those who listened to them and who in doing so heard themselves, their own voice of reason, the voice that said this is the lay of the land. That nothing suppressed that voice, those hitherto quiet thoughts, and that the structures to reject such baseness had ceased to operate became Germany's tragedy.
>
> *This is the lay of the land,* said Hitler, *this is the lay of the land,* said the people and cheered Hitler, and in doing so they cheered themselves and their own. Hitler gave self-righteousness a voice, we could say, but only if we are above that voice, only if our taste is superior, our judgment superior, only then is it the voice of self-righteousness. If one is a part of it, it is righteous. And who is to say where the boundary lies between righteous and self-righteous?

Knausgaard's commentary about *Mein Kampf* and Hitler was written around 2009. Donald Trump wasn't anything more than a rich, preening clod and an American embarrassment at the time—I doubt the Norwegian writer knew much more about the man than his name. In addition, he doesn't write about America and its history or politics at all in *My Struggle*. Yet when I came across the paragraph above, I was stunned: That "then"—in the 1930s—that Knausgaard elucidates is at least somewhat analogous to our American "now."

I've avoided Hitler-Trump comparisons in the past, because as Karl Ove says, it has become rote over the years to compare authoritarians and despots and terrorists—such as Idi Amin or Osama bin Laden—to Hitler, when in truth he exceeded anything they ever did. He did it because of not just his hatred but also because of how he used the language of propaganda in the most simple but effective ways for mass effect to displace Germany's logic with a malignant emotion that became a passion of identity for its populace.

Knausgaard quotes a couple of paragraphs from *Mein Kampf* that get right to the essence of Hitler's thinking on how to overcome the mind and conscience of a nation and fill it instead with terroristic reasoning, with violence and mass slaughter.

The more I've spent time with this difficult but fascinating portion of Knausgaard's book, the more I've been riveted and knocked on my ass by the correlations between—dare I say it?—Trump and Hitler. Also, reading this at a time when Trump is advocating racism and violence against people who want the knee of oppression off their necks, well, it's been unsettling, to say the least. As Knausgaard wrote, Hitler was so sure of himself when it came to the potency of propaganda that he felt he could afford to reveal his recipe. Hitler referred to propaganda as a weapon, "a frightful one in the hand of an expert."

Knausgaard then quoted those brutally revealing *Mein Kampf* paragraphs I mentioned above, about Hitler's credo of propaganda. I'm not going to reproduce them directly myself—because I'm queasy about quoting anything from *Mein Kampf*—but I'll paraphrase because Hitler's reasoning is central to what I'm after here. Here goes:

Whom should propaganda be addressed to, Hitler asked, and answered: always and exclusively to the masses. The art lies in doing this skillfully and effectively enough that everyone will be convinced that the fact—the claimed fact—is real.

You must aim its effect at the emotions and only to a small degree at the intellect. The more exclusively you consider the emotions of the masses, the more effective a propaganda campaign will be.

Another way of saying this, Hitler proclaimed, is that the art of propaganda depends on understanding the emotions of the masses and using that understanding to win their attention. You have to remember that the intelligence of those masses is small—you need to limit propaganda to a few points and harp on your slogans until every member of the masses understands what you want him or her to understand. If you sacrifice your slogan you will piddle away your effect because the masses can't digest more. Follow a simple line and your propaganda will be psychologically sound. (Here I'll allow myself to quote Hitler briefly, when he declared: "What good fortune for those in power that people do not think.")

I still feel uneasy about Hitler-Trump analogies but there's a similarity between the latter's brute force use of propaganda and Hitler's formulated approach: appealing to the emotions of the masses by heightening prejudice against minorities and the disenfranchised while disregarding reason. The dissimilarities, of course, are important. Hitler gave a lot of thought to his tenets; Trump, probably very little, operating on instinct instead. If this should sound like I'm saying Hitler was smarter than Trump, it's because I am. Others have pointed out that we're fortunate for that, because a smarter Trump would likely be more effective.

Mary Trump has provided a psychological assessment of her uncle in *Too Much and Never Enough*, offering the blueprint for how he has extended his familial dysfunction to the American family. Mary Trump's book is valuable for many reasons, not least in explaining Trump's denial of the pandemic, coupled with his increasing propensity to despotism. These two things merge for disastrous effect.

Trump's what I used to call, when I was speaking during readings about my family years ago, the Bad Dad: His authority is all that matters and the family exists primarily for the sake of keeping his image and inviolability paramount. Transfer that to a nation—which is what Trump tries to do all the time, though he's not smart or conscious enough to know it's what he's doing—and you have something worse than an ideology, because Trump doesn't have one.

We are subjected to a man who believes primarily—even solely—in self, who puts self above everything, and it's simultaneously a dominant and fragile self.

Something like that is what happened between Hitler and Germany; Hitler embodied the nation and the nation identified with him. The leader and the people melded into a mass psychosis. Hitler, though, actually had an ideology and a belief in the lost cause of World War I. Trump has only Trump.

Granted, Donald Trump's racism and misogyny are real. In 2016 that animosity tapped into a subliminal American consciousness that now, in 2020, is no longer dormant or concealed but instead out in the open, proud and loud. But Trump certainly couldn't articulate his racism as Hitler did his anti-Semitism; he inherited his biases and antipathy, whereas Hitler studied and sourced his malice.

This is good for us because in addition to being smarter than Trump, Hitler was much cannier. He calculated and plotted and had a true philosophy of propaganda whereas Trump has only the instinct I mentioned, plus opportunists who do have ideologies and know how to exploit his impulses to realize their own wretched creeds and convictions and hopes.

But there are other important differences between Hitler and Trump. One is the variance of time: It is awful that Trump has as much appeal to a mass as he does, and just as awful that he's determined to bend the laws to match his will and ambition, which are one and the same. But whereas Hitler was able to take over the whole of Germany, Trump has not taken over the whole of America, and he never will.

We see mass demonstrations against him daily, and we read acidic criticism and disrespectful cracks about him nearly every hour. It isn't that these things would not have been tolerated in Nazi Germany—though they wouldn't have been—but worse, Nazi Germany would never have produced anything like that because Hitler's persuasive command of the people was total.

America still has a strong liberal tradition—much of it growing more progressive all the time—and that is a saving grace. This is what it means to be an American: Some of us are pushovers but more are not, and those who are not have no appetite for, and increasingly little tolerance of, state violence of the sort in Nazi Germany. If push comes to shove, we will of course shove back forcefully. So Trump is no Hitler, though it's not for want of trying. And Americans—as a national body—will not adopt a fascist mind, no matter how much Trump grows steadily in that direction. In part, we have the law, but also better angels. If they need to be fierce, they will be, but they are not hate-filled, murderous angels.

Hitler could cause a nation to fuse with his mix of psychology and politics into a fascist regime based on the ideology of German nationalism. America doesn't work that way, not in any totality. That leads me to believe it can't actually happen here.

Our guiding myth is not Germany's. No matter how fucked up we can be and how guilty we are, enough of us still have the democratic dream instilled in us, along with the founding revolutionary ideal in our bones, and so we will resist and offset this time of ignominy. But it won't be easy. We are in the middle of a plague (two actually, if you count the presidency) and Trump has abnegated any effective remedy.

That may—and should—cost him his reelection, but in the meantime, his toxic influence has inspired enough of his followers to scorn and flout precautions against illness and possibly death. The question becomes: Is there a way out of this? Well, not for everybody.

There are maddening weeks and seasons ahead, and I'm afraid that countless deaths will attend those seasons, because Trump's endmost instinct is fatality. What's the good of lurching his way into all that power if he can't use it for power's ultimate temptation: to decide when and how to end people's lives?

Which is to say, Trump still has his dreams and we see him reach for them every day. Accordingly, one last passage from Knausgaard's *My Struggle*:

> Nazi Germany was the absolute state. It was the state its people could die for. Watching Riefenstahl's film of the rallies in Nuremberg [*Triumph of the Will*], its depiction of a people almost paradisiac in its unambiguousness, converged upon the same thing, immersed in the symbols, the callings from the deepest pith of human life, that which has to do with birth and death, and with homeland and belonging, one finds it splendid and unbearable at the same time, though increasingly unbearable the more one watches, at least this was how I felt when I watched it one night this spring, and I wondered for a long time where that sense of the unbearable came from, the unease that accompanied these images of the German paradise, with its torches in the darkness, the intactness of its medieval city, its cheering crowds, its sun, and its banners, whether it was something I imposed upon them, knowing how this paradise arose, what it would become and

at what cost, and what happened to it, but I came to the conclusion that this was not the reason, that it came not from what was in me, the knowledge I had of what lay behind the images of those days, but from something in the images themselves, the sense being that the world they displayed was an unbearable world. Not that it was a false world, because this was obvious, its every image meticulously created from scratch for that particular occasion, it was more that this false world, one of the few pure utopias to be established in the last century, in which everything was exactly the way it was supposed to be, was unbearable in itself....

In the Third Reich the voice of human conscience did not say it is wrong to kill, it said it is wrong not to kill, as Hannah Arendt so precisely observes. This was made possible by a shift in the language, displayed in its purest form in *Mein Kampf*, which contains no "you," only an "I," and a "we," which is what makes it possible to turn "they" into "it." In "you" was decency. In "it" was evil. But it was "we" who carried it out.

We will likely never have a unified "we," not altogether for the better and not altogether for the worse. We have learned too many hard truths about ourselves these last few years. But we will never be Trump's nation in the way Germany was Hitler's nation. We will fight to be a better people, and we will fight to determine what a better people is. It will be the fight of our lives.

Who the Fuck Are the Boogaloos?

BLANCHE MCCRARY BOYD

WHY DON'T YOU WRITE BOOKS PEOPLE WILL WANT TO READ, my mother once asked. She's dead now, but she would have hated my final novel, *Tomb of the Unknown Racist.* The narrator, Ellen Burns, is an ex-radical lesbian feminist not unlike myself, just braver and more ornery. Ellen embarks on a quest to find and confront her long-lost brother Royce, an iconic, brilliant figure still lionized by white terrorists. Royce Burns is supposed to be dead, but it's turns out he may be alive and planning renewed destructions. She also tries to save his daughter, Ruby, whose mixed-race children have been reported kidnapped.

Okay, so that's not a cheerful book. In tracking her brother, Ellen uncovers links between the Silent Brotherhood, the white supremacist revolutionary group he had been mixed up with, reportedly destroyed by the FBI in 1984, and Timothy McVeigh, the terrorist who blew up the federal building in Oklahoma City 11 years later. Ellen also discovers the growing presence of vigilantes and organized militias and uncovers evidence that white supremacists might still be operating within our government at all levels.

Tomb of the Unknown Racist may be set 20 years ago, but its warning is raw and painful. My mother had suggested I should write more like Danielle Steele—*Her novels are so lovely!*—but I suspected I was more like Cassandra, given the gift of seeing the future along with the curse of not being believed.

After the pandemic forced us all indoors, I retreated into a peaceful silence, enjoying the lovely presence of my children sent home from college, watching *Killing Eve* with my wife, and reading novels by the Canadian mystery writer Louise Penny. Hillary Clinton said that after she lost the election, she'd been comforted by the novels of Louise Penny, and I thought I had earned some comfort.

Now we have all witnessed the videotapes of a black man named George Floyd being carefully and slowly murdered by four white policemen who seem to be enjoying themselves. Continuing demonstrations and riots here and around the world are a result. Violence is being deliberately exacerbated by the latest incarnation of white extremists, the Boogaloos, so I am sounding the alarm again. Because I get it about the Boogaloos, by which I mean, I know where their beliefs originate.

I grew up in the Deep South in the 1950s, my environment so shuttered and provincial that all I knew about Eleanor Roosevelt was a couple of dirty jokes. I thought Strom Thurmond was a hero and wrote him a fan letter when I was 14. Of course, that was also the year I wrote a letter of consolation to Elizabeth Taylor, upon the death of one of her husbands.

It's hard enough to grow up, especially without context or accurate historical information. I believed Duke was in the north because it was in North Carolina, and, until I got to college, had never met anyone as liberal as a Democrat. I thought Democrats breathtakingly daring because I understood the dangers that had undergirded my upbringing.

I left South Carolina as if it was a burning building, assuming I could somehow escape the dreadful impacts of racism, but it was everywhere I lived: Boston, New York, Washington, and California. I moved back home at 33 to write a nonfiction book called *The Redneck Way of Knowledge*, in which I tried to explore my legacies. My mother remarked, *We learned a lot while you were gone, didn't we.* She meant I had come to understand that white supremacists, conscious or unconscious, were the result of our history of slavery, and they were not an exclusively Southern problem.

The Boogaloos want civil war. Most believe race war is essential, and they want it as soon as possible. Their tactics are deliberately 'accelerationist,' their goal the 'survival' of the white race. They are organized loosely through the Internet, through sources like 4chan, Reddit, and Twitter, and many espouse the apocalyptic predictions of the unidentified figure known as Vox, who may or may not be a real person.

Boogaloos show up at anti-racist events like the one in Charlottesville and recognize each other by their outfits, Hawaiian shirts combined with combat clothes (don't ask), by hand signals, and by "III%" tattoos. Three Percenters believe their small numbers will not prevent their goals because they believe (wrongly) that only 3 percent of American settlers opposed British rule. They may also communicate in ways we don't yet know about.

Online, some Boogaloos allude to *dotr*, 'day of the rope,' referencing *The Turner Diaries*, a novel that recounts a white revolution in which large-scale hangings eliminate all remaining people of color, Jews, and queers. This novel provides quite a popular blueprint among white extremists and has sold over a million copies. One reader was Timothy McVeigh. When he was arrested for the largest incident of domestic terrorism in U.S. history, blowing up the Alfred P. Murrah Federal Building, killing 168, including 19 children in a daycare center, he had with him the pages from that novel containing instructions about how to build a fertilizer bomb like the one he used.

Tomb of the Unknown Racist came out two years ago, but the story concludes in the year 2000, when, according to the Southern Poverty Law Center, there were already more than 100 armed white militias in this country. Now the SPLC estimates that number to be higher than 500. These white 'patriots' have accumulated a large array of lethal weapons. A man wearing a grenade launcher recently went into a Subway and casually ordered a sandwich.

If some of these folks believe race war is inevitable, maybe others simply fear it will happen and want to be prepared. Some might just be a bunch of good ole boys hanging around in the woods playing with their AK-47s. These guns, I am told, are great fun to shoot.

Their decentralization via the Internet makes them harder to track; that is, until they attack. This week three men characterized by authorities as "self-identified" with the Boogaloo movement were arrested making Molotov cocktails they planned to use at a Black Lives Matter demonstration in Las Vegas. All three had served in the military. And false tweets promoting violence purporting to be from Antifa, the left-wing anti-fascist movement, have now been exposed as the work of Boogaloos.

White supremacists and sympathizers are scattered within law enforcement. After a young man named Dylann Roof sat praying with black worshippers in a Charleston church before shooting them in 2015, the white policemen who arrested him took him to Burger King on the way to jail because he was hungry.

Supremacists with badges may or may not be organized, but their presence is provable: The investigative reporting project called REVEAL has confirmed hundreds of law enforcement officers belonging to racist, anti-Islamic, anti-immigrant, and pro-Confederacy groups online. The actual number is almost certainly larger. Sometimes, there's no attempt at obfuscation. A white policeman was caught on video during one of the New York demonstrations giving a white power hand signal and laughing.

To be fair, police officers in many cities have begun to kneel, à la Colin

Kaepernick, in support of the demonstrators, or fist-bump, or pray, or even link arms and march. But the racial fault lines being exposed within our police forces make our civil situation even more volatile. It's probably worth mentioning that many small police departments now have armored vehicles 'donated' to them as military surplus. And of course, we have a president whose political success is built on anger and resentment. He retweets white extremist postings that serve as 'dog whistles.' MAGA devotees might not hear them, but the dogs of war do.

Trump conflates patriotism and nationalism into his promotion of white supremacy, which is only one of the reasons he is so dangerous. We need to understand the fanaticism that can make some of these men willing to die for what they believe in. They heard that 'give me liberty or give me death' line when they were in grammar school and believe they are going to restore the white foundations of our country. The Boogaloos and other terrorists view their cause as a fight for survival.

Timothy McVeigh was the prototype. A Gulf War veteran, McVeigh saw himself as a freedom fighter, a soldier, and he rejected the label of terrorist. He asked to be publicly executed in order to inspire followers, a request that was denied.

In *Tomb of the Unknown Racist* Ellen's brother is an acquaintance of Robert Matthews, the founder of the Silent Brotherhood. Matthews chose to die inside a building the FBI set on fire rather than surrender. Here is the point: these men may be horrific, but they were not cowards, any more than were the pilots who flew kamikaze jetliners into the World Trade Center and the Pentagon. We need to recognize the level of violence our homegrown white extremists can inflict, and the extent of their commitment.

Remember that anthrax that could not be tracked to a source? Cultivating anthrax, a bacteria found in cattle, is simple enough; turning it into a weapon is something else entirely. Not all white supremacists are idiots. That's why Ellen's brother is portrayed as brilliant and messianic, an admirer of Stalin who thinks survival of the fittest in America means white revolution by any means.

Many people think this surge of supremacists in our midst is new. It's not; it just became more visible with Trump's election in 2016. When Trump said he could shoot someone in the street without losing his base of support, he shocked many of us who believe in the values of democracy, but he was absolutely right. The violence he sells is an essential part of his brand, while his own lack of anything resembling physical courage gets oddly dismissed. Trump knows that some of his followers are itching for an excuse to launch into slaughter.

The Boogaloos and accelerationists and all other white supremacist terrorists are the direct inheritors of the Ku Klux Klan. If you have somehow managed not to know what the Klan is, this guerrilla group rose during the Reconstruction Era, after the Civil War ended. Their members wore white robes and hoods, like ghosts of terror, as they burned giant crosses and lynched countless numbers of black men and women and even children across our country, especially in the Deep South, where the population of freed slaves was largest.

Cross-burning, this assertion of Christian righteousness, may seem an inexplicable leap away from the white secularist founders of this country. Membership in the Masons was about as wild as those guys could get, and it's why we have Masonic symbols like that eye and pyramid on the backs of our dollar bills. There is absolutely no talk of God in our founding documents, but, in order to get a buy-in from Southerners about declaring independence from Great Britain, the founders had to justify the country's economic dependence on slavery. They did so by supporting the idea that African men, women, and children were not entirely human.

Tortuous deliberations led to their infamous Three-Fifths Compromise, which determined that each slave was the equivalent of 3/5 of one white person. Michelle Obama, told in high school 'you're not Princeton material,' has pointed out that slave labor actually built the White House. And Harvard historian Jill Lepore, in her astounding history of our country, *These Truths*, calls attention to the fact that George Washington's false teeth included some that he had removed from his own slaves' mouths.

White supremacy got mixed up with Christianity during the Protestant revivalism that arose in the 1800s, as our rapidly growing nation continued to try to solve the contradiction inherent in a country built upon the premise of 'life, liberty, and the pursuit of happiness' while classifying huge numbers of people as beasts, as property that could be bred and sold or worked to death. Economic necessity made the original case for slavery in America, but maybe God could help out too, because slaves were in the Bible, weren't they? And God gave Adam dominion over the beasts, didn't he?

By the 1950s the Klan was considered a low-class organization of louts and rednecks, but it did continue to limp along, and, in the fight over separate-but-equal education, its goals were supported by 'respectable' organizations like the White Citizens' Councils and John Birch Societies, working hard to hold the line against recognition of black human rights.

In Harper Lee's first novel, *Go Set a Watchman,* not published until the end of her life, she presented a raw version of the lawyer character named Atticus Finch, who could defend a black man falsely accused of raping a white woman but nevertheless go off to his White Citizens' Council meetings and speak against equality.

It's no surprise that Lee could not sell this book (and literarily it does have flaws), so she next produced *To Kill a Mockingbird* with its dishonest, romanticized version of Atticus Finch as a white savior, a figure that many white American liberals have come to venerate, love, and sentimentalize. It's no wonder Harper Lee didn't write anything else.

Like Lee and Truman Capote and William Faulkner and Flannery O'Connor and a host of lesser white Southern writers, I grew up immersed in the tragic aftermath of the Civil War. Maybe 'white' and 'colored' bathrooms are gone now and black people can eat in restaurants and sleep in hotels, but we are still living in that aftermath, whether we recognize it or not. Much of my lifetime's work has been an effort to try to unpack some of the damage. A fish doesn't know it's in water, and I have flailed around in this guilty cauldron of white supremacy, this legal and cultural morass of interlockings that often seems impossible to untangle or alter significantly.

"There's something wrong with you," Toni Morrison once said about white people, and "you need to talk to each other about it. Leave me out."

So, white people, let's talk to each other.

We inherit the debts of racism in this country the same way we can, if we should be so fortunate, inherit money and property. We also inherit privileges, no matter what our circumstances. But try telling a white working-class man or woman that they have privileges, and you will often encounter the fury fueling the rise of white supremacy.

We are standing on the bones of black people, I once said to my mother after I first began to understand the culture I'd been raised within. Her face rendered instantly into an expression of anguish as she snarled, *You don't know a thing about my life.*

Eventually I did learn some of it. My mother had been forced to quit school in the eighth grade, a source of shame she hid all her life, and she worked long hours during those teenage years for paltry pay in a tobacco factory, because her father died and it was the Depression and she needed to help her mother survive.

The pains and losses of my mother's early life are not lessened by the fact that, on the floor beneath where she and the other white women and girls worked, black women and girls entered the cigar factory through the 'colored' entrance into the basement to conditions so much worse than my mother's.

But try telling a white man who has worked hard in a manufacturing plant or driven a truck all his life or subsistence farmed or repaired cars or sold shoes in a department store or been a traveling salesman that he has white privilege, and you might get a reaction similar to the one my mother had. Working whites have little to show for the hard labors of their lives, and they are often angry or depressed. Too often alcohol is their cure, and the abuse within families that goes with it. Read Raymond Carver's short stories to get a glimpse of their despair.

So let me make this clear: Many working-class white people do not feel privileged, and they react badly to any suggestion that they have profited from racism. Okay, so maybe they can admit that they don't have to be afraid of the police, and maybe they won't get arrested for driving while black, or thrown into jail for minor or manufactured infractions, and maybe they do get easier breaks for drugs and drunkenness, but it's also true that they get followed around inside stores if they look too poor, and educating their children often remains out of reach.

My father grew up in a house in rural South Carolina without glass in the windows—they'd covered the openings with newspapers to try to keep warm—and his father and brothers supported the family by bootlegging. He graduated from high school without being able to afford any books.

I am proud of my family's working-class origins, of the way my father was ambitious and worked so hard to become a plumber and then started a business and then bought a rickety plantation where my mother could dream about Tara and my father could hunt squirrels to his heart's content, at least until he was killed in a car accident. My parents believed wholeheartedly in the American Dream, in the American promise of renewal and self-invention and in 'pulling yourself up by your bootstraps,' and, luckily, they taught me to believe all that too. If they had not, I might never had found the courage to break free from their racist beliefs and try to reinvent myself, become authentic, dare to be an artist.

But none of that history means that they—and I—haven't been the recipients of many white privileges. For my Irish forebears, America was where you came to escape the famine. It was a land of promise as well as survival. But Africans were brought here in ships as commodities, packed together like fish, and they certainly did not inherit any part of the American Dream.

Instead they endured slavery for generations and then an abrupt emancipation that created a dreadful, confusing mess—read historian Jim Downs' book *Sick from Freedom* to get a sense of it—and they continue even now to persevere through the fleecing of their property by redlining and punitive taxes, the theft of their labor through mass incarceration, and, as we saw so vividly last week with the murder of George Floyd, the very real possibility of being capriciously murdered by law enforcement.

It's easier for me, as a white woman educated at excellent schools, to talk about structural racism and try to figure out ways to take responsibility for it, but the whites attracted to MAGA and to more radical organizations like the Boogaloos, or those who are arming themselves and joining the white militias, absolutely reject my analysis. They feel used, mistreated, co-opted, stained by the relentless encroachments of government into their lives (socialism!), whether by income taxes or social security or even those laws about wearing seat belts.

And now this pandemic? This mass version of house arrest? The loss of their jobs? Wearing masks to go to the fucking store? They are done with it. They cannot imagine that the yokes on their necks are not so different from the yokes holding the people of color below them, that they might have more in common there than they do with rich white people. That's way too threatening.

But these folks, when they're not terrifying, can also be heartbreaking. I once asked a girlfriend from a poor family what she wanted from her life, and it took her many minutes to locate her deepest ambition: "I'd like to own a brick house." She once gave me a gold-plated medallion with my name engraved beside a tiny diamond chip, and she'd even spelled my name wrong. I wore it until the gold came off and the chip fell out, long after she was gone from my life.

No degree of understanding for the plight of the white working class negates white privilege, which is structural and institutionalized. For those of us who understand that, there seems to be no way to reach across the widening gulf to MAGA. So let's face that truth and think what else can we do.

Several events during the demonstrations have given me hope. In Louisville a line of white people—in photos they seemed primarily to be women—formed a human barrier with their bodies to separate the police from the demonstrators. That action has been imitated. Multiple bus drivers have refused to transport people who'd been arrested. And the white police officers who have knelt in front of the demonstrators make clear that they understand their job is to serve and protect. Reports from 'on the ground' inside the demonstrations, reveal mutual kindness and aid among the protesters, medics dispensing aid freely, people bringing food and water and milk that can be used to ameliorate the burning effects of tear gas. In Washington, homeowners opened their doors to shelter protesters trapped on their streets by police.

I never fully understood why Grace Paley kept getting herself arrested instead of writing those great stories, or why Eve Ensler once chained herself to the doors of New York's City Hall, but on Saturday I went to a demonstration, the first in many years where I thought my presence might matter, that my white skin might make a useful statement.

Only one person in the crowd shouted, "We have to arm!" But it is counter-productive for people of color and their supporters to take up guns, and, in any case, it is way too late. The white supremacists are already heavily armed, and they have the implicit support of governing forces. When masked whites with machine guns guarded the doors of a state house during one demonstration, police did not interfere. You don't have to know who the Black Panthers were to imagine what would happen to black demonstrators with automatic weapons.

Our options, as we continue to try to dismantle racism and its horrific effects, can seem puny: voting, running for office, and training for nonviolent resistance. But Gandhi was effective, and, before his murder, so was Martin Luther King. Maybe the Christians submitting to the spectacle of their own murders by lions in the Colosseum wasn't pretty, but it did help trigger the conversion of the Emperor Constantine.

I'm not suggesting anyone kneel for slaughter, just that it's useful to go limp if arrested, forcing police to carry you. Nonviolent resistance is safer and less easily co-opted than rioting, and we need to start employing it again, as demonstrators have begun remembering. Die-ins are a longstanding tactic, and now waves of protesters are lying face down for eight minutes, arms behind their backs as if they are handcuffed, the position in which George Floyd died.

The goal of the Boogaloos and accelerationists is to resurrect open civil war, to continue their fight for white supremacy and freedom from governmental interference in their lives. (Except, perhaps, in the form of VA benefits, or farm subsidies, or paved roads, or cops carrying Narcan.)

They believe such a war is coming and that it will be a race war, and they are enabled both subtly and directly by a president desperate to preserve his power, strutting around declaring Antifa the real enemy, encouraging the abuse of journalists, and demanding a military response to demonstrators. And at night he keeps sending out those tweets.

So listen to me, y'all. Another major outbreak of the War for White Supremacy could get triggered. It really could happen today, or tomorrow, or Monday, or next week. What do you think it would take? Only a few of these self-styled 'heroes' wading into the demonstrators armed with their AK-47s and grenade launchers. Or a bombing in a major city that could be blamed on the demonstrators. And then what? Martial law, even wider swaths of death from the pandemic, a suspended election. Whose interests does that serve?

The god Apollo gave Cassandra the gift to see the future, and, when she rejected him, he could not take back his gift, so he added the curse that no one would believe her. I hope I'm not like Cassandra. I hope I'm just wrong. I want to set aside these fearsome visions and maintain my faith in the frail but steady lights of hope and courage. I do believe absolutely in the goodness of ordinary people, and, like Dr. King, I trust that the arc of history is long but bends toward justice. I insist on believing that.

Freedom Talking: Juneteenth in Montgomery

MICHELLE BROWDER

ALL RIGHT Y'ALL, GOOD MORNING, GOOD MORNING! Black joy! Good morning. Black joy!

Look here, beautiful people! Our ancestors are smiling! Our ancestors are happy, they're happy! Our ancestors are beside themselves this morning!

Y'all give me about ten minutes, you understand. 'Cause this right here, shout-out to the [Montgomery] *Advertiser* that posted the finished piece of art that we did down here. So I'm just going to recap this. I'm going to recap this.

Y'all wanna know how this came about? Let me tell you how this really came about. Remember about a month ago I told you about how I was depressed? I was just depressed because we live in a beautiful city with all of this history, and sometimes we don't milk it like we should. But now with the new museums and memorials open, there's all this new interest. I have been living here for the last eighteen years, what I've relished, what has kept me alive, is this history here in downtown Montgomery, Alabama.

So, a week ago, a week ago today, I'm at home, and I'm like being a creative in a city that has Stockholm syndrome. Okay? The people have Stockholm syndrome, because there are people who should speak up, but they don't because they're afraid of losing their job, or losing their funding, all right? So that depresses me, but a friend of mine calls me up, and literally like, I'm going to hijack something, and put some kind of message, on a building or something, about what's happening for Juneteenth. What's happening with Covid, what's happening with the marginalization of black folks and brown folks, black folks mainly. The matter.

It's the matter of black and brown people that has me a little down and depressed. And so a friend calls and says, Michelle, you been quiet, what are you doing? This lady called last Saturday, and she says, What are you doing? And I said, I'm being quiet because I'm angry, and because I don't want to be inciteful. Because when I say things out of my heart—which is a matter—people vilify me because I speak the truth. Maybe sometimes it's not the right time to speak the truth. But I speak the truth because something happened to me in my childhood which requires me to do that.

So, I was telling her, I was like, you know, sometimes I feel alone in Montgomery, Alabama, because when I speak the truth people don't want to hear it. She says, "Michelle, whatever you want to do, in terms of this of what's happening around the country, around the world people are posting Black Lives Matter, and taking over streets, and just raising this consciousness." She said, we'll get behind you.

And this is a prominent woman, a sister in Montgomery, Alabama. She said we'll put the money behind you. So we started talking about Black Lives Matter in the street, and she said we have to put it up Dexter. I said, No ma'am! We have something that no other city in the Union has! It has history from enslavement of black folks to the Civil War, from Civil War to civil rights. You have Reconstruction, you have the march from Selma to Montgomery. You have Rosa Parks. Montgomery, Alabama, is the place to be! We should be in the middle of this conversation! The middle of the revolution that's taking place right now. And Montgomery has been silent.

I'm depressed! Because I know what we got! But the people that live here don't know what we have. So she says, Do it, I'll get the clearance. I don't know what the sister did, I know what she did, she called some folks, you understand? I called Kevin King—that man is my friend. I called him and I was like, bro, we need to do something. As a creative, we need to do something. I know a lot of folks be scared, but this is not the time to be scared. So I shot him the idea, and he was like, All right, all right, all right!

So I said so why don't I just reach out to all the creative organizations in Montgomery. Some that I haven't worked with before. Like 21 Dreams. And they came on board. Six days later, out of my pocket, out of my youth organization, I got the supplies, Kevin brought the hands, you understand, and one day before we got the call from my girl down at the city planning, she calls me Wednesday, and we got the go-ahead. This thing was funded by the citizens of Montgomery, by private businesses, it was okayed by our awesome mayor, so, I don't know what the negative comments are, on the news, or whatever white people in Montgomery are saying about the Black Lives.

I don't care! Nobody cares what y'all think! Nobody cares that we've had to look at Jefferson Davis. Every picture—when you look at Dr. King, Martin Luther King Jr., giving his speech on the back of a truck, he did it in front of

Jefferson Davis, one hundred years later. Y'all didn't care that a racist was behind him in the picture! When people come to Montgomery, and they take a picture of the capitol, there's a racist, a treasonous backwards racist that's in every photo.

Y'all are mad because we put Black Lives Matter around the square where black people were bought, sold, and traded? That built this city? That nursed your babies? That picked your cotton? Huh? You all mad because Black Lives Matter is around the square? Don't nobody care about that! This is black joy this morning!

Okay, so what happened was, we got the job done, you understand, we got it done, and a lot of private businesses stepped up to pay for it. We didn't get all the funds, but that's not what really matters. Let me tell you about what mattered. We took over space. Downtown Montgomery, where black people were bought, sold, and traded.

Black lives mattered in 1619, because some folks went over and brought about 20 people over here. Went to Africa. The matter was, the British, the French, the Portuguese, and the Spaniards couldn't lift a finger to take care of their damn selves, so what did they do? They went over to Africa, and brought in slaves through Jamestown, Virginia, to till the ground, for your rum, your cotton, your tobacco, and your rice. Black lives mattered, okay?

This is all about joy, this morning! I want you to look at this through a different set of eyes. Black lives mattered when the women from the antebellum South couldn't take care and nurse their babies. It was their mammies who did that for them. Black lives mattered when Quaker Oats needed someone to sell their syrup or their pancakes! Black lives mattered, huh.

Black lives matter today with mass incarceration. When you need your streets cleaned up, when you need buildings fixed up, you go to the prisons for the "work release programs." Black lives matter! Uh!

So I'm just letting you know. When it came down to going to war, in World War II, black lives mattered. It was the Tuskegee Airmen that brought our men home without losing one! Black lives mattered! You see what I'm saying?

So, I don't care that there's some white people running around here talking about all lives matter. Well, guess what, because you don't think that for real, because there's some black lives, and brown lives that are on the border—children!—and they have not been fed. And families that have been split apart, just like they did during Jim Crow and slavery times. Black lives, brown lives, all lives mattered. If it mattered, we wouldn't be the laughingstock of the world right now, because of this idiot president that y'all have.

And please believe me! I am not asleep, by no means. I know the cradle of the Confederacy is upset, but guess what? The cradle is crumbling because black lives matter!

Black lives mattered so much that in 1861 white men were willing to kill each other, for the black lives and the peculiar institution! Black lives mattered so much that somebody would sit down, after Reconstruction, they would sit down and come up with Jim Crow laws to keep us oppressed. Black lives mattered.

So what's the matter? What's the matter? When you ask people what's the matter, the matter is that black lives are disproportionately marginalized, imprisoned, degraded, sodomized, mutilated—hung. Black lives matter.

Black lives matter so much that a white man would be willing to put on a cape, and hide his face—cowardly—and hang a man in the trees. All these hangings going on? You don't think we know what's happening?

This is all about joy—this is still all about joy. And the design for this was a design I did months ago. Months ago! And because we ran out of paint, Deborah Cedric came and said, why don't we do this, and Milton said, Milton Madison, who's a gifted artist, both of these people are gifted artists, came and said why don't we add a little patch here, and that hatched a design that I had already. And the reason why I'm saying this is because black folks came together! And we put our heads on how we are going to get this thing done.

Can we not do it again in 2020? Can we not come again together to do this in 2020 to reclaim our spaces?

You can keep Jefferson Davis, if y'all want to! Keep him! Keep him! Keep James Marion Sims who raped and mutilated children, and then when they turned women he used them as subjects. Keep him! Because black lives matter downtown in Montgomery, Alabama!

And if the city decides that they want to cover it up, that's fine! We'll go buy us, we'll go purchase our own property and put up our own black lives matter.

But I'm so grateful for what they did, we didn't have to navigate the racist folks who was left in the administration to stop people from being creative and bringing life to our city. Have you all seen the light? We're in the midst of Covid, and people are happy. You can see the smiles through the masks! Black joy!

Can I tell you something? Can I be honest? Can I be transparent? Let me tell you, when I first heard black lives matter, I looked at the organization, and I'm like, I'm not really into the whole thing. But I started listening to more and more people saying black lives mattered to me, it was changing this narrative and this mindset that we have been indoctrinated to think about black people! What is the matter with that?

We've been taught that we're savages, that we don't take care of our property, that we're lazy. That we're thieves, and murderers, and drug dealers. And niggers, and bitches, and hos. That's the matter. Right? And now we have this positive affirmation that says, "I matter!" Black lives matter! We mean something. Our culture matters!

Why? Because black lives matter, with our culture. Without it, you don't have Elvis! Without black lives matter, you don't have Hank Williams! "I saw the light/Praise the Lord/I saw the light." Where do you think he got that from? Black lives that mattered.

White folks have taken everything that's great about culture, from us. Apple pie, too. You better go talk to Uncle Ben! Black lives matter. We matter so much we'll sell your watermelon skins, your pickaninny signs. Black people mattered so much that people actually took time to write laws to degrade us. And y'all mad because the people that built this city were black lives.

The only time black lives didn't matter was when they were fallen out from picking cotton from sunup to sundown, and you find a hole to throw them in. But you wanted to protect your property, so that's why we have the Confederacy right now today, because of your antebellum homes and nursing your babies, and raping the wenches, the negresses, when white women couldn't give it up like a black woman could, they'd go out to the field to find them a black woman to have sex with. Black lives mattered.

So I'm just saying—I'm breaking my silence because a spirit of heaviness broke off of me because I was able to exercise my creativity in a positive manner that spoke to the ancestors who were the commerce along with King Cotton. White folks, y'all know that you weren't going out there to pick that there cotton. It took a whole day to take the seeds out of the cotton. Y'all know you ain't got that kind of patience to do that. So you had to go and get you some black lives. Because they mattered.

Don't tell me that we ain't worth it. You ain't no gifted nothing. Black lives matter! What's the matter? So the next time you say, "What's the matter?

What's the situation?" Black lives are still being destroyed by systemic racism. So all of you white folks, all my brothers and sisters, don't get me wrong. I grew up with you—in my first community, right? Don't get me wrong, but everybody wants to be educated. Everybody wants to know, how can we do better? Put on the glasses, honey. See it through a different perspective on how black lives mattered.

And we still matter. Still! 'Cause if you think about it, there's nothing in the American culture that hasn't been engrafted. You can't go to a stoplight without a black life that mattered. You can't iron your clothes without a black life that mattered. You cannot even turn on an air conditioner or have open heart surgery without a black life that mattered.

So now we have the National Memorial for Peace and Justice, where there is no peace and there is no justice. But because they're putting it out there that there's going to be peace and justice? Here's your peace: When they open up, make sure you go out and support. And then you can see all of the black lives that mattered.

Businessmen that lost their lives—Elmore Bolling. Because he was a successful businessman. We see that happening today, with Island Delight, and how they're trying to kill black business. And black business that matters.

I just had to get this off my chest, because people don't want to be associated, or they don't want to say that this was an idea that God gave me. The Bible says, to write the vision, make it plain, and those that read it will read it and run with it. And that's what happened. Those that saw it, read it, ran with it. Kevin King, ran with it. All of the artists that saw it? Ran with it.

So anytime y'all want to run around, the next time that somebody says, oh, my God, the cradle, all lives matter? No they don't. Only your white lives matter. Because if all lives mattered, y'all would close Guantanamo Bay, and you would open up those borders, you would get those kids in cages—like you did with enslaved African gifted people...

If all lives really mattered...get out of here with that! Get out of here with that! All lives do matter! Except for black lives. So what's the matter? Black folks are waking up to the greatness, that we matter, that we have a contribution outside of mass incarceration. We have a contribution other than nursing your children.

The help? The help mattered. Black joy this morning! I am no longer depressed.

And I know, there's a big old target on my back.

I grew up with formerly incarcerated murderers, thieves, hookers. Y'all don't scare me. Grew up with the KKK. Don't scare me. So, with that being said, to the bougie black folks, when I find myself at your table, and you say I don't belong there? Black lives matter. To the city folks who say, she's too radical, she's too this—I don't care! My artwork? My ideas, my God-given ideas, to God be the glory? They matter. So many black children were so happy yesterday. And I will continue to say that we are not niggers, bitches, and hos. Because black lives matter. Without us, you're nothing. So, with that being said, the spirit has left me. Thank you so much.

The Letter

"One day, may we all meet together in the light of understanding."

—Malcolm X

THE AUTOBIOGRAPHY OF MALCOLM X, AS TOLD to the writer Alex Haley, was part of the Sixties canon: *Soul on Ice, Revolution for the Hell of It, Steal This Book,* and later, *The Female Eunuch* and *The Dialectic of Sex.*

Few of these books are still widely read. The Malcolm X autobiography is an exception, often taught in schools, where it is discovered by new generations of students fired up by Malcolm X's story, one which traces the history of black liberation in the United States.

Malcolm X, then Malcolm Little, was born in Omaha, Nebraska in 1925. His parents, Earl and Louise Little, were followers of the pan-African, black nationalist movement founded by Jamaican-born Marcus Garvey, a charismatic if controversial figure whose Back to Africa message set one of the templates for the black liberation movement. The youngest of eight, Malcolm was a bright student. Later he would tell his daughters that his eighth-grade teacher discouraged his ambition to become a lawyer because it was unrealistic for "a colored boy."

Malcolm's father died in 1931, reportedly in a streetcar accident, but the family often discussed whether Little was murdered because of his political beliefs. After his mother, Louise, an educated woman from the island of Grenada, entered a mental hospital in 1939, her children bounced around relatives and foster homes. In his teens, Malcolm made his way to Harlem, where he became a pimp and a numbers runner. After going to prison for larceny in 1946, Malcolm became the student he had wanted to be as a boy. Reading voraciously, he joined several of his siblings in the Nation of Islam, the black pride movement headed by Elijah Muhammad.

The Nation preached black empowerment, but its leader, Elijah Muhammad, also taught that whites were "blue-eyed devils" created by an evil scientist thousands of years ago. After his release in 1952, Malcolm X became close to Muhammad, helping to build the Nation of Islam into a national organization, and gaining a following in his own right as head of the Harlem mosque.

Integration versus separatism was a major intellectual debate in the 1960s. Unlike Martin Luther King, Jr., Malcolm X and the Nation preached black separatism. In fact, he expressed contempt for King, thinking him naïve and calling King's march on Washington, the "Farce on Washington." As this clever line suggests, Malcolm X was a talented orator. Today, he sounds like a cross between Jay-Z and Cornel West: "We didn't land on Plymouth Rock, my brothers and sisters. Plymouth Rock landed on us!"

In 1964, after returning from a pilgrimage to Mecca, Malcolm X moved away from wholesale denunciations of whites, embracing a more humanistic approach to fighting oppression. Nonetheless, he never recanted the anti-Semitism that had tinctured his remarks, including one statement that the Jews had brought the Holocaust on themselves. At the same time, Malcolm X was liberal when it came to gender; apparently he had affairs with white men as a teenager and refused to consider this aspect of his personal history in a negative light.

Yet Malcolm X could be rigidly moralistic. When John F. Kennedy was assassinated, Malcolm X said he considered the death as "chickens coming home to roost" blaming Kennedy for coups in Vietnam and Congo, both believed to be CIA-backed. And after discovering that his mentor Elijah Muhammad had fathered illegitimate children in contravention of Islamic teaching, he broke with the Nation of Islam, starting his own sect: the Muslim Mosque and the Organization for African-American Unity.

The 2020 film *One Night in Miami* shows the struggle between Elijah Muhammad and Malcolm X for their most iconic convert, Muhammad Ali. Ali chose Elijah Muhammad, a decision he later regretted.

On February 14, 1965, someone threw a Molotov cocktail at Malcolm X's home. He immediately made a statement accusing Elijah Muhammad of ordering the attack.

> My house was bombed. It was bombed by the Black Muslim movement upon the orders of Elijah Muhammad.
>
> Now, if they had come around to... they had planned to do it from the front and the back so that I couldn't get out. They covered the front completely, the front door. Then they had came to the back.
>
> But instead of getting directly in the back of the house and throwing it this way, they stood at a 45-degree angle and tossed it at the

window so it glanced and went onto the ground. And the fire hit the window and it woke up my second-oldest baby. But the fire burned on the outside of the house. But had that fire, had that one gone through that window, it would have fallen on a six-year-old girl, a four-year-old girl and a two-year-old girl.

And I'm gonna tell you, if it had done it, I'd have taken my rifle and gone after anybody in sight. I would not wait! And I say that because of this: the police know the criminal operation of the Black Muslim movement because they have thoroughly infiltrated it.

A week later, gunmen shot Malcolm X dead in Harlem's Audubon Ballroom. His wife, Betty Shabazz, pregnant with twins, shielded her daughters from the hail of bullets.

Malcolm X was 39.

Three men were convicted of the murder, all Nation of Islam members thought to be acting on orders from Muhammad. But it turned out that the story wasn't that simple.

On February 22, 2021, members of Malcolm X's family made public a letter they said was written by Raymond A. Wood, a former New York undercover police officer. According to the letter, the New York Police Department and the FBI had recruited Wood to infiltrate civil rights groups between 1964 and 1971. In the letter, Wood stated that he drummed up a conspiracy among the Black Panthers and members of Malcolm X's security detail to blow up the Statue of Liberty. The goal was to arrest Malcolm X's security men so he would be unprotected at a speech at the Audubon Ballroom.

Several people were wrongfully accused of complicity in the plot, Wood wrote, including Afeni Shakur, the mother of slain rapper Tupac Shakur. She was part of the group that came to be called the Panther 21.

According to his cousin, Wood wrote the letter in 2011 shortly after being diagnosed with stomach cancer. He insisted that he did not want his involvement to be made public until after his death. He died on November 24, 2020, after a summer of mass protests over George Floyd's murder.

While there was little doubt that Elijah Muhammad, perhaps with the tacit approval of heir apparent Louis Farrakhan, ordered Malcolm X's death, possible FBI involvement remained murky. In *The Dead Are Arising: The Life of Malcolm X*, winner of the 2020 National Book Award for Nonfiction, co-authors Les and Tamara Payne reported that by the beginning of 1965, there had already been five attempts on Malcolm X's life. They wrote that Elijah Muhammad had set an absolute deadline for Malcolm's assassination: Febuary 26, designated as Savior's Day by the Nation of Islam. They called the hit on Malcolm X "the worst-kept secret" in Muslim circles.

On the last day of his life, speaking at the Audubon Ballroom, Malcolm X accused Muhammad of engaging in violence against blacks, but never against the white power structure. And he promised to name names in the coming weeks.

Minutes later, he was dead.

Three members of the Nation of Islam were quickly convicted of the murder: Khalil Islam, Muhammad Aziz, and Mujahid Abdul Halim. Islam, who spent 20 years behind bars for the crime, insisted always that he was nowhere near the Audubon Ballroom that day. Halim, the only man who confessed to the murder, also known as Talmadge Hayer or Thomas Hagan, backed up Islam's claim, insisting that the others convicted of the killing were innocent.

On November 18, 2021, 50 years after the death of Malcolm X, Aziz and Islam were exonerated. A review initiated by the Manhattan district attorney found that they had not received a fair trial. The investigation also found that evidence pointing toward their innocence had been withheld by some of the country's most prominent law enforcement agencies, and that at least some was suppressed on the order of the longtime FBI director J. Edgar Hoover.

"I do not need this court, these prosecutors or a piece of paper to tell me I am innocent," said Aziz. "I am an 83-year-old man who was victimized by the criminal justice system."

Khalil Islam had died in 2009, after spending 20 years in prison and being paroled in 1987.

The question of who pulled the trigger remains important, not only for the sake of history, but to determine whether not just Elijah Muhammad but federal law enforcement had targeted Malcolm X. The FBI's counterintelligence activities against the Black Panthers, the American Indian Movement, the Ku Klux Klan, and the antiwar movements of the 1960s are well documented. It defies logic that a figure as radical and charismatic as Malcolm X wouldn't have attracted similar attention.

When Wood's letter surfaced, the question could no longer be ignored. Or so it seemed until Raymond Wood's daughter told a different story. While she acknowledged that her father had worked undercover on the Statue of Liberty case, she refuted the contention that he had been present at the Audubon Ballroom or directly involved in the assassination.

"My father is a hero," she told a TV reporter, adding a message to the family of Malcolm X: "My heart goes out to you. I am so sorry because I know what it feels like when you want answers."

Her uncle disagreed. He told a sad story of a police officer tormented by conflicting loyalties, a black man who felt he had betrayed his people. Wood said that his cousin isolated himself, fearful that if the story surfaced, he would be targeted by both police and radicals. For the sake of their safety, he kept his family at arm's length until he became ill.

In his isolation, his nephew reported, Reggie Wood had to face his own conscience. "He felt guilt and remorse for that for 56 years."

The Shabazz family, buffeted by their own history of pain and loss, and confusion, hired attorney Ben Crump, who represented the family of George Floyd and in early 2023, prepared to sue the FBI and NYPD. Crump made the connections across history.

"Malcolm X is Black Lives Matter," Crump said.

While Crump's words resonate, the overturning of the convictions of Aziz and Islam, and vigorous prosecutions of hate crimes and racially motivated police murders in the wake of Floyd's killing, may be signs that the arc of history does indeed bend toward justice.

But not quickly enough for Khalil Islam and George Floyd. Or, for that matter, Malcolm X.

—The Editors

The Poet

KEITH DONNELL JR., WHO WROTE THE POEM "EULOGY Delivered by Ossie Davis at the Funeral of Malcolm X," grew up in Philadelphia—Philly, he calls it, sounding like a true native son—where his grandparents had a portrait of Malcolm X in their living room.

In his poem, Donnell riffs on the stirring eulogy delivered by actor Ossie Davis at Malcolm X's 1965 funeral. In his words, "I break down, warp, swap out, and reorganize the original words and sounds to create new meanings and associations."

One of those associations is unexpected: the Donner Party, settlers stopped on their way to California by heavy snows in the Sierra who resorted to cannibalism. Cannibalism, of course, is a tried-and-true trope of the "primitive." But the Donner Party were God-fearing Christian farmers. They were white. And they were cannibals.

"I read this Joan Didion book, *Run River*," Donnell said. "She talks about the Donner Party. People believed that the Donner Party failed because there was something internally that was wrong with them. The obligations that they shared among each other were wrong. So I was bringing in this idea of community, the obligations we have toward one another."

Donnell has immersed himself in history, both as an undergraduate and while studying for a master's degree in African-American literature. His approach to the Malcolm X poem, along with a collection that will be his second, represents his sense that to truly eliminate anti-blackness requires nothing less than entirely remaking society.

"I want to create a voice that is singular and at the same time, multitudes that talk over each other, connections between now and then," he said.

"I contain multitudes?" we asked, teasing him about his ambitions matching the famously bombastic line of Whitman's. Whitman, of course, was talking in the voice of America itself.

Donnell laughed, self-deprecation implied. It's not quite that, but something like it. Donnell says he's trying to channel our time: "the confusion, the echo chamber, how history bears upon the present."

"I'm trying to capture a language of this moment," he said.

Eulogy Delivered by Ossie Davis at the Funeral of Malcolm X

KEITH DONNELL JR.

Faith Temple Church of God
February 27, 1965

Here, at this final hour
In this quiet place
Alarm has come.
Dim lit stairwell
Torn from it
Sober eye test hopes
Extinguished
No wind
Gone with us, forever.

Four-alarm is here.
We were kids wandering
Strung lead and fog –
His home of bones
Where his heart was sand
Where his people are –
And ISIS.

The reform lost footing
That we're meat once again
In alarm – to shard these
Last monuments

Rhythm

Four-alarm

A sewer bin grace
Use to those who have lost air

Half-volt
He ran, dove
Defended air
Donners
Eaten to the death.

It is night in the memory of man
That this drinking gourd
A fortune faked
But, nonetheless, proud
Co-immunity
Half sound
A braver, more gallant
Young sham
Peon.

Then, this Afro-American
Holy before sun
Conquered still eyes.
Say the word again.
Wood ash wants me, too.
Afro-Amor. Icon.
Afro-Amori. Kin.
My clone, who was a mass tear
Wash my stem
Too cool
Us
Just words
No known body returned
A knee to power
Wars

Half off remains of men.

My clone had stopped being a 'Negro' years ago.
It had becloned too small, too puny
To wreck a word form.
My clone was badder than that
My clone had becloned
An Afro-American
And he wanted – soul disparity
That we, that all his people
Would beclone Afro-Americans 2.

The roar of those
Who wall
Consider it their duty
As friend zone, still,
We grow
People total us.
To revive hymn
Tough lovin' from the prisms of memory
To save ourselves by riding harm out of history
Of our turbulent times
Money will ask what alarm fires
To Donner in this
Stormy
Controversial
And bold young craps hand –
And we wall miles.

Many wall Sister away
Airway.
Frame this man
For he is not a man
But tandem:
A sermon, a subverter, and anemone
All that Black man –

And we wall miles.

They will say that he is half ape
An attic fan, sun-kissed
Whole canon liberating evil
Tooth decause fork wrench stew rubble
And dwell
And swear
And dismay. To them:
Delude every tattoo, Brother, my clone
Delude every touch.

Humor, have harm smile at you.
Did you ever really glisten to him?
Did he ever di Amin thing?
Wash me over
Hymn Sale
Assassinated with violins
Or any public disco dance. For if you do you
Were now him, and you
If you knew harm, you, widow
Wide
We missed so near him.

Malcolm was our human donor
Our loving main back road
This was his meaning to his people
And in honoring him
We honor the blast out our cells.

Laughter from a rich hero
To the sewer dystopia
Friends!
Our journey!
He slays, is all mist, undead
And I laugh a much-braided rope.

Scan when eyes start to doubt
Which eyeball's evil
Odd new life
And demand siphon
Tour struggle for free
Demand honor and dig
Not in these lights.

I am writing to set hinges soft
In your wall
No artifact
The dream in dust
Some paths end up port
Wade among we African strays
Forearm. Human rights
Strangled.

The main thing is that we keep a unit fronted here
In our most volatile time and memory.
Wall not to be washed
Filleting each other, however, we may
Dream deferred within
Our wrist
We're shackled
Reboot him
And his value as a man
Light his going from us
Sever only to bring us together
New.
Consign these mortal remains
To earth
The common mother
And fall.
Seek core in the knowledge
That what we lace
Pinned to gown

ICE no more
Now
Amen
But acid wash
After the winter of our discontent.

Wall came forth again
To me, dust
And we will know him then
For what he was
And is –
A brick
Our own Black shining brick!
Who didn't hesitate to fly
Because he loved us so.

Night, Donald

MIKAL GILMORE

I HAD TO LAUGH WHEN MY WIFE, ELAINE SCHOCK, WROTE recently that we live in an alternative universe. We write lying in bed next to one another, and sometimes it feels as though ideas travel between us before the words are formed. A thought had been eating at me the last couple of days, a terrible and perplexing one.

Remember Bizarro World? It was a fictional planet, Htrae (which is "Earth" spelled backward), populated by reverse counterparts to characters in DC Comics' Superman mythos.

Htrae was cubed rather than round, see? People said and did things the opposite of the way normal reality (even superhero reality) should work. They said "goodbye" when they greeted each other, "hello" when they parted. There was a Bizarro-Aquaman—he couldn't swim. A Bizarro-Marilyn Monroe—the ugliest person on the planet. My favorite was the Bizarro-Batman, Batzarro, the World's Worst Detective.

For me, though, the Bizarro World stories were too much of an absurd thing; they strained credulity (even in, as I say, a superhero mythos), and their cleverness was exhausting. How could it be anything else? Sometimes, though, they could be damn funny.

I hadn't mentioned to Elaine that I was thinking about Bizarro World—I'd be surprised if she knew what it was; comic book enthusiasts were usually prepubescent boys and the early incarnations of Bizarro were better than the later ones that she would have seen. The earlier Bizarro had a certain pathos. Bizarro was evil, yes, but he had an endearing clumsiness, as if he was confounded by his own chaos.

But what put me in mind of Bizarro was the same thing that Elaine was feeling about the mind of TrumpWorld: What's up is down these days, what's down is up; what's good is bad, what's bad is valorous. This isn't merely absurd—I mean, we all like to laugh at Trump when he asserts some grand claim about himself that is manifestly antithetical to what is true about him. (He boasted in Tulsa about how good-looking he is.)

No, it isn't merely absurd. It's worrisome, sometimes depressing, even

scary, increasingly so. I watched the video of the three women haranguing Miami's city commissioners, claiming that masks kill people; one telling a doctor that the doctor doesn't know medical science because she believes in cautions about Covid—and maybe it isn't deadly after all, but some myth, a plot for control?

Another woman stood with her Bible, upset that more people don't stand with Bibles in their hands in the face of Covid and the onslaught of masks.

The exchange was an ugly laugh relief—truly ugly, because two of the women speaking were hectoring the commissioners, one threatening them with citizen's arrests. I was astounded that one of them just didn't say, "Shut the fuck up and get out of here—and wear your goddamn masks on the street outside or you'll get a fine!"

Then there was the woman at Starbucks who got crazily offensive with a barista who asked her to wear a mask. She threatened to come back with the police.

Those are WTF displays. Contemptible, powerless dolts looking for power—maybe because they're afraid of what could be coming their way. But the inverted reasoning is getting bigger by the day, reaching a tipping point, conflating with other craziness, spreading like a contagion all its own: anti-maskers raging at the same time that Trump and his hordes rage against Black Lives Matter, against Obamacare, against immigrant children, against, I'd say, life itself.

As all these matters have grown politicized, they've assumed an amorphous form of ideology and religion that is dangerous and, well—may as well say it—kind of...evil. It isn't merely stupid to ignore precautions—masks, distancing, staying home as much as possible—it's menacing, a means of spreading the twin viruses of Covid and proud ignorance, like a threat against the welfare of the American community.

The frantic need to fend off intimations of mortality is expressed not only by a desire to offend the people who are trying to do the right thing but to jeopardize or terrorize them. An increasing number of health officials have been resigning lately because of threats on their lives. People whose work is to save lives are afraid for their own lives.

What do you call an evil afraid, for its own sake, of the harm it does? Hypocrisy, certainly. From CNN this morning: "When he travels to locations where the virus is surging, every venue the President enters is inspected for potential areas of contagion by advance security and medical teams, according to people familiar with the arrangements.

"Bathrooms designated for the President's use are scrubbed and sanitized before he arrives. Staff maintain a close accounting of who will come into contact with the President to ensure they receive tests."

But surely hypocrisy is the least of it. Mary Trump's book calmly constructs a psychological portrait of an almost-sympathetic sadist in a padded cell. "Donald has, in some sense, always been institutionalized, shielded from his limitations or his need to succeed on his own in the world," Mary Trump writes.

Lack of accountability cemented the man's pathology, but Donald Trump, like all of us, is a creature of his time. The failures of accountability that have been invading our public life since the Reagan years are now forcing us to live on Donald's Trump's cellblock.

I see a correspondence between the anti-health factions and the defenders of racism and police violence, the Confederacy advocates. The right thing for a good nation is to look out for the health of its citizens. The right thing for a good nation is to banish excessive uses of force and bigoted speech and actions. The right thing for a good nation is to promote compassion. Social benignity is the reason government exists.

But in Trump's Bizarro World, what's good is bad, what's bad is valorous. The effect of all this goes beyond a surge of ugliness and instead posits a new norm, a new morality that proclaims death is due, kindness and tolerance are blasphemy, and the future's only acceptable direction is backward.

These are crazy fucking times. More than once when I've been sitting in the backyard at night, looking at the fairytale glow of the lights, playing with the dog or listening to Bob Dylan on my earphones or watching Elaine and my stepdaughter Claudia cherish the new baby, I feel like I'm in a citadel, a refuge of safety, a household of sanity, a kindred way forward.

America's true reopening won't begin until the morning after November 3rd, when we can begin to walk again the streets of a land that believes in promises better than death and cruelty. I wonder if others feel something similar at times.

Goodbye.

Hello.

The Seer

Reporters with international experience know a coup attempt when they see it. We called it a coup among ourselves, in low voices, tentatively, as shocked as everyone else. But the notion sounded so outlandish to most Americans that we needed confirmation.

So we hustled to get in touch with national security and law enforcement sources. They confirmed our gut reaction, but most insisted on speaking to us only on deep background. One—let's call him Deep State Throat—was willing to be quoted, if we withheld his name. Looking back at our conversation, it's striking how accurately he predicted what would happen over the next several years. The interview ran on January 16, 2021.

∿∿

What went wrong on January 6? Very simple, the president of the United States who was in charge of security for the capitol didn't want to stop [the insurrection]. Trump wanted the thing to go forward. He wanted [the Capitol] understaffed, he wanted it undefended. It was his last desperate attempt to stay in power. Nobody's pointed out that Mike Pence did not have the authority to call out the National Guard. He overstepped his authority when he did that. Thank God he did.

Chad Wolf resigned as acting head of the Department of Homeland Security on January 11, five days after the attack on the Capitol. Do you know why Wolf resigned? Disgust with the president's inability in the last few days to come to the realization that he's lost the election.

So nobody's in charge? Nobody's in charge.

That has serious implications. Doesn't that leave the U.S. undefended? Pretty much. Most people will still defend against foreign attacks. That happens automatically without presidential intervention.

What about domestic attacks? Let's start with the threatened attacks on the state capitols. The problems in D.C. are unique to the federal government. The states are run by the governors, so they can call out the National Guard.

If Republican governors are willing to do that, and they don't sympathize with the insurrectionists. Now to the immediate fear: the inauguration. Will Joe Biden and Kamala Harris be adequately protected? I think that the pros in terms of securing the White House and the other key buildings do a very good job. Obama was never shot, never killed. The danger is if somebody comes in, and they've acquired weapons of mass destruction from the Middle East or someplace. If somebody were going to try to coordinate with Al Qaeda or the Taliban, these people are trained terrorists. They have access to toxic chemical weapons or dirty bombs. Who knows what happened to the nuclear weapons from the former Soviet Union?

Shouldn't they just cancel the inauguration ceremony? Why have it at the Capitol? They may have already decided to move it and they just haven't told us. Right now, there are 20,000 National Guardsmen guarding the Capitol. You don't want the Boogaloos going somewhere else. You want them to try to take out 20,000 National Guardsmen. That's how it works with covert operations: classic misdirection. You don't telegraph the punch.

All you need is one person on the inside, right? There are people in the middle level of the military and in police forces who were sympathetic to the rioters. Two off-duty cops from Virginia got a slap on the wrist for participating in the attack. One, Thomas Robertson, is an Army veteran and trained sniper. The other is a member of the Virginia National Guard. There were Seattle police officers, and a Philadelphia police detective and even more disturbingly, a number of ex-military folks. And we all saw the infamous "selfie" one Capitol police officer took with the rioters. A few military people are defending it and a few cops. But the true pros are all over it. There was the letter from the ten former members of joint chiefs, saying we're not going to follow illegal orders of the president. And Liz Cheney is telling the world that she's ready to vote for impeachment.

Which is pretty much the military saying it. In some ways—I hate to say this—there really is kind of a "deep state." They're not trying to take over anything. They're trying to maintain the status quo. They're rounding up the bad actors.

Who's the lead agency? The FBI? The FBI. Secret Service on specific things.

This threat isn't going away anytime soon. Do you get a sense of how enforcement will be ongoing? One person I communicated with was a former U.S. district attorney for the D.C. court. He thinks it's going to take two years to build the cases against all these people. There will be long-term Justice Department and FBI engagement.

In the meantime, there's a mad shuffle now going on, belatedly, from Facebook's stunningly inept attempts to control "political speech" to the shutdown of platforms like Parler because the January 6 insurrectionists were organizing through social media. Are the government's cyber resources adequate to track domestic terrorists? Yes. The NSA (National Security Agency) is feeding information to the FBI. But we don't know what we've missed. We're watching the Proud Boys, the Boogaloos, the 3 Percenters, all the people in the Southern Poverty Law Center database. We're seeing where they're going. We're quietly keeping an eye on them. But I think that there will be people there we don't know about.

How are they dealing with that uncertainty? It's macro defense. Twenty thousand National Guard is three times as many people as we have in Afghanistan and Iraq combined. They've shut down all the roads. D.C. is in lockdown. We haven't seen anything like this since 9/11. It just tells you, everyone is assuming they're not playing psychological warfare but they don't have specificity of targets. They're extending the perimeter around D.C., and they don't want anyone coming into the city. They've flooded the zone, because they're acutely aware that before the Capitol attack the government wasn't prepared.

That's comforting. Try this: the inauguration will be a TV event. So anybody who wants to get their message across will see that as an opportunity.

This is America

MATT COOPER

THE NIGHT BEFORE ELECTION DAY, I DROVE through downtown Washington, D.C. The city had been tense for several days, not just because of the election but because of protests following the death of a young African-American Washingtonian who was pursued by police. He had been using a rideshare electric motor scooter. He crashed and died. He was 20. There had been some boarding up. Now it's everywhere.

When I drove past, *National Geographic*'s headquarters was boarded up. Defenders of Wildlife was defending itself with plywood. Any number of unions and pharmacies were, too.

A week ago, just a few stores had been closed. Loro Piana, the fashion staple of the casual rich, had taken all of its inventory and stashed it someplace. The $2,250 Fillmore Cashmere men's sweater was safe.

This is America. A middle-aged man in a mask driving on empty streets wondering what would happen next, listening to electric drills and hammers.

Even if Joe Biden wins, no one expects the Trump years' mendaciousness or vulgarity to simply disappear. Leave aside the question of whether Trump would accept defeat after an almost certain attempt to reverse a loss through litigation. The QAnon cult will still be here. So will the pandemic. Fox News and Facebook disinformation aren't turning down the volume. Everyone will remain siloed in their information and geographic bubbles. Priuses and Whole Foods on one side, F-150 pickups and Dollar Generals on the other.

I had hoped that when Trump left, the fever would break. That's what happened with Joseph McCarthy. When the Republican Senator was training his fulminations and lies on the U.S. Army, he had gone too far. The anti-Communist who had done so much to help Communism quickly collapsed along with his cause. Soon he was censured by the Republican and Democratic cowards who had abided him. A few years later he was dead.

Salem's witch-hunters had a brief run in the 17th century, too, but their mania faded. In *The Plot Against America*, Philip Roth's book and not the HBO movie, the Nazi-appeasement and polite anti-Semitism of President Charles Lindbergh ends when Lucky Lindy's plane goes missing. There are a few gasps of Lindberghism without Lindbergh, but they fade quickly, within hours. It's over.

We're in for a longer season of madness, I fear. The ties of public schools and doctors' house calls that kept this dynamic, polyglot society together in my youth were famously frayed before Donald Trump and it won't end with him. That is true in my Washington. As corrupt as they are, the political parties were once a moderating influence, far more than the whack-job special interest groups that dominate primaries and enjoy unlimited Citizens United money.

In Congress, the old Schoolhouse Rock process of regular order tended to keep the crazies on the backbench instead of in control. The slow, normal process gave everyone an incentive to at least fight things out in a controlled fashion. Now, the House and Senate are cage matches of brute power: ramming through Amy Coney Barrett or the insane brinksmanship of shutting down the government.

We shouldn't complain, I suppose. Compared to the Civil War, thugs cos-playing as soldiers aren't an existential threat. The Black Lives Matter uprising is like a TED Talk compared to the Draft Riots of 1863 when Irish mobs protesting conscription in New York City lynched blacks and burned down Brooks Brothers. We usually get through our darkest periods. For every Selma, there's a John Lewis and for every Father Coughlin an FDR. At least we hope.

Still, I'm not sure the bad feeling will be easy to put behind us. As a nine-year-old in New Jersey, I knew which neighbors were for Nixon. My parents must have planted the scorecard in my head. We thought it was weird anyone would back Nixon, but my friend's parents did, and the elderly couple next door, and the people three houses down. It felt highstakes in my house, as I recall. My parents worried about the Vietnam War going on ad nauseam. But it didn't feel as weird as this.

I politely talk to my Trump-voting friends. I'm genuinely perplexed, pissed that the Putin embrace and kids in cages and corrupt appointments doesn't rile them. Some friends just like him for the tax cuts. Others to own the libs.

Driving in my Washington, I try to take comfort in other things. This is still an enormously free and dynamic society without the sclerotic malaise of European economies or the klepto-authoritarianism of Russia. Immigrants want to be here for a reason. We're still an assimilation machine, a world away from the bleak segregated suburbs of Paris or the shootings in Nice. Go to Dearborn, Michigan and Paterson, New Jersey, and see the thriving Arab communities, and you'll have hope. As James and Deborah Fallows recently wrote, the politics of many of America's small towns and cities are often normal, productive, and kind, just as Washington politics are toxic.

I don't know what will happen on November 4, the day after the election, or January 21, the day after the inauguration. If Trump wins, his worst tendencies will be unleashed without the constraints of reelection. Goodbye, Fauci. Maybe, goodbye NATO as we knew it. Trump's pathologies will only be exacerbated by age and, quite possibly, the still mysterious lingering effects of Covid. I can't say things won't get worse.

Driving down K Street, the famed lobbyist row, where restaurants and law firms alike were hidden behind wooden boards, I remember the times I've tried to explain to my 22-year-old what politics used to be like. I try to explain the Clinton-Dole race in 1996 or the Carter-Ford race in 1976, where the choice did not feel existential. You didn't think the other team winning was good, but it wasn't the apocalypse. And you didn't know the results could be stolen by the Supreme Court or Moscow or the Postmaster General. Remember, even Nixon showed gallantry when he refused to contest the ultra-close 1960 presidential election.

I think in a few years we'll come out of this, sooner if Biden wins, much longer if Trump does. Maybe in 2022 or '23, we'll stop wearing masks. Billions of refrigerated vaccines will have been distributed, and the anti-science post-rationalists of the left and right who refuse to take them will be few enough that we can go back to funerals and football.

A more normal politics might emerge by then, driven by wily but sane politicians who understand the market for not crazy. This plague won't be a year, to cite Daniel Defoe's book or this publication. It will be the Plague Years, but I think, like the sounds of plywood going up and the dank smell of a cloth mask worn all day, it will end.

The Trump Presidential Library

TED MOONEY

Covfefe (/koʊˈfɛfi/ koh-FEH-fee, /kəvˈfeɪfeɪ, koʊˈfɛfeɪ/) is a nonsense word, widely presumed to be a typographical error, that Donald Trump used in a viral tweet when he was President of the United States. It instantly became an Internet meme.

I HAD A VISION. I SAW THE DONALD J. TRUMP Presidential Library. It was a little one-room outbuilding, in a bad part of town, never mind which town. Not much signage, little in the way of memorabilia, and just one display. I saw, lit by its own light, his greatest accomplishment—his Twitter feed, on endless loop on a very small screen, there for history to savor, without filter, forever. No more, no less. *Covfefe*!

THERE ARE
NO ACCIDENTS

One of the great triumphs of the Biden administration's early days was the passage of a pandemic relief bill. Economic inequality in America had become increasingly dire and when Covid-19 swept through the nation inequities became a matter of life and death.

One of the first articles we ran at *Journal of the Plague Years* was an investigation of the shortage of hospital beds in New York City. As it turned out, New York was not so different from the rest of the country. Privatization and corporate consolidation meant that hospitals in poor and rural communities had been closing, one by one, for several decades. Letting the profit motive remake American health care had left the country unprepared to save the lives of its citizens in an emergency.

The result was a disproportionate number of deaths among blacks, Latinx, and rural white Americans whose pre-existing conditions included poverty.

Desperation of one kind or another had seeped through America until it touched almost everyone. The pandemic forced us to confront it.

Stick Built

MIKE MEDBERRY

This song is a soulful riff on saxophone with a piano interlude, a tragic samba oiled by wealth and aspiration, a song about dying and attempts to live well. There is beauty in the music and when I hear this song I find myself flowing in that dance, moving with the sadness and joy of a crumbling economy.

THIS IS THE STORY OF A HOUSE BUT IT STARTS with the more fragile structure of a human body. I had a stroke at 43, more than 20 years ago. In the beginning I couldn't walk, talk, think, write, or remember my mother's name. Over a few years of hard work I recovered roughly 95 percent of what I'd lost—physical and mentally, that is. Financially, I was a wreck.

After my mother died, I inherited enough for a down payment on a house. This was after the 2008 housing meltdown and banks had tightened lending requirements. Like a lot of folks with spotty credit and patched-together employment, I couldn't get a mortgage. So I bought a piece of land with cash and acted as the general contractor to build the goddamned house, which may or may not have been cheaper than hiring someone else to build it. I had to beg and plead and hustle but now I have lived in my little stick-built house here in Boise for five years and I have few complaints.

I thought life had reached a kind of benign stasis. But in those five years the whole world, and my world, changed. We've had a pandemic, the prices of homes in Boise have risen more than 70 percent, the climate has taken a turn for the worse, my girlfriend left me, the U.S. bailed out of Afghanistan, my friends fight over masks and vaccines, and I've gotten just a little bit older.

And again, I was feeling quite broke. Some things never change, it seems. I'd spent most of my career as an environmentalist working for statewide groups and feisty locals, not the big national organizations, so there was no talk of matching retirement savings as if I'd worked for, say, Walmart. Or, hey, a union.

I'd left that vocation to get an MFA in creative writing—yeah, I know: great financial move. I'm a boomer and when "follow your bliss" changed to "cover your ass" I missed the memo. After the stroke, I've been a carpenter, a solar installer, and now I work at a winery. But, yeah: a writer. Broke.

So when my friend's son and his wife needed a cheap place to stay while they looked for a more permanent place to settle, I decided to rent them my house. I could move into the garage. After all, I'd spent a big portion of my life camping. The garage was more or less finished, with real walls and a roof. Their parents and I had been friends for years; I'd been drinking buddies with Lee's dad and I had worked with Lee's mom Helen, whose quirkiness and passion I admired. Like many of us, they'd been solidly middle-class, but fallen on hard times. They couldn't give Lee and his wife Cindy the cash they'd need for a down payment in Boise's insanely skyrocketing housing market.

Lee and Cindy were still in their twenties but they already had two boys, 4 and 1. As I got to know them, I could see that Cindy was the most creative, in-control character in the room—or perhaps in the whole damned city. Blonde, attractive, she was the energetic one.

Lee worked hard but he didn't have what you'd call a career. He was a house cleaner, working in expensive homes in the upscale parts of Boise. But he didn't earn enough to make the rent on a regular basis. He was handsome, dark to Cindy's blonde, and he spoke with the exaggerated certainty of a man who knows, deep down, that he is undecided.

I knew they were struggling, so I had set the rent for about half of market rate, $750 a month, with the caveat that I would be using the kitchen, bathroom, and shower when I needed to. I'd given them a one-year lease, so they got a cheap place to live, for a while.

Mostly, it worked. Cindy and Lee were very kind to me and I attempted to be a decent landlord. However, there were tensions—things like late rent and police cars following Lee home and ticketing him for reckless driving—but they were easily forgivable. Cindy had become a dog trainer. She gave me cookies and helped me with my unruly dog. But the place really wasn't set up for two separate living spaces, and definitely not for five people.

I probably was around the house too much, but at their age, they were mellow about people coming and going. The wood stove stopped working, the garage got frigid, and the water that had once flowed from the outside faucet became solid ice. Until the wood stove was repaired, I was in the main house regularly, more like a roommate than a landlord. I banged around in the kitchen making coffee. I wanted to sleep on the sofa but I found their friends or Lee sleeping there, or I'd find a week's worth of dirty dishes to clean before I could make breakfast.

Let's face it, I was growing old. When I noticed marijuana smoke billowing out one window of my living room, I kept peeking out toward the city police office which was and is across the street because Idaho still has repressive laws against smoking pot.

Toward the end of the year's rental contract, I decided that Lee and Cindy and the kids would have to find a new place to live—I was exhausted. It was the house that I built and I couldn't live in it. Around this time, Lee's dad told me that Cindy was pregnant again. I gave them three months to find a new place.

During the year they had lived in my little green house, the rental market had grown more forbidding. Boise, once a backwater, was making national news. Tech had come to town a few years before, and the pandemic ramped prices up from there. Real estate articles made me reach back to high school math classes to remember the precise definition of exponential. In a state where the minimum wage was $7.25 an hour, the rent for a two-bedroom apartment was $1,400 to $2,100. Rent at the lower end added up to $16,800 a year. A minimum wage employee earned $15,000 a year. Even a writer can do that math.

To put it another way, a Massachusetts Institute of Technology study calculated the living wage for two adults with two children in the county at $32.03 per hour. I knew enough about their jobs to realize that Lee and Cindy didn't come close. So they moved into Lee's parents' house. They had no choice.

Thankfully there were no hard feelings about my asking them to move out. I still saw Lee's parents, and occasionally I'd see Lee and Cindy and the kids. Still, I could tell that they were all under stress.

After Lee and Cindy left, my modest 1,100-square-foot house felt palatial. But I was broke again. Here's the thing: being broke isn't a big thing for a single guy who owns his house. For a young man with two kids and a pregnant wife, an uncertain wage, and no good place to live, it was quite another.

Lee and Cindy had left a few of their possessions in the house: food they'd gotten from a food bank, the metal fire pit, a dresser, and some painted rocks left by the older boy. Right before Cindy delivered her third child, I drove over to their parents' place, thinking they might need some of the things that they had left and to deliver the mail that hadn't managed to follow them. I knocked at the door. No response. I knocked again.

Cindy's car was parked in front of the house, so I figured they were there. I opened the front door and heard her shushing the children. I didn't want to intrude so I left the mail on a side table, saying softly: "Mail's inside."

I did some errands and headed to a wine bar to taste their wares. As I sat drinking a glass of Tempranillo, I listened to my voicemail. Lee's mother had left a message. In a wavering voice, she said, "Mike, I've got to tell you that our son is no longer alive. I'm sorry."

Here's the odd part. She added, in a strangely formal, almost stately locution: "I can receive your condolences and sorrows."

When I learned that Lee had killed himself, I realized that Helen hadn't been able to say it. The death of a child is impossible under any circumstances. But suicide leaves behind an abyssal guilt, a sense of helplessness, and sometimes a parent is drawn to suicide themselves in the aftermath. The stilted, awkwardly juxtaposed words shielded her, in her shock, from a grief that was ungovernable.

Without Lee, his sons and wife could be living in his parents' small house for months, maybe years. What had Lee been thinking? Did he fail to see any hope? Maybe not right away, but a few years down the road? He loved his kids. He loved Cindy. He might have been adrift in certain ways, but he was a good man, a good father. The third child would be named after his own father.

I've read that there are eight million people in the United States who are behind on their rent. As I sorted through the complicated feelings after Lee's death, I understood that, despite my own difficulties, an accident of birth lands me on the lucky side of a very stark equation.

I'm only there, still, because I'm disciplined, and determined not to let the bastards beat me. I took out a reverse mortgage and I'm using the cash to finish the house. I have to be careful, because the reverse mortgage debt doesn't just evaporate. I'm not required to make payments, but if I don't, in 20 years I will have to relinquish my home.

My house recently appraised for $370,000, which gives me room to maneuver, and as I said, I've been the beneficiary of the last dregs of mid-century affluence, including a decent education that equips me to think my way out of desperation, or try. Nothing more. But what will the many trailer home residents in the Garden City section of Boise do when their rents increase and landowners choose to build more profitable condominiums or apartment complexes on their land?

Did I do enough for Lee and Cindy? I assuage my guilt by thinking that the forces that crushed Lee, and hurt three generations of his family, are beyond any individual's influence.

The pain is global: London, Paris, Berlin. In Seoul, South Korea, the average price of an apartment has gone up 90 percent since 2017. Studies show that the lack of affordable housing is determining the outcome of elections, and some believe it influenced Britain's wrongheaded decision to leave the European Union.

What I remember is the day when Cindy and their older boy, Chad, did an art project. That was when he painted those rocks they had left behind. The paint was blue and white, the colors of clouds and sky. She set the stones around the front yard and they circled the green, making it a small landscape contained within the bounds of home.

"Build a bonfire!" she told Lee. He laughed but he dragged the metal firepit out to the front yard and built a fire, right there on the sidewalk. It was almost certainly illegal, but clean enough and contained. The air had a chill and the fire was bright and warming. We told stories and ate marshmallows.

What I remember most clearly is how Cindy and Lee loved each other and how tied they were to the kids. The younger boy, Donny, kept toddling toward the flames. Lee pulled him back each time, long before Donny got too near the fire. Lee was close to his own father, and they had been planning to climb Mount Lassen together, something they'd done when Lee was a boy.

It's been four months since Lee committed suicide. I think about Cindy and her young sons' future. Shelter is one of the fundamental needs of a human being, second only to food and water. Are we already in a society where we are jettisoning the weak to save ourselves?

The house is quieter now, and I can't say I don't luxuriate in the peace. The Boise River is a block away. I walk there almost every day. It's beautiful with its channels, clear pools, and riffles; wildlife is abundant: osprey, mink, beavers. Cottonwood trees shade the banks and it's not unusual to see someone fishing.

But it's an urban river. Homeless people have tree forts and camps. Like me, they have chosen to live by the river. It's beautiful there under the cottonwoods but in the winter, it is unendurably cold.

What $50,000 Loan Forgiveness Would Look Like

ESSENTIAL WORKER ZH43DFC

IT APPEARS THAT BIDEN'S THINKING OF forgiving $50,000 of everyone's student loan debt. A friend calls me with the news last week when I'm driving home from work. I don't run off the road from excitement. My heart does not leap for joy. My student loan debt has hit an even number this year, so it's easy for me to do the math inside my head. I deduct 50 grand from what I owe, pencil in the new balance and think, okay.

What's for supper?

It is raining. It's a Thursday. Thursdays are good because teachers get to wear jeans every Friday. I've been back inside a classroom since August. By 3:30 every day, teachers are pretty much shut down in the emotion department. Pretty much in survival mode.

My student loan turns 31 years old this month. My student loan and me—it's been a long and rocky road. We've lasted longer than some marriages. Some business ventures. I'm not even sure what my life would look like without it anymore.

There've been wild and desperate hopes across the years that I would be able to pay it off. That was back when I just owed $100,000. A while ago. There've been regrets that I had to make it in the first place. Wishes that someone would have thought it a bad business venture to loan an English major who was planning on being a teacher—and what is worse, a writer—that kind of money. There has been anger. Fear. There has been some sorrow.

The worst part was that time I went into default. That was pretty awful. Although, if we were sitting here on my couch, just you and me, a couple of drinks, I could make you laugh. I could make it a warm and funny story.

Because at the end of the day, it's just money.

Sometimes mornings, before daylight, when I'm commuting to work, I have bright ideas for paying my student loan off. There are YouTubers earning six figures. Maybe I could live in a camper for a while? Get on a tiny house show?

A funny story. One summer almost 20 years ago when things were not going well for me in the house or the money department, I ended up crashing one night at the house of my friends who'd gone off to their other house in another country.

Their house sitter was this guy I knew from around town. Back in his day, he'd partied pretty hard. But by this time, he was all kindness and brotherly. He made me a steak. I told him I owed the government one hundred thousand dollars.

I got a little teary because I'd had one glass of wine too much.

He laughed and said, "If it makes you feel any better, I've snorted that much coke up my nose." I have to say—that night was a real turning point for me. Someone having the guts to admit something like that gave me real hope.

You have to trust me when I say that, for me, making student loans was unavoidable. The government wanting me to pay them back, understandable. At the end of a long day inside a pandemic classroom and 31 years, it's just inscrutable numbers on my Credit Karma.

It's just money.

And, I cannot pay back the money I borrowed to get a degree to do the thing I do by doing the thing I do for money—teaching high school. So you would have to be better at math than I am to figure out the solution to this problem.

Ice Station Larry

PAUL CULLUM

Here's to Daddy Claxton, may his name forever stand
And always be remembered in the courts throughout the land
Now his earthly race is over and the curtains 'round him fall
We'll carry him home to Dixie on the Wabash Cannonball.

—Roy Acuff

FOR ROUGHLY TWO YEARS, FROM THE SUMMER of 1994 to the spring of 1996, I had the signal pleasure of working for LFP, i.e., Larry Flynt Productions—pleasure in the sense of having seen active combat and survived unspeakable carnage, with the freedom to dine out on those experiences for the rest of my life.

I was the Managing Editor of *Film Threat* magazine—"We are the mammals who eat the dinosaurs' eggs!"—the clearinghouse for all things film geek, in those last few moments before the Internet rendered such enterprises a growth industry.

Larry had recognized in *Film Threat* founder Chris Gore a like-minded sensibility, one that could terrorize L.A.'s single-industry town if hyper-capitalized, and so he offered a tiny suite of offices in a glass tower at the corner of Wilshire and La Cienega and turned the hooligans loose on Hollywood's powermongers, who were the real pornographers after all.

The bi-monthly *Film Threat* had a budget of $5,000 per issue, all in—staff, articles, office supplies—so I was forced to subsidize my income as a copy editor. My high-minded principles prevented me from working on such porn titles as *Beaver Hunt, Barely Legal,* or the workhorse *Hustler,* and so I opted instead for the fetish digests like *Modern Gun, Fighting Knives* and something we affectionately referred to as "Celebrity Death Watch." Overseen by a woman named Linda Cauthen (we secretly referred to her as "Linda Coffin") these were one-off, standalone memorial tribute issues dedicated to show-biz icons who, based on our careful actuarial calculations, could reasonably be expected to pass away in such a time frame as might justify the investment.

Having been frozen out of self-respecting bookstores and newsstands (the all-night mega-stall at Cahuenga and Sunset notwithstanding) Flynt had cobbled together a distribution apparatus that comprised virtually every porn arcade and liquor store in America. As such, he was uniquely situated to target a particular demographic, one susceptible to bad judgment born of strong drink or curdled desire, just as certainly as the gangsters and pro-to-fascists at American Media (*National Enquirer, Star*) had ascertained how to leverage incipient hunger and the impulse sugar buzz of the supermarket checkout aisle to reveal untapped strains of schadenfreude and grievance. I was responsible for large chunks of our Frank Sinatra, Bob Hope, and George Burns commemorative volumes. At the end of the day, I felt altogether better about myself.

Born in the Shadow of the Peabody Coal Company

Larry Claxton Flynt, Jr.— presumably the same Claxtons whose lineage Roy Claxton Acuff, just across the state line in Maynardville, Tennessee, appropriated for his third verse of "The Wabash Cannonball"—was born in the coal hollers of Magoffin County, Kentucky, the same despoiled backdrop as the Butcher Holler of Loretta Lynn's "Coal Miner's Daughter" (song and movie) and the Muhlenberg County of John Prine's "Paradise." My friend John Patterson, who was a Flynt minion for roughly the same period I was and (spoiler alert) authored the "Letters to *Hustler*" column (before becoming a beloved film columnist at the *Guardian* of two decades' standing) summarized this biography succinctly: "Larry Flynt was born in the shadow of the Peabody Coal Company, and adopted wholesale its approach to both human resources and the environment he inherited, as well as the raw materials of his profession."

Just before I got there, Larry had sold multiple commercial real estate holdings in Beverly Hills and purchased the Great Western Bank Building at 8484 Wilshire Boulevard. in which to house his empire—primarily, I'm convinced, because of the large sculpture of John Wayne on horseback that graces the entry plaza. Carpooling in from our hipster redoubt of Los Feliz every morning, then turning at its crest onto La Cienega, this ten-story, 225,000-square-foot black barrel-shaped tower at the bottom of the hill, just catching the morning sun, looked exactly like the conning tower of a giant submarine rising out of the lower depths of Beverly Hills. We nicknamed it "Ice Station Larry."

This was also when Larry bought his first Gulfstream jet, and around the time it was announced in the trades that *The People vs. Larry Flynt* finally had been greenlit, after a long dormancy, and despite a rumored budget shortfall of $10 million. It's tempting to see this as the sudden impact of what was diagnosed as manic depression, although I asked director Milos Forman once if Larry had kicked in a big chunk of the budget himself, and he said no. But he might as well have.

Surreptitiously conducting interviews without an option on Larry's life rights, Forman told me that he and the film's screenwriters, Scott Alexander and Larry Karaszewski, received a phone call from the man himself. (At least I think it was Forman; 25 years later, the provenance is a little murky, and Milos, like they say in Hollywood, is no longer with the project.)

"This is Larry Flynt," came that signature elongated drawl—if you've ever heard William Burroughs speak, that's pretty close. "I understand you want to make a movie about me." After some vague attempt at a noncommittal answer, followed by an uncomfortable pause, he said, "Well, I guess you better come and see me."

The three of them dutifully showed up at Ice Station Larry and were escorted to his private office on the tenth floor—essentially, the entire tenth floor, done up in that special Clampett Revival-meets-Palace of Versailles interior design style that we christened "Larry XIVth"—authentic Tiffany lamps and flea-market knockoffs co-existing side by side. After keeping them waiting a suitable amount of time, Larry was wheeled in by an attractive female attendant. Implacable in his gold-plated wheelchair (having been gunned down by a white supremacist sniper in Lawrenceville, Georgia, during a break in his 1978 obscenity trial) he settled in behind his massive desk while they awaited the wrath of God.

Instead, he told them, "I'll answer any questions you want to ask me. In addition, I'll open up my archives and you can look through any of my papers you want. You can call anyone who knows me and interview them, and if they won't talk to you, you tell me and I'll call them and tell them to talk to you."

They sat waiting for the other shoe to drop. Larry nodded and the woman wheeled him away, and they were escorted out. Down in the parking lot, they were practically giddy: Had they just hustled one of the legendary hustlers? It wasn't until the Oscars, with Larry Flynt seated on the aisle, being welcomed by host Billy Crystal, that they realized what they had created was a form of

Renaissance portraiture. Whatever stories they told about him, they could never be worse than the ones he told about himself. And he would be remembered in their romanticized version forever.

The Man Who Loved Women. (Sort of.)

Larry Flynt was the most misanthropic person I think I ever met. And that's not just because he killed *Film Threat* right before the premiere of *The People vs. Larry Flynt,* no doubt assuming—correctly—that we were plotting some unauthorized takedown, incapable of not biting the hand that fed us. He liked Althea, his former employee and fourth wife, a woman whose life story was so volcanic it required Courtney Love to play her in the movie. (They once filmed a re-creation of the Kennedy assassination at Dealey Plaza using rented limos, replete with Althea scrambling out over the trunk.) And he apparently liked Suze Randall, the first female staff photographer at both *Hustler* and *Playboy.* After that, it was a pretty steep drop-off.

Old-timers there told of how when Althea was still alive (she died of a drug overdose in 1987), and profits fell below an acceptable level, the two of them would scan the salary list of executives, peel the high-earner off the top and summon him to their office, then fire him on the spot. This was presented as some kind of sport, Althea reportedly cackling, "We had that guy shitting in his pants, man!" (This and all the anecdotes related here are either secondhand or burnished in memory, so take them with a grain of salt.)

Flynt offered anyone the opportunity to succeed—exuding a kind of class-averse populism—but he would happily chop your head if you failed. My crew saw him as the Roger Corman of journalism, enabling those who would later stairstep to greatness, but that might have been aspirational on our parts. Novelists Jerry Stahl and Lydia Millet came before us, and the *Big Brother* crew came after. This was *Big Brother* the skate magazine, not the totalitarian game show, and it launched Spike Jonze, Johnny Knoxville and the *Jackass* brain trust.

We made do with the likes of *Futurama* writer Dan Vebber, *Pandora* show-runner Mark Altman and Dominic Griffin from *The Real World.* There also seemed to be an equitable distribution of men and women in staff positions, and I certainly saw none of the future #MeToo-style behavior that characterized, say, the *Chicago Tribune.* But for all that, the work environment was fairly acrid, if not outright toxic. Jay Babcock, an editor at *Sci-Fi Universe* (with which we shared a suite), and someone I later wrote for at *Mean* and

Arthur, posted a similar observation on Twitter:

"I worked inside Larry's empire on non-porn titles for three years, 1995–98. He was a tacky, cruel tightwad who hired well, offering gainful employment to at least three generations of smart, extremely witty misfits and bohemians, whose talents he dutifully and heartbreakingly squandered."

You'd talk to him once in a blue moon, whenever he made a point to wheel through and ask you how it was going, but he was a ubiquitous presence in the *Hustler* offices (which I was perched just outside of), and particularly what we referred to as "the Hall of Shame." This was a conference room dedicated to the presentation of "girl sets," those featured model layouts that appeared multiple times in each hardcore publication every month, all grouped by title and pinned to the walls, so that Larry could bask in them and accurately judge whether they rose to his rarefied standards.

Some mornings, summoned to the back shop on a production matter or to deliver page proofs, not yet fortified with coffee or industrial resolve, you might unwittingly catch a glimpse of this out of the corner of your eye, or be drawn to peek inside even as your conscious mind told you not to, much as you might a traffic pileup on the freeway, and then be suddenly pitched into a swirling sensorium of autonomous vagina, lapping seas of the stuff, as it caught you in its thrall and you slipped inexorably into its immutable vortex. Every job has its challenges.

America's Nether Regions

There was another anecdote I heard, also possibly apocryphal, which has stayed with me and seems to speak to a higher truth. At some point, long after *Hustler's* breakout success and its uneasy adoption of a corporate patina, Larry was persuaded to commission a marketing survey of magazine subscribers, in the interest of formulating an advertising strategy. Perhaps in the spirit of all working narcissists, who imagine the universe constituted in their own image, he had assumed his ideal reader was like him—rural, blue-collar, come from the working poor—even as he had systematically removed all of those conditions from his own life.

Except that the survey revealed the opposite: The average *Hustler* reader was middle- to upper-middle-class, financially better off than average, with expendable income. For them, its sniggering misogyny and abject vulgarity was a feature, not a bug.

Larry Flynt himself never lost or even muted his rabble-rousing politics; he remained an unrepentant, fire-breathing radical to the very end, less Roosevelt than Robespierre. At the height of the Clinton impeachment, he forced the resignation of an incoming Republican House Speaker with the threat of publishing embarrassing photos—less outraged by the man's politics than his hypocrisy—and he remained locked in mortal combat with televangelist Jerry Falwell and his Moral Majority for a quarter of a century.

But his enduring genius was this silent demographic, which he alone recognized and insisted upon—perhaps even before it recognized itself. I don't think we've seen the last of it.

Larry Flynt died February 10, 2021 at his home in the Hollywood Hills. The cause was reported as heart failure.

Vaccine Priority List

BY DAVID GALEF

Phase 1A

high-risk hospital workers

low-risk hospital administrators

big risk-takers: gamblers; those who text while driving

EMS workers

ESM, SME, and BDSM workers

healthcare providers

careful providers: Amazon executives

providers who care: Mummy, Daddy

essential doctors

doctors specializing in cosmetic enhancement

even optometrists

opportunistic relatives of doctors

long-term care residents

correctional facility residents

over my dead body

Phase 1B

law enforcement personnel

law enforcement victims

firefighters

other fighters (for social justice and truth)

people with co-morbid conditions

people who think morbid thoughts

those over 75

people who look over 75

people who claim to be over 75 to sell their makeup line

Phase 1C

essential workers (transit, food—even the 7-Eleven clerk with the purple faux-hawk) workers who are essential depending on your point of view

first responders

second responders

third-rate responders

second-party vendors

the party of the first part

educators with tenure

for adjunct instructors, see Phase 1Z

Phase 1D

nice people, including but not restricted to

the volunteer crossing guard who always waves hello

the neighbor who looks after your cat when you go on a trip

adults who throw back your ball after it lands in their yard

people who seem as if they're important

Porsche drivers

those who shop at Vera Wang

Phase 1E

psychics

ghosts, phantoms, ghouls

extraterrestrials

Republicans

tenth-raters

people who tell waitresses to unmask, honey, so we can see your pretty face

Phase Zero

Florida residents convicted of throwing an alligator through a drive-through window

Florida residents pardoned by Governor DeSantis

Governor DeSantis

VI:

HISTORY
LESSONS

As Yale historian Frank Snowden documented in *Epidemics and Society,* people have responded in similar ways to plagues throughout history. Hysteria, denial, magical thinking, scapegoating, cheating, lying, profiteering—the worst of human nature parades itself when the plague doctor comes knocking.

Our magazine was named after perhaps the most well-known account, Daniel Defoe's *A Journal of the Plague Year*, published in 1722. Defoe's book is an archetypal account of the rumormongering and myth-making that attends plague. He wrote it in the first person, as if the author was on the scene, but when scholars did the math, they realized that Defoe was a mere lad of about five in 1665–1666, when the bubonic plague killed 100,000 inhabitants of London.

Yet Defoe vamped a bit, writing as if the book was a genuine contemporary account—sort of. The title page states that it consists of: "Observations or Memorials of the most remarkable occurrences, as well public as private, which happened in London during the last great visitation in 1665. Written by a CITIZEN who continued all the while in London. Never made publick before."

To be fair, he credited the book to HF, later understood to be his uncle Henry Foe, who lived through the plague in London. Foe may have left a journal but there's no question that the writing style, which holds up today, is his nephew's. Reading the book, though, you feel as though you are with HF on the streets of London. It's that vivid, that immediate.

Defoe also claimed that *Robinson Crusoe* was written by a man who lived on a desert island for 28 years, and that his book about the celebrated thief Moll Flanders was written "from her own memorandums."

Breaking the fourth wall was Defoe's specialty. In our own time, the pandemic did that, casting us into a netherworld where Death stalked us. Many of us lost our balance in a maelstrom of heightened emotion. Fear infected us, it drove us. Too many of us resorted to a digitized version of the magical thinking described by Defoe.

It's one thing to identify the reactions to plague, quite another to figure out how to use this information. One hopes to discover remedies, but perhaps the best we can hope for is insight.

These authors took on the task of viewing the pandemic through an historical lens. They examined the nature of history and its retellings, of evil, of art and mortality, and the tenuousness of civilization's hold.

The Last Great Visitation

MICHAEL BROWN

BEING OBSERVATIONS OR MEMORIALS, OF THE MOST REMARKABLE OCCURRENCES, AS WELL PUBLICK AS PRIVATE, WHICH HAPPENED IN LONDON DURING THE LAST GREAT VISITATION IN 1665.

Written by a Citizen who continued all the while in London.
Never made publick before.

In early April of last year, a package arrived: the Penguin Classics edition of Daniel Defoe's *A Journal of the Plague Year*. The gift note attached read: "Be careful with this. It might hit close to home." The book came from my partner's mom, who has three daily newspaper subscriptions and a Nook well stocked with British literature. She was right. It did hit home. As we mark this our second pandemic year, *Plague Year* describes scenes at once utterly bizarre and strikingly familiar.

Plague Year presents itself as the detailed record dutifully kept by one "H.F." in 1665, when the "Great Plague" invested London. So compelling are H.F's observations, so methodical the tally of mounting dead that it was long believed that Defoe had been in London when the plague hit. In fact, he was but a wee lad in 1665. As scholar Frank Bastian writes, H.F. may instead "be identified with Defoe's uncle, Henry Foe, with complete certainty."

Whether *Plague Year* is history, fiction, or hoax has long been debated, but at least some of Defoe's tale may have sprung from his eyewitness uncle. Defoe could also have drawn upon contemporary reports—as he published in 1722, plague was just loosening its grip on Marseilles.

Three years ago, if you had read not this *Journal of the Plague Year* but Defoe's, with its heaps of corpses, wails of lamentation, and smell-o-vision-caliber noxious fumes, you might have concluded that the past was clearly worse than the present and that, notwithstanding many strains and cracks, the great Enlightenment ideal of progress holds, if only on the medical front.

That was before 900,000 dead—and counting—in this wealthy nation of ours. It was before refrigeration trucks became mobile morgues and food-cupboard lines stretched around the block and over the horizon. It was before shoppers assaulted store clerks in the name of going unmasked. It was before crematoria became front-page photos and obituaries crowded out the usual news.

At some point in 2020, Defoe's pages began to read less like dispatches from a safely distant history and more like stories ripped from the headlines. If ever it was possible to read *Plague Year* as a smug modern, it no longer is.

In July of the first pandemic year, Feilding Cage, a visual editor at Reuters, produced an interactive exercise called "Why time feels so weird in 2020." Living amid the "pandemic has heightened our awareness that time is subjective," Cage concluded. The hours feel longer when, instead of the usual harried round of things, we are in Covid isolation. But it's not just our subjective perception of time that shifts—the difference, for example, between "time flying" when we're having fun and slowing down when we're depressed. It's also the nature of historical time and how we locate our experience in it.

The pandemic evokes the pioneering work of mid-20th-century French historian Fernand Braudel. In the 1920s, Braudel accepted a teaching position in Algeria. Thinking back across the water to his native France, he began to see that traditional national histories—accounts of what kings, ministers, or generals said and did in throne rooms and on battlefields—were simply the surface layers of time, beneath which deeper, slower currents moved.

Braudel's historical imagination shifted from the geographic unit of the nation-state to a larger, older, and more rhythmic domain: the Mediterranean itself. Captured by the Germans while serving with French forces in 1940, Braudel eventually became a prisoner of war in Lübeck. There he trained his mind on a scale of history wider than the terrible episodes through which he was living. In prison camp he drafted a sweeping account of the Mediterranean world in the expansive age of Spanish and Ottoman rivalry.

Braudel's sense of historical time was cultivated not in plague years, but in a time of war. Yet his notion of history looked beyond the drama of a stochastic event. A precursor of systems theory, Braudel gave us a sense that history is plural. Some historical temporalities are brief and *allegro con moto*—the length and pace of a presidency, for instance. Others are very long—like the Little Ice Age—and both literally and figuratively glacial.

Across a range of temporalities, we and Defoe's Londoners are separated by epochal divides; the Stuart England of the Great Plague and the Georgian England of *Plague Year's* publication are both long gone. But in terms of human mortality, and particularly mass death by disease, we and Defoe's people occupy the same temporality. From that basic commonality, others emerge.

Among them is the recognition that, to quote Cyndi Lauper, whose parti-colored costumes evoke the wise fool of 17th-century England: "money changes everything." This, too, was noted by Defoe, and it can hardly be missed when you look at the disparity between white-collar people fretting over their backgrounds for Zoom calls and the dangers faced by frontline workers. To take but one example: in stark numbers from San Diego County, California, farm workers' share of the Covid death toll was 612 percent higher than their share of the working population, according to data reporting by the Voice of San Diego. Often, the less a job pays, the more physical danger it poses. The pandemic didn't start that dynamic; it threw it into sharp relief.

Such disparities were not lost on Defoe, whose ups and downs were as dramatic as the plots of his novels. At one point, he was forced to declare bankruptcy and did time in a debtor's prison. As his raucous novel *Moll Flanders* amply reveals, Defoe was acutely aware of the divide between rich and poor, and he was no friend of the former.

So it is no wonder that Defoe's *Journal* notes the details of inequity with seemingly scientific precision, compiling a record of how the burden of plague falls upon all, but its distribution follows that of wealth. At the outset, when the plague reaches London, Defoe's narrator, H.F. sees that "the richer sort of people, especially the nobility and gentry from the west part of the city, thronged out of town."

It's not exactly Airbnb in the Catskills, but "all that had friends or estates in the country retired with their families." The exodus includes H.F.'s elder brother who advised his younger sibling to do the same: "In a Word, he was for my retiring into the Country, as he resolved to do himself with his Family; telling me, what he had it seems, heard abroad, that the best Preparation for the Plague was to run away from it." (His warnings went unheeded or there would be no *Journal of the Plague Year*.)

The emptying of London described by Defoe calls up images we've seen more recently, both real and doctored: painterly scenes of empty city streets, dolphins leaping in Venice canals. Defoe wrote that when "one would have thought the very city itself was running out of the gates, and that there would be nobody left behind; you may be sure from that hour all trade, except such as related to immediate subsistence, was, as it were, at a full stop."

Those left behind had recourse to tactics also familiar: outsourcing risk and hoarding supplies. Londoners employing servants sent them to market in their stead, the Instacart of their day. And many wealthier Londoners, "foreseeing the approach of the distemper, laid up stores of provisions sufficient for their whole families, and shut themselves up...so entirely that they were neither seen or heard of till the infection was quite ceased." In contrast, "the poor people could not lay up provisions, and there was a necessity that they must go to market to buy."

Like the epidemiological burden, the economic one falls most heavily on poorer folk. Many trades and what we would call service sector work were no longer viable, driving those employed in them from subsistence to lack of it. Economic necessity begets increased risk. Among the 17th-century counterparts of Instacart workers running to the market, "a great many that went thither sound brought death home with them."

Viruses are indiscriminate, risk inequitable.

A plague that afflicts all requires more than individual action, one might think. How did Defoe's government respond? The magistrates of London perform like the most principled politicians of our own time, and rather better than most, if Defoe is to be believed.

City officials put in place measures "for the general safety, and to prevent the spreading of the distemper," H.F. tells us. "I shall have frequent occasion to speak of the prudence of the magistrates, their charity, their vigilance for the poor, and for preserving good order, furnishing provisions, and the like, when the plague was increased."

When shutdowns arrive, they fall heavily on the entertainment sector, for which the decree is made "that all plays, bear-baitings, games, singing of ballads, buckler-play, or such-like causes of assemblies of people be utterly prohibited, and the parties offending severely punished by every alderman in his ward."

Restaurants are shuttered too, with an element of economic justice. The order goes out:

That all public feasting...and dinners at taverns, ale-houses, and other places of common entertainment, be forborne till further order and allowance; and that the money thereby spared be preserved and employed for the benefit and relief of the poor visited with the infection.

Bars likewise:

That disorderly tippling in taverns, ale-houses, coffee-houses, and cellars be severely looked unto, as the common sin of this time and greatest occasion of dispersing the plague.

Reasoning, like contemporary mayors and governors, that nighttime is the right time for incautious conduct, London officials set last call to inhibit transmission of plague, resolving that: "…no company or person be suffered to remain or come into any tavern, ale-house, or coffee-house to drink after nine of the clock in the evening."

The most stringent measure in Defoe's London is quarantine in the form of household confinement. When plague is found in a residence, all who dwell there are locked in (literally, as opposed to our figurative "lockdown") to contain contagion. By 1665, there would have been 300 years of precedent for such a measure: Milan dramatically reduced its death toll from the Black Death of 1348 by bricking up the homes of the infected.

In Defoe's London, those "so confined made bitter lamentations" and brought their complaints to the Lord Mayor. Some do more than complain. Just as cities and states today have hired contact tracers, so London authorities appoint "examiners" to seek out cases of plague and "watchmen" to stand guard at the sealed homes of those found to have it. The latter is a particularly fraught employment, as "several violences were committed and injuries offered to the men who were set to watch the houses."

We have in our time seen viral (indeed) videos of store employees being physically attacked by those who refuse to comply with mask requirements—a provocation hardly comparable to being locked in a house. Contemporary measures, like "shelter in place" orders, look mild compared to the "the shutting up of houses, so as to confine those that were well with those that were sick."

As we might imagine, this arrangement "had very great inconveniences in it." Just as Americans have fought public-health measures today, those locked down in Defoe's rendering of London "broke out by force in many places," resulting in "frequent scuffles and some mischief."

Others proceed in more covert ways, as people employed "all manner of stratagem…to get out" of the magistrates' constraints. We have seen stratagems too, not so much to break rules—little strategy in that—so much as to work creatively within them. The drive-in theater and the outdoor pop-up enjoyed a booming year. So did all manner of outdoor dining configurations and socially distanced socializing. The drive-by birthday was an event. But these accommodations did not satisfy everyone, and, as Defoe writes of London, so with us "confinements made many people desperate, and made them run out of their houses at all hazards."

Hazards indeed, for in *Plague Year* as in our year, those who circulate propagate. Defoe makes that especially true of "those that did thus break out" of quarantine, for they "spread the infection farther by their wandering about with the distemper upon them." Just as now, the afflicted in Defoe's world carry the illness to others, often as unwitting accomplices.

"The infection," H.F. observes, "is retained in bodies apparently well, and conveyed from them to those they converse with, while it is known to neither the one nor the other." Anyone for whom the term "asymptomatic spread" sends a shiver down the spine will recognize how Defoe's people became "exceeding shy and jealous of every one that came near them"—once they knew "that the infection was received in this surprising manner from persons apparently well."

The plague that struck London in 1665 and that was burning out in Marseilles as Defoe published in 1722 was bubonic. While our coronavirus can take weeks to move from infection to severe illness, bubonic plague works quickly. The interval from seeming health to painful death could be brief, and few who fell sick recovered. Perhaps the most unusual Covid symptoms are the loss of taste and smell. Bubonic plague is relatively unsubtle, with swollen pockets called buboes appearing on the body—"mortal marks," as Defoe puts it. Such illness was plain to the naked eye.

I am fortunate that in my locale there has been periodic free, rapid testing for asymptomatic people. Last winter, my partner and I took our socially distanced places in a high-school cafeteria, watching those in front of us receive their nasal swabs from personnel wearing the now-familiar full regalia of PPE: face shield, mask, gloves, surgical-style gown. When my turn came, the swab tickled my sinuses and I reared back for what felt like an irresistible rhinal revolt.

"Sneeze!" shouted the PPE'd attendant who had given me the swab, as if she were saying "Fore!" or, indeed, "Bomb!" Some ran for distance. Others ducked and covered. Thankfully, I was able to defuse without detonating.

Reflecting their own understanding of viral spread, Londoners reacted not so much to imminent sneezes as to offensive smells. When in Aldgate Church a parishioner "fancied she smelt an ill smell" indicating the presence of plague, she communicated her fears to those nearby and set in motion an exodus from "the two or three adjoining pews."

Our understanding of viral transmission has advanced since Defoe's day. And yet, like Defoe's Londoners, we have our rituals for protecting ourselves in public. Many of these habits are consequential, providing real benefit. Others, however, may be more reassuring than genuinely prophylactic. Today and in *Plague Year*, there is an emphasis on "hand hygiene," as Dr. Fauci puts it, and the peril of "high-touch" surfaces. At London markets, H.F. relates, customers buying "a joint of meat…would not take it off the butcher's hand, but took it off the hooks themselves." For their part, butchers "would not touch the money, but have it put into a pot full of vinegar." All "carried bottles of scents and perfumes in their hands," as I my trusty sanitizer.

Have you ever put sanitizer on other than your hands? H.F. describes one woman who subscribed to the precaution of "washing her head in vinegar…and if the smell of any of those she waited on was more than ordinary offensive, she snuffed vinegar up her nose and sprinkled vinegar upon her head-clothes, and held a handkerchief wetted with vinegar to her mouth." That degree of vinegar use puts into perspective why sanitizer was sold by the 40-ounce jug at my corner drugstore—and frequently sold out. For every practice that provides actual safety or ritual that merely provides comfort, there is a sham, peddled by those seeking to translate suffering and uncertainty into profit. In Defoe's London, "the posts of houses and corners of streets were plastered over" by advertisements from those "quacking and tampering in physic." They peddle "Infallible preventive pills against the plague" and "Sovereign cordials against the corruption of the air."

Such nostrums gain traction as much—or more—from the panic of the buyers as the hucksterism of the sellers. In a pandemic, people are wont to believe in miracle cures and infallible remedies. That we wish something were true does not make it so, but it does supply the will to believe. That will may overpower any checks supplied by reason and evidence, particularly when quacks and putative authorities put their fingers on the scales of belief in the service of their own narrow economic (or political) interests.

The desire to believe in, as H.F. puts it, "mountebanks, wizards and fortune-tellers" is not only a form of wishful thinking; it is an alternative reality to pit against what, in a pandemic, can be so frightening as to be unassimilable: reality itself. To place fake cures and powerless prophylactics in the light of reason is to acknowledge how truly vulnerable one is before the raging virus.

So strong may be the impulse to deny this truth that it drives people not only to drinking bleach or ingesting light but, Defoe writes, "even to madness."

What does madness look like? Desperate people take to "wearing charms, philtres, exorcisms, amulets, and I know not what," H.F. records disapprovingly. They act "as if the plague was not the hand of God, but a kind of possession of an evil spirit...to be kept off with crossings, signs of the zodiac, papers tied up with so many knots, and certain words or figures written on them, as particularly the word Abracadabra, formed in triangle or pyramid."

As evidence of the "the insufficiency of those things," H.F. relates how many who wore them "were afterwards carried away in the dead-carts and thrown into the common graves of every parish with these hellish charms and trumpery hanging about their necks." We know a thing or two, ourselves, about hellish charms and Trumpery.

Plague is a more vivid word than pandemic, but both terms conjure worlds where illness and death have slipped the boundaries normally imposed upon them and intruded visibly, urgently, and jarringly into everyday life.

The sudden awareness of mortality, the rush of fear, all are familiar to a reader of Defoe; the solecism bursting in on our ordinary days like the comet that "appear'd for several Months before the Plague" in H.F.'s account. Defoe's narrator tells the reader he could "almost" dismiss the superstitious beliefs that comets portend God's judgment.

Poised between the Irrational and the burgeoning hegemony of scientific thought, H.F. hedged his bets. In a masterpiece of political speech, he juxtaposes the fear of God's judgment to the "natural causes assign'd by the Astronomers for such Things," which have "their Motions, and even their Revolutions...calculated, or pretended to be calculated; so that they cannot be so perfect call'd the Fore-runners, or Fore-tellers, much less the procurers of such Events, as Pestilence, War, Fire, and the like."

We, too, remain, in large part, strung between the rational and the visceral. The first impulse remains denial. When rumors of plague first emerge, H.F. reports, "the Government had a true account of it, and several councils were held about ways to prevent its coming over; but all was kept very private."

Among the public, consequently, the "rumour died off again, and people began to forget it as a thing we were very little concerned in, and that we hoped was not true."

We had such reassurances ourselves. "It's one person coming in from China," the president said of Covid in January of 2020. "We have it under control. It's going to be just fine." A month later, he predicted: "It's going to disappear. One day—it's like a miracle—it will disappear."

Flourishing in tandem with our denial—not only Donald Trump's politically motived strain, but the everyday denial of mortality that makes it possible for us to function—an insistent optimism—call it hubris—may be why we were not prepared for Covid. And it is why, the next time plague scythes the population, we may, once again, be unprepared.

Nearly four centuries have passed since the Great Plague of London about which Defoe wrote, and though *Homo sapiens* has in the intervening years set foot on the moon, we have not put an end to such mass afflictions. As I write, the number of infected in the United States alone exceeds 75 million; the number of dead is soon to reach 1 million. *The New York Times* reports these numbers in a chart under the heading "Coronavirus in the U.S.: Latest Map and Case Count."

Plague Year, too, has its charts and counts. Defoe referred to them as "bills of mortality." All this counting (as well as undercounting, which Defoe points to and which we see today, both in the U.S. and elsewhere) signals a potentially strong resonance between his time and ours: the illusion of control by measurement, as if the enormity of a thing could be contained by quantifying it. To put it more bluntly: Statistics give us the illusion that death can be managed.

Defoe's reconstruction of the plague year—even if as much the product of his imagination as his research—shows Londoners acting then in a manner resembling us now. Viruses mutate. Our response to mass illness, it seems, less so.

The notion of history that lives in many of our heads here in the United States is a linear one. The trajectory reflects some of our deepest assumptions about the nature of history, including not only its linear character but also its direction. We are moving forward such that each passing second provides increasing distance from every point in the past. For many of us, that distance is a measure of moral as well as temporal change. It is Progress.

The alien world of the past—the strangeness of Defoe's imagination and the London it limns—affirms this concept of history. Olde and plague-ridden England is a place where terrified people aver that "a flaming sword held in a hand coming out of a cloud" has its "point hanging directly over the city," and a man called Solomon Eagle roams the streets, hurling down "judgement...in a frightful manner, sometimes quite naked, and with a pan of burning charcoal on his head." Our world is unlike that one. The distance we have from it is a mark of our progress. Or so we assumed until QAnon transformed our neighbors.

If the differences between *Plague Year* and our own years of plague harden our assumptions about history, time, and progress, then what do we make of the striking similarities between our time and the text? The unmistakable resonances between Defoe's plague and our pandemic may leave us searching for a new model. Gone is the straight line. Instead, a cross-sectional image of the planet Earth comes to mind. There is a relatively thin crust along which all our building, talking, doing, and living takes place. Beneath that surface, there are strange depths that we see only seldom and about which we know very little. What we do know is vaguely menacing. What we do see—earthquakes and eruptions—is terrifying. Life on the crust has changed dramatically since Defoe's time. We think differently, live differently, and are in many ways a new kind of people. But the vulcanian stuff below that crust does not so much change as simmer. From time to time, it surfaces.

The past is a foreign country, but the substratum beneath all countries is this ur-experience—of living, dying, and fear—to which plagues summon us. Like comets that cross the sky once a century lest we forget the vastness of the dark that surrounds us, plagues that come once a century (only once, we hope) recall us to a deep sense of fragility, casting us back into an experiential realm known, also, to those who lived long ago.

In *La Méditerranée et le Monde méditerranéen à l'époque de Philippe II* (1949), Braudel asked readers to think of time as layered. One temporality was that of events—the headlines of the day, the latest TikTok dance craze. A second layer was a longer, more cyclical kind of time—the duration over which political dispositions shift or an economy arcs from boom to bust. A third layer, the *longue durée*, was a deep kind of time. It had an environmental rhythm to it, measuring the long horizon of interactions between geography and humanity that results not so much in events or governments as societies and cultures.

These layers of time co-exist, such that we presently live in the hubbub of headlines, the long run of economic and political cycles, and the underlying, almost tectonic reshaping of human experiences all at once. In the briefer two of these temporalities, we exist in different eras than Defoe's Londoners did. They were neither concerned with Joe Rogan versus Neil Young on Spotify nor with the broader rise of digital media. Those preoccupations are for us.

But when I fall through the topmost layers of time and history to land on what is—apart, maybe, from cosmology or liturgical time—the bottommost sort of duration, the one where humanity is beset by plagues, then I am startled to see there beside me the dwellers of 17th-century London.

Journals of the plague year are, then, perhaps a misnomer. The striking resemblance between our experience and the one Defoe presents suggests that we are not living in a plague year, but a plague age.

Déjà Vu All Over Again

UNKONDA RASHEDA SAWYER

IN DECEMBER 2013, WHEN THE EBOLA VIRUS broke out in West Africa, I was in Burkina Faso. I'd finished my service as a Peace Corps volunteer and extended my stay so I could gain more work experience with international aid organizations. What I witnessed over the next few months was something I never thought I would see duplicated in the United States. Yet here we are, nearly ten years later, and all I can think of is the phrase "déjà vu all over again."

I should explain a little about my background. I'm descended from formerly enslaved people repatriated to West Africa in the 1800s. These former slaves, called Creoles, dominated Liberian politics for roughly a century; in fact, my uncle was acting president of Liberia in the 1990s. Years earlier, when the country had fallen into civil war, my parents fled, taking us to the United States. I was five years old.

I admit that, to some extent, I bought into the idea that Liberia and its neighboring countries—Sierra Leone, Guinea, Cote D'Ivoire—were deficient when it came to civil society, especially in contrast to America. For us, in many ways, the U.S. had been "the shining city on a hill." I wouldn't say this was a conscious assumption on my part; neither was it completely untrue. I grew up living in Maryland. I went to good private Catholic schools. My family was secure.

I could not have conceived that America would look so much like Liberia, which, even after climbing out of the deepest part of the crater its big men dug in the '90s, still has only a thin skin of governance. But as I lived through Ebola, and six years later, Covid, I realized how naïve I had been.

Ebola was shocking enough. I don't mean simply the disease, which was awful: a hemorrhagic fever that kills 90 percent of the people who catch it. The disease was bad, but the reactions to it were, in a certain sense, more unsettling. I watched as government officials and individuals responded to a crisis with denial, and citizens acted out with rage, superstition, scapegoating, and, sometimes, bar-hopping. It wasn't all bleak. There were acts of generosity and even heroism.

But mostly there was hysteria and really, really bad information.

The News By Any Other Name

It was December 2013 when the news arrived to us in Ouagadougou that cases of Ebola had been detected in Guinea. There was no official announcement that the disease was Ebola. But the Africans I knew were very aware of it, because Ebola had been identified in the Democratic Republic of Congo in 1976 and periodically resurfaced after that. The symptoms were not subtle. Terrible bleeding and rapid death.

In Burkina Faso, we listened to the radio news intently to find out whatever we could about how Guinea was handling it, tuning in to international channels such as France 24 and BBC Africa, and local channels such as Radio Television Burkina (RTB) or Radio Omega. We were desperate to find out whatever we could about how Guinea was handling the outbreak. Basically, the Guinean method seemed to consist of pretending it wasn't happening. It wasn't until March 2014—more than three months after the outbreak started—that the Guinean government even acknowledged the problem.

That's not to say we didn't get information. We had a different way of being informed. To understand the way information traveled, it is important to understand that Liberia, Sierra Leone, Burkina, Guinea are linked geographically, historically, politically, economically, and culturally. National borders, drawn by colonialists, are extremely porous. Personally, I remember that Burkinabé mercenaries were sent to Liberia during Liberia's civil war. And I had always heard how Liberia's ex-president, the U.S.-educated warlord Charles Taylor, was a frequent presence in Burkina Faso. He had a home there and at least one of his children attended the International School of Ouagadougou.

In 2013, news traveled along with commodities like tomatoes or tires. Gueckedou, Guinea, is a regional trading post, so merchants and commercial vehicles traveled to and from Liberia regularly. By Christmas, even though media outlets relying on the official reports weren't giving us the information we needed, people in Burkina Faso were already discussing what actions could be taken if Ebola came nearer. I recall a conversation with a friend who said, "Bon, on attend pas les blanches pour nos informations." Loosely translated this means "we don't wait for white people for our news."

Even though it would be months later when an Ebola outbreak was officially declared, the Burkina Faso government had already begun taking action. Everyone around me comforted me that everything would be fine, that measures would be taken to stop Ebola before it reached us.

Perhaps I should have worried about my own safety but what was troubling me was the way Liberia would respond. I may have been reacting to my early memories. My Uncle Amos had been an outspoken activist, along with Ellen Johnson Sirleaf, Africa's first woman president, who was in office when Ebola broke out. In 1983, Amos became one of the founders of the Liberian People's Party. I was a toddler when his home was set ablaze and he was clapped into jail, along with Sirleaf, for protesting government policies.

To the outside world, Ellen Johnson Sirleaf's election seemed to put an end to Liberia's troubles. But no single person could be a panacea for a society that had been in ruins. As reports of Ebola's brutal toll surfaced, I worried about my aunts, uncles, cousins, and friends. One of my college roommates had moved to Liberia, too, and several cousins had moved there. I was a wreck.

My friends in Burkina couldn't understand why I was so upset. I had to explain why I was so convinced that my friends and relatives were in peril. Liberia shares a border with Guinea. Liberia imports goods from Guinea and movement across the border is very fluid. An outbreak in Guinea would be an outbreak in Liberia.

And as I anticipated, the virus soon spread to Liberia. It moved through the country at warp speed.

A Strange, Unknown Enemy

Despite the warnings, my relatives complained that the government wasn't taking measures to combat the disease. Nightclubs, markets, and football stadiums were packed. In rural areas, people believed Ebola was a curse. Traditional death rituals of washing and cleaning the dead spread the disease, but it was difficult to convince grieving relatives to abandon their loved ones.

And when fears rose, so did traditional religious beliefs. Wild rumors spread that doctors and nurses were harvesting the organs of the dead. These rumors were not confined to Liberia. In Guinea, aid workers from Médecins Sans Frontières, Doctors Without Borders, were forced to evacuate a health center because of the threat of violent attacks. In 2018, when Ebola cycled through Congo, the same scenario played out.

My relatives and friends had no choice but to isolate themselves. They asked friends not to visit, hoping they would understand. They worked at home. My cousin set up a hand washing station outside his house for people who didn't have ready access to clean water. I listened to complaints. Most Liberians were not taking the outbreak seriously. Yet Ebola killed 90 percent of those infected and the deaths were devastatingly painful and grisly.

Ellen Johnson Sirleaf later would call Ebola "a strange, unknown enemy" and admit that the government didn't know how to respond. In her defense, she would later tell the press that the country had only two ambulances. Doctors and nurses were afraid to work; those who did were swiftly killed by the virus.

It was chaos.

That's why I couldn't believe it when I learned that the Independence Day celebrations would still be going on. Here's what I read in a newspaper:

MONROVIA, LIBERIA: JULY 26, LIBERIA'S INDEPENDENCE, DESPITE THE EBOLA TRAGEDY SOME CHOSE TO CELEBRATE LIFE WHILE RECOGNIZING THE NEED TO BE AWARE OF THIS VIRUS. THE PLACE TO BE WAS THE DAY PARTY AT THE SKYBAR.

Party at the Skybar? Really? I was outraged. Where is the government, I remember thinking. What are the protocols, what is the national response? Some of the people who attended some of these gatherings later contracted Ebola and died. I began to wonder how we could keep Burkina safe if Liberia's outbreak spread across our borders.

I remember my family in Liberia and the United States asking what measures the Burkinabé government was taking. Burkina stood in sharp contract to Liberia. Police went around to street vendors to verify they were not selling or cooking outlawed foods such as bushmeat. People were advised not to travel. At the borders, guards did temperature checks and verified departure and arrival information. If a visitor was coming from an infected country they were not permitted to enter.

A full-fledged awareness campaign took place over the course of several months. Businesses, hospitals, schools, and all public places were to train, emphasize, and display prevention measures.

Finally, in September 2014, Liberia marshaled the resources to fight the virus. Initially, Sirleaf went hard, using the military to close the country's borders. Inevitably, she was criticized for this, just as she had earlier been criticized for failing to act.

What made the real difference was help from the outside world. It took the death of a Liberian, Thomas Edward Duncan, 42, in Texas to galvanize a response from the U.S. Given the historic relationship between the two countries—the Firestone tire company had dominated Liberia's economy for much of the country's existence and Liberia is often called a colony of the U.S. in all but name—one might argue that help should have come sooner. But at least the world had become aware of the threat posed by Ebola.

I was in favor of all of it, of course, both in Liberia and Burkina. But my principles faltered when it came to my wedding, which I was planning for December 2014. I hadn't anticipated that a hotelier would ask if any family members would be coming from Liberia. It was hard to know what to feel. I was offended, but I, too, had concern that if people came for the wedding we might end up getting Ebola. It felt like something out of a horror movie.

Between an epidemic and civil unrest in Burkina Faso, we could have made a tragicomic version of a rom-com. We went ahead with our plans, and like every wedding, it was perfect in its imperfections.

By the end of the Ebola outbreak nearly two years later, Liberia had suffered the greatest number of casualties of the region's four countries. Nearly 5,000 people had died by the time the Liberian government declared it Ebola-free. I was immensely relieved that none of my friends or relatives were of that number.

The Failed State of America

During the Ebola crisis, that term "failed state," which had come into parlance in the 1990s, resurfaced. Ellen Johnson Sirleaf had been a figure of salvation but Ebola nearly destroyed her reputation. Even if Sirleaf had acted more rapidly, Liberia's public health infrastructure was so poor that a high death toll was inevitable. People were using makeshift barriers made of garbage bags and cloth to get by on a daily basis. Liberians in the U.S. were signing petitions, asking the Obama administration for help, and setting up GoFundMe campaigns for personal protective equipment for the home country.

The correlations to what I saw in the first year of Covid are astonishing. The United States of America couldn't secure and supply enough medical-grade masks and gloves to healthcare workers. Corpses piled up in parking lots. The president shouted denials. Misinformation was rampant. Hysteria reigned.

This was the *United States*, not Liberia, a country ranked between Angola and Libya in Transparency International's Fragile States Index.

And in the later stages of the pandemic, the U.S. resembled Liberia in another way: the country had been crippled by the public's loss of faith in government, along with many of the country's social institutions. A study published in *The Lancet* indicated that countries whose citizens trust the government achieve much higher vaccination rates, even without mandates, and lower death rates overall. While more cohesive countries had vaccination rates as high as 90 percent, the U.S. was stuck at roughly 70 percent.

In Liberia, public distrust of government clearly contributed to the breakdown of public health measures. Liberia had long had its struggles with corrupt leaders, civil unrest, civil war, coup d'états, and mass displacement of the population. A failure to respond during the Ebola outbreak was just the last in a long line of failures, solidifying what Liberians have known for years. But the United States? This was the place my family had found safety, the rock of my childhood.

Double Vision

In 2019 I found myself living in Zanzibar. My husband and I and our young son had left Burkina, fearing that the instability was making the country too dangerous. What did I say about déjà vu all over again? Not long after we arrived, I started hearing word of a virus in China. Remembering SARS and H1N1, my first thought was here we go, another virus coming from China. My second thought was I hope it doesn't reach Zanzibar, which has a large Chinese transient population of workers and investors plus tons of tourists.

By February, European countries were seeing outbreaks, and it was clear that Zanzibar would not be spared. It felt a bit eerie that I was hearing nothing about the U.S. combating the spread of coronavirus, either domestically or internationally. I hadn't heard a single concrete measure the U.S. government was taking. The country seemed to be acting as if it was business as usual.

Even though the United States, the country where I am a naturalized citizen, had a president who was bizarre, to say the least, I was sure that our other institutions would take the lead in fighting the virus. That was what I was used to as an American.

March came and went. Still there was no direction coming from the United States. In Zanzibar schools and businesses were considering when it would make sense to close and for how long. On March 18, 2020, the official message came from the Tanzanian government that schools were closed for a minimum of 30 days. At that point I started paying closer attention to the American news.

Of course, I was speaking to my family in the States. My mom is a teacher. Her school had closed, too, and she was uncertain when she would go back to work. On the night the Tanzanian government made its announcement, I decided to listen to the White House briefings on the Internet. I assumed that although the Trump administration was inept, for a pandemic they would pull themselves together and mount a presidential response.

I listened that night to the White House briefing, and came away even more confused. But I also was scared. The president sounded like someone who had no clue what was going on. What was worse, there appeared to be no plan for dealing with a virus that seemed quite dangerous.

I watched the White House briefings for a few more nights. I was convinced that something would eventually come of them. As the nights went on, I grew more and more fearful. Listening to the president of the United States speak so incoherently was giving me a grimmer outlook, both of the future of the virus and of America's future.

Trump sounded the same as leaders of tragically failed states. Maybe worse. By March, like many others, I discovered New York Governor Andrew Cuomo's press briefings. I stopped watching the White House press briefings and tuned in to Governor Cuomo's briefings every single day.

As the months went on, I watched how governors scrambled to get personal protective equipment. I watched a federal government that was more hands-off than I had ever witnessed in America. I yearned for leadership. Mostly I felt sad.

Over the next months, I experienced a kind of double vision. I saw the government's denial that a crisis was threatening the lives of the American people. I watched panic and superstition spread with the reach and alacrity of the virus itself, fake news and conspiracy theories that made so little sense, I couldn't believe the people I had lived with for most of my life could take these mad ideas seriously.

As hospitals broke under the strain, I saw wild parties, not at Monrovia's Skybar but at the Bonnaroo music festival.

I saw individuals taking action, but for a long time, only that. Nurses, doctors, emergency medical technicians, all working unbelievable shifts as the bodies piled up.

Later I would hear the same "blame for the messenger" rhetoric that had done so much damage in West Africa. There was nothing more shocking than the threats of violence—crafted with tissue-paper-thin deniability—by Fox

News talking head Jesse Watters against Dr. Anthony Fauci. It was unthinkable that, in the United States, an 81-year-old doctor who had devoted his career to fighting disease suddenly needed bodyguards. In traditional West African religions, unconventional women were called witches and blamed when misfortune befell a community. The same had happened in colonial days in the U.S. And I remembered when the Médecins Sans Frontières personnel had been run out of Guinea. This couldn't happen in contemporary America, I thought.

An unbearable sadness took over as I realized that nobody was in charge. America was no longer a global leader. Nobody was looking to us to do anything. I was seeing a great nation, a country I still believe can be great, reduced to something close to a failed state. Our public services were overwhelmed and the poor were dying at greater rates than the rich. The Trump administration had institutionalized corruption. There is no more powerful corrosive force. To my disgust, the pandemic did not slow down the graft or influence-peddling.

Later, Americans would point to the events of January 6, 2021 as an example of how close the country came to a coup d'état. I believe the decisive moment was earlier: June 11, 2020, when General Mark Milley appeared with Donald Trump at Lafayette Square after the administration had brutally dispersed protesters. Thankfully, Milley later apologized and the Joint Chiefs of Staff issued a statement asserting that the military leadership would remain loyal to the U.S. constitution—not to a demagogue.

Military interference in national politics and an ineffective judicial system are the last elements of failed states. Calling active-duty soldiers to disperse peaceful protesters and failing to charge and prosecute police officers who murder citizens were steps toward that final dissolution. I invite you to look up the social indicators of a failed state; if Trump is re-elected, we can guarantee that America will join the ranks of Yemen, Syria, and Iraq.

I am concerned. The country's divisions continue to deepen. Remember, Liberia's downfall had started with civil war.

Everything is Connected

What capped it all off for me was the civil unrest when citizens protested the death of a black man killed tragically by police: George Floyd. Learning of Floyd's death, I remembered that in 2014, while Ebola was raging, the racism hit home to me, again from a distance. That was when police killed Eric Garner, a black man in New York, one of a long list of Black American citizens murdered by police on a regular basis in the United States. These outbreaks of plague accompanied by widespread fear and hysteria became associated for me with the murders of black men.

We have moved from mass enslavement to mass incarceration, and between those two, murders at the hands of police, and other racist whites calling themselves vigilantes. Americans cannot overcome threats to the country's national integrity if racism persists. Racism is intricately tied to the demoralization that seeps into the populace when a government does not protect its citizens.

During the coronavirus pandemic it was another high-profile death that ripped off the thin scab we had grown on racism. George Floyd was yet another black man that met his fate at the hands of, or rather at the knee of, a white officer who kneeled on his neck for 8 minutes and 46 seconds. He died on camera and the world watched. Anger spilled through me. I was proud to see people protesting.

During the lockdown, I was secretly happy that fewer people would be out and there would be fewer chances for black people to get killed by police. But I was scared too, because I was thinking that just because you don't hear about or see a killing on video, doesn't mean someone didn't get murdered.

As more states opened, stories of gun violence multiplied. I can't forget the tragic and horrible story of Ahmaud Arbery, a 25-year-old black jogger murdered by three white men in Georgia in early 2020, but there were more, too many to list.

The pain of racism is so deep, it burns and literally makes it so you can't breathe. The story of my family spans the history of black Africans and their relationship with America. I want better for the United States. I want better for all of us.

Prague — & why I could not get there

BETH ALVARADO

ON A WALL IN MY APARTMENT THERE IS a black-and-white photograph my daughter took while we were in Prague. I looked at it every morning last summer, trying to get in the mood to write. It is, I would say, an iconic photo of the west end of the Charles Bridge. The building you are facing is white, a church. The photograph is peopled with statues, most of them on the roofs, most of them, I'm assuming, saints. Kathryn must have taken it on one of our early morning walks when the streets were empty. St. Nicholas Church, I think. There is something that looks very Eastern, a turret in the background that goes up to a spire. If the photo were in color, the turret would be the green of weathered copper.

Since the lockdown started, I had been writing about travel—previous travel, of course—to escape my trackless days and keep a record of them during the pandemic. Once we got to August, I found writing more and more difficult until, finally, I stopped.

The menu of days in August and September, then, went something like this: research on psoriatic arthritis, doomscrolling—(police violence against Black Lives Matter protesters eclipses the plague)—feel guilty, donate $20, work, take a walk with my daughter and her family, lunch with her twins, play school with the twins, work, Zoom class, more doomscrolling—(the coming election eclipses the plague)—feel worried, donate $20 (should I choose "monthly" because this wasn't going to be solved overnight?), Zoom meeting, another walk, drink a cocktail, help Kathryn make dinner, eat dinner, hug and kiss twins good night, drink wine while reading, more doomscrolling—(wildfires begin to eclipse the plague)—feel despair, long to go to Norway. But why Norway? When I wanted to write about Prague?

∿

Kathryn and I had gone to Prague in 2006. On the surface, we went because of a conference on writing and photography. When I told Kathryn I was going, over the phone, she'd said, "Oh, I want to go." Such wistfulness in her voice, such longing. I didn't yet know she was planning on leaving her first husband.

I told Kathryn, "Apply for a fellowship in photography and we'll figure out the rest." My parents had divorced when I was in my early thirties, but my mother didn't leave my father for another ten years. As soon as the divorce was final, my mother took herself to France. I remember my mother saying that when she felt the plane lift off, when she was finally on her way, leaving him below on another continent, she felt all the burden she had been carrying fall away. At that moment, because she felt free of him, I suppose she also felt the full weight of him. She said that to really leave someone, you had to put an ocean between you. My mother paid for Kathryn's plane ticket. She must have suspected what I did not.

Kathryn was escaping her marriage and I was escaping my mother. This might sound cruel. My mother had a fracture of her spine. That was the immediate crisis. But for years, pulmonary disease had diminished her lung capacity. I'd been taking care of her and, before that, helping her take care of her bedridden sister Dorothy. It felt like for years, this caregiving, although it might have been only six. Or seven. Or eight.

By 2006, my mother was terminal. For years, she had told people, "I have a terminal disease," confusing the word "terminal" with "chronic," a distinction that, in the end, made no difference. Really. So why did I insist on correcting her? When you die, you die.

I knew she might die while I was gone. She knew. But she wanted us to go. She made me promise not to let Kathryn out of my sight—she was worried about sex slave traders—but not to bring her home early, no matter what happened. I made her promise not to die. This was in her hospital room, the night before we flew out.

In Prague, my mother stayed in the periphery of my vision—as we were deposited, jet-lagged, at the door of the flat we would be renting with my friend Barbara; as we ascended with all our luggage in the creaky wire cage of an elevator; as we went out, crossing crowded Týn Square, Kathryn tucking my arm under hers because she could feel my disorientation. I wasn't quite there, my mother hovering, as the dead sometimes do, although she was not dead and would not die until after I returned home. She hovered as we passed the brightly lit shop fronts full of Bohemian crystal, amber earrings, and garnets like drops of blood; as we came around a dark corner to an opening, a street, trolleys rattling by; as we saw the Charles Bridge, the black statues silhouetted against the light sky at dusk, just as you may have seen in the postcards; as we wound our way, later, back through narrow cobbled streets, coal dust still graying the walls of buildings; as, even later, I stood in the classroom looking down on the Jewish cemetery's thin, toppling headstones.

My mother hovered as Kathryn and I toured Terezín, a holding camp, not a concentration camp, the guide was careful to tell us. Those who died there, mostly children and the elderly, were not liquidated, she said, but died, instead, from the conditions or else they were sent from here to concentration camps.

My mother hovered as we heard numbers so incredible, I knew I'd never remember them, one hundred, four hundred? slept in this room? The wooden platforms, where they slept, had no mattresses, no blankets, only so many centimeters allotted for each person.

She hovered as we learned about the cold showers, the elderly prisoners made to walk naked, wet, emaciated, starving, across snow-covered yards, from showers to bunks, weak, but not liquidated, not yet. Liquidated. How many times could this woman say this word in reference to human beings without her voice, her lilting voice, cracking? I could not help but picture my mother, her frail bones and thin blue veins, her sun-freckled skin, her modesty, my mother, her back hunched over from osteoporosis, arms cradling her breasts, walking naked through the snow.

∿

In my apartment now, next to the photograph that Kathryn took of the Charles Bridge, there are watercolors painted by a great-uncle, a botanist. I could not go outside once September came—because of the smoke—the West was on fire—so I found myself substituting them for the pine forest, outside yet untouchable. The paintings, ca. 1900, were landscapes from his travel around the world to paint exotic plants for textbooks; they used to line the walls of my aunt Dorothy's house in Carmel Valley. I wondered if her house was still standing or if it had been burned in this current conflagration. A 100-year wildfire, climatologists tell us, and yet only the beginning of more to come.

My aunt and uncle once had to bury these very watercolors in the yard to save them from fire. But that was over 40 years ago. This fire, this conflagration, has been a long time in the making.

Also in September: around four in the morning, every morning, I wake up with tightness around my heart. Was it my lungs? I'd been diagnosed with a mild case of bronchiectasis, the damage to the lungs that had eventually killed my mother and would complicate everything if I came down with Covid. How did I get bronchiectasis? I'd quit smoking when I was 19 and pregnant with Michael—but maybe it was my lungs. I'd had pneumonia twice. Or was it my heart? Worry over the fires? The coming election and armed self-appointed "patriots"? The state of our divided union?

I was worried about our democracy, it is true. And Michael. Michael, in Boise. He'd been ill since March and I was sure it was the allostatic load, the adaptation to chronic stress, that had tipped him over. Finally, a diagnosis: psoriatic arthritis, which is an autoimmune disease. Not good in the middle of Covid.

I worried, of course, about other things as well: Michael is Mexican-American, his wife is Jewish and very visible in her work in social justice, one child looks white but is nonbinary, the other looks Mexican. All four of them, therefore, possible targets.

Michael's income has gone down by half and he is homeschooling the kids. Boise, where, by December, the Anne Frank Memorial will be defaced with swastikas, and where, with an infection rate of 50 percent, people with guns will surround meetings and the homes of public health officials to protest wearing masks. It is easy to foresee danger, easy to worry about such things in advance.

Michael said it felt like his body was eating itself, and Kathryn said, It is. Some mornings, he could not walk.

I wanted to write about Prague, but I couldn't get there. I kept saying that on Zoom, "I can't get to Prague," and people would look at me: "Of course, you can't." I meant in my head. I couldn't even get there in my head. They say when you're depressed, your memories flatten, become generic, lose their particularity. Is this what was happening?

The rest of the photos Kathryn had taken were in a box high on a shelf in the garage. Why hadn't I thought to get them down? I skimmed an essay I'd written about Prague soon after the trip, but I couldn't remember anything beyond those words, nothing around the edges. It felt like the paralysis of grief.

There was fire on the coast, fire in the passes between here and the coast, fire to the south in California and to the north, up near Portland. When I stood looking out my window to the west, I could see the mountain and one ribbon of blue between the mountain and the clouds, but they were not clouds—it was smoke, heavy and dark.

We were not worried about fire. We could not go outside. But we didn't have to duct-tape our windows and doors shut like they did in Portland, although the smoke was seeping in, burning our eyes and dulling our minds, carrying tiny particulate matter that settled in our sinuses and lungs, maybe like splinters. Never good. Oh, the tender tissues of the lungs, especially worrisome, now, with small children, in the middle of a pandemic, just before flu season.

Was there smoke in Boise, I asked Michael. There was.

How much more can we bear, I wondered, not Americans only, of course; all of us—but I know people always bear more. It's what we do. How we do it, that seems to be another matter.

∿

Do you know there are very few movies on Netflix set in Prague? When we were there, we watched a documentary about a Jewish man who had escaped the Nazis by clinging to the undercarriage of a train. We were sitting in an airless auditorium as we watched, midday—it was hot and humid that summer—and I was still jet-lagged and sleep-deprived from having taken care of my mother. I'd been sleeping in the bedroom with her in case she had to get up in the middle of the night—I didn't want her oxygen cord to get tangled in the wheels of her walker.

That was who I was in that auditorium, a traveler between here and there, not fully present, but I do remember that film, even though my eyes kept closing from the heat and the weariness of travel. I remember: the color blue, a young man climbing beneath the train leaving Prague, the black boots of the Carabinieri as the train arrived in Italy. He is sent to a prisoner of war camp. Later there is a hillside village, people in a town square, a girlfriend. The man who wrote the voiceover for the film and who is narrating it is in the auditorium as we're watching.

One recent evening, I googled "film about Jewish man who escapes Nazis by clinging to undercarriage of train" and I found *Fighter*, director Amir Bar-Lev. No record of it on IMDB, but I could stream it on YouTube.

Arnost Lustig, the narrator, is Jan's friend, a writer and also a Czech émigré. He had not escaped the Nazis. Instead, he survived three concentration camps and only escaped going to Dachau when the train he was on was strafed by the Allies. He is the man who was sitting in the auditorium that afternoon in Prague and whose story is woven, almost as a counterpoint to Weiner's, throughout the film—although, as I strained to remember it, I found that Lustig's story had receded entirely from my memory. It is the morally fraught and ambiguous story of the man in the audience I recall.

The story begins with the two men, decades older, poring over maps as they plan to retrace their divergent lives. Lustig teases Weiner about all the Italian girlfriends he must have had after the war ended, one a nun in Palermo.

The film shifts back to 1938, archival footage of Czech troops marching off to stop the invading Germans, only to be withdrawn after the Munich Pact. In exchange for a promise of peace, Germany, Italy, Great Britain, and France forced Czechoslovakia to surrender its border regions and defenses to Nazi Germany, not understanding that the promise meant nothing. Jan Weiner and the other soldiers were sent home, "broken by shame," to their countrymen, who heckled them in the streets.

An old woman calls him up to her apartment. "Go," she says, "This will be a horror. Go away while you still can." He does, leaving his mother behind, visiting his father and his second wife in Slovenia. On the eve of the Nazi occupation, his father tells him, "Tonight I will die," and then calls him into his room and asks him to lie on the bed with him. "I have taken the pills already," he tells him, "hold my hand." On the next bed, his wife is already dead. She was not Jewish.

Weiner tells this story during the first stop in his and Lustig's journey to retrace their lives. They are sitting on a bed in the father's room in Slovenia. "She must have loved him very much," Lustig says of the stepmother.

Pointing out the window at the cornfields Weiner tells us that he remembers thinking, "I will live," and then silently urging his father, "Die fast. So I can run and save myself."

Lustig tries to comfort him. "He gave you the freedom to go. The three of you would not have made it together."

Weiner responds, "I could not leave my son alone in this hostile world."

Throughout the film, this will be the contrast between the two, their visions, Lustig always weighing possibilities, imagining inner conflicts and motivations, while Weiner insists that our actions alone define us.

ᴧᴧᴧ

After Kathryn and I left the camp in Terezín, we wandered around the town. We bought ice cream from a small store, an ordinary and easy pleasure. A stray thought left by the place we'd left intruded: I remembered reading Hannah Arendt's book *Eichmann in Jerusalem,* and how surprised I was when I first read that Eichmann had been a vacuum cleaner salesman and that his wife was half-Jewish. Why had it been so hard for me to believe that ordinary people were capable of such things? And the hypocrisy of a man married to a Jewish woman was unfathomable. "The banality of evil," Arendt famously called it. But what does that tell us, really?

I remembered my mother telling me that her friend, Susie, a war bride from Germany, swore that she and her family knew nothing of the camps. Yet they could see one in the distance as they were working in the fields. Susie, my mother told me, never again wanted to see a potato.

Kathryn and I were sitting on a bench. I kept looking at the walls of the museum across the street. The pale yellow seemed incongruous, but why? Maybe because it was the color of the kitchen in the house where I grew up and so reminded me of my mother and her stories?

What am I trying to get at? My own discomfort, for one thing. Susie never wanted to see another potato? Of course not. But did I really think she would tell my mother she never wanted to see another concentration camp? Another Gestapo? Maybe "potato" represents a constellation of things she couldn't bear to remember or maybe, literally, the worst thing about the war for her was that she had to eat so many potatoes.

That was the source of my discomfort, I think, the collision of the ordinary with extremity. They are not so far apart as we might wish. The concentration camp was less than a block from the ice cream shop. Kathryn and I had just "toured" it. We had disembarked from a tour bus, tickets in hand.

Inside the museum, we had seen the paintings made by the children who passed through Terezín from 1943–44. Their teacher, Friedl Dicker-Brandeis, saved their paintings, 4,387 of them, in suitcases that she hid in the children's dormitories. Many are of things children always paint, flowers, butterflies, children holding hands. There are quite a few entitled "Memory of Home."

Some are of things that should not be ordinary for any child: lines of people carrying bags, families huddled together, climbing into the mouths of box cars. Next to each painting, on a slip of paper, the title, the child's name, the birth and death dates. The death date for almost all of them was 1944. In the autumn of that year, Dicker-Brandeis and most of the children were transported to Auschwitz.

∿

I hit pause, wrote a few scattered notes, took a slug of wine. How could I have forgotten the scene where Weiner tells Lustig of his father's suicide? Or the one before that, when the two of them visit Terezín? This is where their roads had diverged. Lustig, who had not escaped, who had not been told to go by his father, was held in the camp until he was sent on a train to Auschwitz.

I try to remember my own visit to Terezín in relation to this viewing of the film. Which came first? The visit must have. Otherwise, I would have imagined them there, looked to see if there was a painting by Lustig. As it was, I felt myself resisting the lilting voice of the tour guide as she assured us that this was merely a transportation camp. "No one was liquidated here."

In the film, the tunnel is precisely as I remember it, and just as Kathryn captured it in her black-and-white photographs, narrow and dark, textured stone, the door at the end, a bright archway. I remember feeling the presence of those marched through that tunnel, their fear, their knowing that they were approaching their deaths. The doorway opened onto a bright field where people were executed, where fathers and sons were ordered to attack one another.

Weiner and Lustig stand in a room with faded walls, chipped terra-cotta paint. This is the room, Weiner tells us, where his mother was beaten to death. He mentions having brought his daughter there. "It is difficult to take," he says. I feel as if Kathryn and I entered that room. I remember the windows. A wall of windows. Like in the room with the showers. Huge, gray exposed pipes overhead. There are archival photos of children being offered slices of bread from platters, singing in choirs, being tucked into beds out of doors in the summers, a Potemkin village for the benefit of the Swiss Red Cross.

"A theater was played here," Weiner says, "[but it] was a railroad station to the gas chambers." He and Lustig are now standing in green, like a meadow, and Lustig shows us the tracks he and the other boys helped build. He mentions that he liked being outdoors building them, because "here is some possibility of going far into the distance...."

Later, in a café, the two men eat lunch. In the background, we see a younger man filling steins of beer and, all around them, people eating. Lustig tells Weiner about things that happened in Auschwitz and Buchenwald—a friend who had worked with him to build the tracks, for instance, his frozen legs were amputated "without any injection." After the war, the friend's father wanted to know how he died. Lustig says he didn't, couldn't, tell him. He told him, instead, that before the son was sent off on the train from Terezín, his friends had procured for him a prostitute. "A very beautiful woman, an artist in the circus, a horseback rider."

As Lustig tells the story, Weiner's hands, in a close-up, shake. He is worrying a piece of paper. Lustig said to us, earlier, of the camps, "If you will be sensitive to everything that deserves your sensitivity, you will go mad."

∿

As I watched *Fighter*, I kept waiting for the movie I'd seen in the auditorium to begin. When was Weiner, as a young man, going to climb beneath the train? When was the train going to begin moving? I remembered, so clearly, the sound of the train, the boots of the Carabinieri. Where was the black-and-white of the archival footage, the muted colors of Weiner and Lustig, as old men, remembering, when was all of that going to burst into the Technicolor of escape to southern Italy? Where were the people Weiner met there? The girlfriend? Where was the real story? Was this a different film? Maybe this was a documentary about making that film?

And then we come to the moment when Weiner shows Lustig the rusted undercarriage and I realize that there, in the hot auditorium, in the hypnagogic state hovering between sleeping and wakefulness, I'd dreamed a parallel journey based on small details. The movie I remembered did not exist.

In reality, Weiner had clung to a filthy steel plate attached to a toilet hole to escape. The trip took 18 hours. If the sky was blue, it did not matter. He could not see it. He took with him some bread and milk. Did he eat while he was under the train?

Yes, he says. It is clear it was as disgusting as we imagine. And then, in Genoa, the head of the Italian police, after hearing the story of his father's suicide, sends him to a POW camp in southern Italy instead of back to certain death in Prague.

Of the prisoner of war camp, not much more is said. We see old black-and-white photos. Weiner and the other prisoners are young, handsome, shirtless, smiling, and I thought of so many of the pictures I'd seen of my father and his brothers, also soldiers in that war. Weiner and a Polish prisoner decide to escape together. They have nothing, not even shirts, and he remembers knocking on the door of an old man who says, "Step in. We are all sons of Christ."

Returning, decades later, to the old man's village, Weiner approaches a table in the village square. He asks for the address of the old man's daughter. A man with his back to us turns out to be her husband. Weiner is shooed away. The two men visit a family in their home. Adult children sitting around a dining room table tell Weiner they don't remember him. We see the place where the POW camp used to be. His past has vanished.

∿

In the Bohemia Internet Café, I opened emails from my husband who, with my sisters, had been taking care of my mother. He tells me that on morphine, in the hospital, while recovering from an operation to stabilize her spine, she kept dreaming that she was on Saipan where she and her first husband, a Marine officer, had been stationed after the war. 1947.

In her morphine dream, the Japanese soldiers who'd been left behind were surrounding her. My older sister and brother were still infants and she had to protect them. Her husband was on night duty and she was sitting, revolver in her hands, her children tucked in behind her, listening for the soldiers, for their footsteps coming through the jungle.

Long ago, she'd told me that she and her husband had taken a jeep up into the hills to see the caves where the Japanese soldiers had hidden and the cliffs from which they had jumped to their deaths rather than be taken prisoner. She didn't tell me, then, that their wives and children had also jumped. I found out later. She must have known. How could she have not known? We're talking about thousands of bodies broken on the shore below, the cliffs now a memorial.

The sacrifices so others go on. After living in the Southwest for years, I knew that Diné women had wrapped their arms around their children and jumped from cliffs in Canyon de Chelly to escape capture by Kit Carson. Jews hiding from Nazis had sometimes inadvertently smothered their crying babies, trying to save their families. I knew about the designated survivor, how the most Aryan-looking Jew in a village was chosen to pass and sometimes ordered to load his own family onto the trains as a "test" of his identity. The designated survivor: one person left to tell the story.

Was I thinking about all of this in beautiful Prague? Such a charming city, a paradoxical grace and weight in the architecture, the weather not bad at all. Did these unthinkable choices linger in the light outside the café where we ate with Barbara and our friend Cynthia, behind the glass shop where the chandeliers still looked molten, where the fan was turning turning turning but never cooling us off? I don't think so.

I drank wine and went to hear writers reading their work below the smoky bar. Afterwards, we talked of the fragment and its relation to the whole, which always, it's true, reminded me of Picasso's *Guernica* and the power of abstraction. A fragment can be a word. The word "liquidation" for example.

"In the struggle between yourself and the world, you must side with the world," Kafka said, but I don't think Kafka had children, or could have imagined, even in his darkest hours, Theresienstadt.

Prague, a charming city, has a history that is unsettling. The streets in Prague, where Kafka grew up, are made of cobbles and in the cobbles, of Old Town Square, there are 27 inlaid crosses, one for each martyr beheaded upon that spot. There are memorials everywhere if you know how to see them, if you've heard the stories.

When I visited Prague Castle, I was told that the word defenestration comes from *fenêtre*, "window" in French, but defenestration, the term, was coined in Prague and means to throw someone out of a high window, especially during political upheaval, as in a coup.

Later, when I looked at Kathryn's proof sheets from Terezín, there were so many windows—windows and doors that led nowhere, windows and doors behind bars, doors the texture of tombstones, tombstones shaped like doors.

A memorial is a way of seeing. "The first step in liquidating a people," the Czech historian Milan Hubl said, "is to erase its memory."

～

One historical period does not equate in a 1:1 fashion with another. Yet there are lessons we can learn. Tearing apart the fragile carapace of a civilization can be as quick as ripping a piece of silk. On the time it takes to mend it, if it can be mended at all, I believe the jury is out.

Better to stop it from happening, always. If one can. In 1945, at the age of 19, Arnost Lustig, primed by his experience in the camps, returned to Prague and took part in the uprising against the Nazi occupation. Jan Weiner joined Britain's Royal Air Force.

In 1946, when Weiner returned to Prague, the name of his neighbor's son was on the door of his family's apartment. "You lived?" the son asked when he saw him on the threshold. The son had become a member of the Czech Communist Party. The Party was then in the process of consolidating its power. Under its rule, Czechoslovakia would become an oppressive totalitarian state. "Here is your home no longer," the son told Weiner.

Weiner next visited the Nazi official he'd had to petition for an exit visa; he credited his hatred of this man for his own survival: he often felt that he had lived only in order to return and kill him.

Weiner found him in the same office: third floor, fourth door on the right. The official did not remember him. He, too, was now a member of the Party. Weiner had a pistol cocked and ready but when he grabbed the man by the lapels, the man said, "Please don't. I have family." And Weiner couldn't kill him.

He thought, at first, it was "a weakness" that caused him to spare the man and leave him with only a beating. He had wished his father dead so he could escape; a weakness, too, perhaps. And yet he had escaped, and served, bravely, one supposes, in Britain's Royal Air Force.

After leaving the man's office, Weiner recalled feeling enormous relief. "On those stairs, I finished WWII."

I have a friend who says, "As you are in one thing, you are in all things."

After the war, Weiner would not join the Party, and so he became a non-person. Unlike Weiner, Lustig joined the Party. He believed that if Weiner had been in the camps, he, too, might have reacted by becoming an apparatchik in what soon became a repressive one-party state.

Instead, Weiner was interrogated as a British spy, as were many other fliers who'd joined the Royal Air Force, and then endured five years, from 1950–1955, in Klodno Forced Labor Camp, the skeleton of which still exists. So, in the end, he did not escape. He survived.

As he and Lustig are standing in the camp's shadow, he rests his hand on Lustig's shoulder and says, "So tell me, what did you do while I was in prison?"

There is some back and forth between them, with Weiner interrupting Lustig and Lustig insisting that the Communist Party, at first, until the Russians took over in 1948, was idealistic, full of young people who studied the U.S. Constitution and wanted to make a society "more democratic than capitalism, more tolerant, more just…"

"Did you know?" Weiner asks. "You must have known….the fliers were locked up."

Admitting that he had a "comfortable life," during those years, Lustig insists, "I tell you, on the heads of my children and grandchildren, the day I found out that I am with a regime which has concentration camps, I felt sick of my stomach, I couldn't sleep, and this was the end of my belief and I ended as an exile. But if I learned something….I learned it through horrible mistakes. Being a Communist, I believed I am equal to being a Nazi."

As Weiner watches Lustig, his expression betrays nothing, not disbelief, not compassion. Lustig goes on to explain that when he worked for Radio Prague, he was only 20 years old. They had fired everyone over 25. They didn't want people with memory, with knowledge, experience. They wanted blank slates, young people who knew only that their society had been torn down and who believed it could be built utterly new.

All that had happened to Lustig before the war ended: the time in the camps, escaping nearly certain death in Dachau only because the train carrying him and the others was strafed; all that before he was 20 years old.

"Everyone should ask themselves these questions: how many did you denounce, how many did you harm, how many did you beat, how many did you kill? I didn't denounce, didn't harm, didn't beat, didn't kill. My hands are clean," he says to Weiner.

After this scene, Lustig is walking through the streets of Prague alone. He watches a teacher leading children in exercise in a park. To the camera, he confesses something quite different. "I am not judging people, after my life experience, too fast. I tell you what I was asking myself in camp, one question, very secretly, all day I was dreaming that I am a Gestapo man. I was a slave, I was freezing, but I said if I would be a Gestapo man, I would have good shoes, a good coat.

"But then I was asking a real question, which really haunts me today. What would happen to me if I would be born as a German boy? And if I wouldn't be Jewish, if I would enter Hitler heaven, how many people would I kill? This was a very good philosophical question because it made me almost happy that I was born as a Jew and that I became a slave, someone only to be killed."

I'm afraid I am giving this essay over to Arnost Lustig. But all the things I don't remember him saying while I was sitting, half-awake, half-asleep, in that hot auditorium suddenly feel so important. He seems to me a man with empathy, which maybe allowed him to survive his memories, whereas Weiner, even the way he carries himself, is rigid with pain.

∿

In extreme historical circumstances, there may be no way to escape responsibility, even by inaction. A Nazi official becomes a Communist official and, as Lustig points out to Weiner: "Because you didn't kill him, he became, again, a killer of Jews." As well as of others.

After the war, ethnic Germans, mostly women, children, and the elderly were forcibly removed from Czech areas where their families had lived, sometimes for centuries, where that home was the only one they'd ever known, where they had intermarried. While some had joined the Nazi party and welcomed the German occupation, others had occupied confiscated property or been sympathizers simply as a matter of survival. Many were innocent of ties to Nazi Germany, and had fled to central Czechoslovakia because they were Jews or Social Democrats or Communists or anti-fascists or simply identified as Czech citizens, no matter their ethnicity. After the war, no distinctions were made.

Ethnic Germans were required to wear white squares with the letter N, *Nemec*, the Czech word for "German." From 1944–45, during the "wild expulsions," they were terrorized, raped, sent to labor camps, forced to migrate without food or adequate clothing, tortured, and murdered. The infrastructure created by the Nazis to exterminate the Jews was repurposed so easily, so quickly.

The Allies were guilty of not intervening—their sin of neglect committed, essentially, for political reasons: they did not want to seem "soft" on the Germans and they did not want to antagonize the Russians. At the Potsdam Conference in July 1945, it was agreed that there could be further expulsions but only if they were "orderly and humane," which, given the circumstances, was a series of words untethered to actual behavior or events.

Some historians call this forced migration the largest instance of "ethnic cleansing" to date: between 12 million and 14 million were expelled from Eastern European countries and, because there was no planning or oversight or funding, 1.5 million died, most of exposure or malnutrition. Their treatment in Czechoslovakia, however, stood out as deliberate and sometimes vicious; not surprising, I suppose, given that Hitler had purposefully exploited existing tensions between the two ethnic groups for his own political gain.

∿

My mother's first husband was killed in the Korean War and then she married my father, who had served in the Navy in the South Pacific in World War II. Yet none of this felt like my war, not like the war in Vietnam, my generation's war, until I read reviews of *Orderly and Humane: The Expulsion of the Germans After the Second World War* by R.M. Douglas, a history professor at Colgate

University. As a young woman, I had believed the war had solved everything. That war. I believed, and still believe, that World War II is an example of a Just War. There was no alternative but to fight it. Only recently, have I read that perhaps the principles of Just War Theory should also be applied to the aftermath of a war, to the reconstruction which, I suppose, is exactly what Douglas is positing.

I was curious. Were others as surprised by the many atrocities committed against these ethnic German refugees as I was? I read the comments below the reviews about the 2012 book, which had won many prizes. Many in the States were as disturbed as I was but many were grateful for the book, saying they had heard these stories whispered in their families about what their grandparents had endured before emigrating.

There were those in the UK who knew the history but thought the book was an important analysis of it. And there were those who claimed that these ethnic Germans had been oppressed in Eastern European countries for centuries and that this was why Hitler had invaded, to save them from oppression.

Even given the complicated history of the region, it takes a particular point of view to see Hitler as an altruistic liberator when the truth is that the ethnic Germans were collateral damage, victims of his aggression and political ambition even if they weren't his intended victims.

Still, the age-old questions: What does it take for neighbor to turn against neighbor or, even, to turn a blind eye? What does it do to a person—both James Baldwin and Toni Morrison pose this question—to not be able to see another's humanity, to not be able to empathize? And what about whispers of stories that are suppressed for whatever reasons, what does that silence feed?

"The struggle of man against power is the struggle of memory against forgetting." Long before going to Prague, in the early '80s, I'd read Milan Kundera's novels. *The Book of Laughter and Forgetting* begins with a description of the Communist leader Gottwald stepping out onto a snowy balcony in 1948 to "harangue" the citizens. Next to him, one of his comrades, Clementis, puts his hat on Gottwald's bare head and a picture is snapped. Clementis, four years later, is charged with treason, hanged, and erased from the photograph. Of him in that moment, only the hat remains.

When I thought of Prague before I went to Prague, I always imagined the dark sooty land of the Communists, probably because that was my mother's fear: why, she wondered, would we want to go to a country that had been behind the Iron Curtain? My awareness of the Czech Republic began in 1968 with Prague Spring, because I was alive when that happened. Those black-and-white images of students surrounding Russian tanks? They looked very much like my friends at protests here, like the photographs of students in Paris and Madrid. Czechoslovakia before 1968? I was barely aware that it existed. It was a word. A fragment.

I remember now how we walked through the city very late one night so Kathryn could try out a new lens. There was a full moon. The gates of the Kinski Palace museum were still open when we got there. A guard watched as we walked in but did not stop us. Above the gate, on each side, a huge statue. On the right, a man about to smash the head of another man prostrate at his feet; on the left, the soon-to-be victor had a long dagger raised above the head of his opponent. The guard's boots echoed against the cobblestones. Some of the gargoyles hanging from the stones of the cathedral looked like gruesome simians, their faces tortured, tongues jutting out. I sat looking at them for a long time while Kathryn took photographs. The gargoyles were really men, not mythic creatures, not simians, but men, their faces distorted by rage or anguish, and I realized, then, something that many people already know: the most frightening thing in the world has a human face.

In Prague, at night, all of my mother's fears came alive in me. I was not quite there, sleep-deprived because I worried when Kathryn often went out with her friends to clubs and, because her friends were staying in student housing on the other side of the river, walked by herself through Old Town to get to our apartment. She said if men approached her, she answered them in Spanish, and they would leave her alone. Besides, she said, I'm taller than they are.

This, I think now, might be a drunken logic, but I had no logic at all. Logic had left me. I was a tuning fork for grief: grieving history, grieving my mother's approaching death, and grieving in advance the eventual deaths of my husband and children. I stood in front of the long windows of our apartment; I parted the curtains and looked up and down the street. It was 3 a.m. I kept dreaming of my mother, emaciated, helpless.

I could not fall back to sleep. I stood before the long windows in my night-gown. Across the street, men stood next to their taxis and waved at me. Teenaged boys celebrating the World Cup ran through the streets, waving flags and calling out *Deutschland, Deutschland.* Everywhere we go, a friend tells me, we're confronted with the ugliness of history—but what is it that unveils the truth in any given journey? I was in a country where I didn't speak the languages, I couldn't sleep without dreaming of my mother suffering, and my daughter, where was she? I didn't know. I stood in the window and watched for her until she came home.

Dear Reader: I'd been thinking about *The Book of Laughter and Forgetting* as I tried to write about Prague, as I thought about a president who erased even the recent past, calling it "fake news" and inventing, in its place, a reality that suited him. Could I imagine that, in a televised debate, the president, when asked to denounce white supremacists, would say, "Stand back and stand by, but I'll tell you what, I'll tell you what, somebody's gotta do something"? Who encouraged armed men and women to invade the U.S. Capitol and who, then, along with them, appeared to derive perverse pleasure from it?

Why, yes. Yes, I could. In fact, I was waiting for it.

Danse Macabre

CHRISTINE KIESSLING

DURING THIS PLAGUE YEAR, I'VE BEEN infected with memories of a strange song I discovered as an exchange student in Italy. The song has roots in the arts and history of Bergamo, the epicenter of Italy's Covid-19 outbreak. In the spring of 2020, more than half of the city's inhabitants tested positive for the virus, but not before the Regione had been so overwhelmed with the death, grief and exhaustion that funeral homes, mortuaries and cemeteries could not contain it all.

In the 1970s, a conservatory-trained practitioner of the questionable genre of progressive rock named Angelo Branduardi drew on Medieval and Renaissance themes of love and death. His muse, if you will, was the time of plague in Italy. Not the recent plague, but the bubonic plague, the Black Death that ebbed and flowed for an astonishing 500 years.

We mock prog rock now, and even back then a lot of the music was, shall we say, a tad histrionic. But Branduardi was the real deal, a virtuoso violinist and composer. He possessed a peculiar vision that limited his audience but led to high-octane collaborations with British rock royalty, including Paul Buckmaster, the musical polymath who arranged for everyone from David Bowie to the Grateful Dead.

Onstage, Branduardi was a madman. This was in keeping with the times: the 1970s and early 1980s. (Remember Ian Anderson?) But Branduardi's music suddenly seems not only relevant but necessary. He evoked not only the words and melodies of the Plague Years, but archetypal themes. The plague years that stretched from the 1300s to the 1800s was a time of grief and madness not unlike our own.

I would never have encountered Branduardi if I hadn't spent my junior year abroad studying art history in Padua in 1981–1982. I was living in a house with American students and everyone was going to see Branduardi. I was on the third day of a migraine, but I was damned if I was going to miss a concert with so much buzz in the household. The pain was such that I could not imagine it being worse and I figured that it was only going to last three days anyway, so it didn't matter. You think these kinds of things when you are

20 years old. So I went, and it became a touchstone of my year in Italy, which shifted my life's foundations.

Even for those of us without migraines, there was some question about the advisability of attending the concert. Within walking distance of the concert venue, a kidnapped U.S. Army general James Dozier was chained to a steel cot. The Red Brigades, a Marxist-Leninist organization committed to revolution through armed struggle, had snatched him from a nearby U.S. Army base. Americans should take extra care in their movements, or so the U.S. Department of State had warned.

Before this audacious action against the U.S. military presence, the Red Brigades had shocked the world with the kidnapping and killing of Aldo Moro, a much-loved former prime minister of Italy. This was part of a grand plan to thwart the creation of a center-left coalition linking the Christian Democrats, the Socialists, and the mainstream Italian Communist Party.

The Red Brigades and Black Shirt fascist sympathizers were engaging in dueling atrocities. Fortunately for us, the previous director of our study abroad program had worked out some kind of agreement, apparently still being respected by the local Marxist cell, that University of California students remain unbothered.

Once arrived and safe from possible drama in the streets, the evening delivered the kind of concert that stays somewhere between your ringing ears and throbbing solar plexus. As much as I had done everything "wrong" for my migraine, the staging of the concert was identically wrong. The concert hall's acoustics were that of an airplane hangar and the show's conceptual design was atrocious: the stage was too low and all you could see was a black hole punctuated by spotlights heaving into the gyrating audience.

And yet the mastery of the compositions, the musicianship, and Branduardi's manic energy exceeded the horrendousness. Branduardi's synthesis of pop with Medieval and Renaissance themes and musical styles was irresistible. I had a wonderful time.

When I returned to school in Davis, California, I played my Branduardi albums incessantly. I was trying to prolong...something. They say that the culture shock when you come back to America is worse than the culture shock when you're abroad: everything is the same yet feels different. I found that to be true.

Branduardi was my therapy. What rose to the top in my music rotation was

Fresco at Clusone.
The Disciplini.

"Ballo in Fa Dieses Minore, Dance in F Sharp Minor" from the 1977 album *La Pulce d'Acqua,* The Water Flea. The song stood out for its ancient melody and what felt like a compelling dialogue to a young woman questioning her identity—Branduardi played two roles: Death and an artist appealing to Death.

What made this song so compelling, was what it was not. It was unexpected, commanding, even joyful. It had the kind of cool that leads students on the Grand Death Tour of Europe, the one with stops in Rouen for the plague house carvings of skulls on half-timber buildings, the Death Strip of the Berlin Wall, Paris' Musée Carnavalet's stuffed monkeys and models of guillotines, Roman catacombs, and other exuberant and excessive corpse dispositions, like random gruesome themes in frescoed churches and in art museums. Death is attractive when you are young enough not to feel its fetid breath upon your neck.

Living in Padua, the largest city on dry land that was part of the Venetian empire, had led all of us students to develop a fascination with 18th-century Venetian decadence, when people wore masks of the Commedia dell'Arte characters on visits, in the streets, going about their daily lives. The Venetian genre artist Pietro Longhi chronicled this world of the masked surfaces, or, better, "la facciata," simultaneously mundane and excessive in the celebration of obvious falsity associated with life in a city of mirrors and watery main thoroughfares. Of course, the coolest masked character was the one seen out and about signifying Death and the effort to keep it at bay: the Plague Doctor.

Plagues and echoes of plagues. Growing up in California, I was more accustomed to disasters of the tectonic and conflagatory variety. I had no idea that plague had been a nearly constant feature of the human landscape for millennia.

Starting in the Nile Delta in 541 A.D., a plague thought to be typhoid swept through Europe, particularly the Mediterranean, and until it faded around 755, killing between 20 and 50 million people. The second great plague, the infamous Black Death, lasted from the 1330s until the 1830s.

Just as the coronavirus is breaking apart political economies worldwide and reconstituting them in new forms, successive plague outbreaks throughout history affected every aspect of society. Plagues changed the outcome of wars. Epidemic illness exacerbated the slave trade and the atrocities of the Middle Passage. Typhoid defeated Napoleon in Russia, and drove his armies out of the New World, resulting in the Louisiana Purchase that doubled the size of the United States, making the new country a force to be reckoned with globally.

It's certainly no surprise that such an overwhelming and poorly understood destructive force led to an outpouring of piety. Yet the randomness of plague's choice of victims also generated what Yale historian Frank Snowden calls "a powerful undertow" in the opposite direction. "The result was not so much atheism but a mute despair," he writes in *Epidemics and Society: From the Black Death to the Present* (2019).

By virtue of its central place on Mediterranean trading routes, Italy was among the first countries to be ravaged by the bubonic plague. No wonder, then, that there is an immense number of Last Judgments plastered in churches. Jesus Christ returns to separate the blessed and the damned, bodies emerge in decay from their graves. What was already "nasty, brutish, and short" was made visible according to received spiritual wisdom. At least, that was one of the ways the Black Death played out in sacred art.

Not far from Bergamo is the little town of Clusone, famed for its Oratorio dei Disciplini, part of the Basilica of Santa Maria Assunta. On the Oratorio exterior wall is a remarkable fresco depicting The Triumph of Death painted by Giacomo Borlone de Burchis in 1485. Nothing can prepare you for the force of Triumphant Death, a living skeleton, crowned and wearing a richly embroidered cloak spread over her victims of plague, the great and powerful, the paupers, the developing mercantile class, the religious, the irreligious, the just and the unjust.

This is not the Grim (and abstractly masculine) Reaper. The representation is La Morte, the ancient feminine Queen of Death. In her bony hands are the ends of two unfurling scrolls declaring her power. The only wealth she knows are lives.

She is flanked by two skeletons who fire at their earthly mortal targets, one with an elaborate bow and the other on the right, with an early arquebus, the long gun of the Ottoman Empire. At her feet are the corpses of a Pope and an Emperor sharing an open stony sepulcher, together with snakes, frogs and scorpions. Below her are "powerful" figures, a cardinal, a bishop, a king and a philosopher, beseeching her with useless riches and gifts in a hopeless effort to avoid the fates of the dead around them.

Below the crowning register of victorious Death is a band of figures, mortals alternating with skeletal guides. This is the Dance of Death, a Danza Macabra, arrayed in a calm and regular manner, not "dancing," but walking in a meta-phorical "dance." Their pace is measured and orderly. Death cannot be avoided. We must accede to Her demand. The Oratorio's fresco leads us, through its doors to the interior, to find our hope in more conventional art, renderings of Christian doctrine and penance and piety.

How does mass death affect us? This fresco tells one tale. The Oratorio and its complex was the home of the "Disciplini Bianchi," a lay confraternity of prayer, penance, and self-flagellation. Their practices arose in response to the devas-tation caused by wars between the Papacy and Holy Roman Empire from 1048 to 1257, and to the recurrent disease and plagues brought with warring armies.

Barring self-flagellation, what can stay Death's hand? Even for a brief while? Branduardi's inspiration for the "Ballo in Fa Diesis Minore" was Ingmar Bergman's *The Seventh Seal*. In the influential 1957 film (*pace* Woody Allen) the Knight distracts Death long enough to allow a minstrel and his family to escape. It is this minstrel who has the film's last words, as Death leads the Knight and his other victims out of life. Music survives. Art lives on.

Branduardi said he was influenced by Bergman, but the song's material goes back further. The lyrics for "Ballo in Fa Diesis Minore" were set by Branduardi's wife, Luisa Zappa. She collected the original text from a fresco painted in 1539 on the church of San Vigilio in Pinzolo, a small town in the Italian Alps to the northeast of Clusone. The fresco on the church's exterior shows a Dance of Death, complete with skeleton musicians, presaging Mexico's Day of the Dead. The words painted on the wall are an exhortation concerning Death's power over all:

Io sont la morte che porto corona
Sonte signora de ognia persona
Et cossi son fiera forte e dura
Che trapasso le porte et ultra le mura
Et son quela che fa tremar el mondo
Reuolgendo mia falze atondo atondo
O uero l'archo col mio strale

I am death and wear the crown
I rule over everyone
I am proud, strong and hard
I pass through doors and over walls
I am feared by the world
Swinging my scythe round and round
oh true the bow with my arrow

For the melody, Branduardi chose an oddly upbeat "Schiarazula Marazula," a medieval northern Italian folk tune claimed to have a reputation for accompanying exorcism rites that had recently been recorded using ancient instruments. Confronting death doesn't normally bring to mind a jaunty dance tune. Was Branduardi exorcising death or celebrating it?

The finished song exceeded the original texts collected by Luisa Zappa. It did not end with Death's aim being "true," à la Elvis Costello, but changed from a minor key to a major one and made a different claim:

You are the guest of honor
at this dance played for you
Put aside your scythe and
dance a round and a round
the twirl of one dance and
then still yet another
and you will no longer be the
Queen of Time

Branduardi's "Ballo in Fa Dieses Minore" was noted by fans in comments and blogs that arose during the terrible spring of 2020. The association of Death and her crown were seen in the virus as a "corona."

Yet Branduardi was not viewed as having been part of a terrible link in a chain forged again and again in Bergamo. He was not foretelling the horror of an eternal return of plague in an ancient plague ground, but was instead a prophet of *sopravvivenza*, survival.

As a much younger person it was easier to see, or believe in, immersion in art as life's *primum mobile* against Death—a promise of immortality, if only in theory. If I were my younger self perhaps I might still believe that. My current self asks whether art is enough. Is any art powerful enough to transcend the unholy marriage of human pathology with a plague whose randomness is enough to drive anyone mad? Perhaps that's always what we've been doing all long, distracting ourselves from the one real certainty: Death.

I hear something different now, when I listen to Branduardi. The mad dance leaves us somewhere else, drained, down to essentials. Beauty is still resistance, but the resistance requires everything we have and more.

Taking a cue from Bergman's famous scene whereby the Knight abjures the artist to slip away when Death's attention is elsewhere, Branduardi and Zappa added text and music that provided a way to distract Death by persuading her "to put down [her] scythe and dance a round, and a round." In this way, one might escape her embrace long enough to perform a "meaningful deed," that will allow others to survive.

Unlike the film, in "Ballo in Fa Diesis Minore" Death is not simply looking away briefly to allow an artist to steal away with his little family. Seduced by Branduardi's whirl, Death is called to join in with the living. She feels the music course through her body. She dances.

VII:

TURN, TURN, TURN

Of all the unexpected things that happened in the first years of the pandemic—even as I write those words, I realize they convey the assumption that the pandemic will never end, or will go on until such time as we cannot imagine—as I say, of all the unexpected things that happened, perhaps the most surprising was a major writer giving a startup magazine the chance to publish a novella-length work of nonfiction. Steve Erickson's *American Stutter* was the first major literary effort to emerge from the pandemic.

Erickson has been called one of America's greatest living novelists. Early in his career he worked as a journalist in Europe and the U.S., writing for publications including the *LA Weekly* and *Rolling Stone*. Reviewing *American Nomad*, an account of his time on the campaign trail in 2008 in *The New York Times*, Barbara Ehrenreich wrote: "At best, Mr. Erickson functions like some high-tech psycho-medical sensing device inserted into the ravaged soul of American politics."

Between the pandemic and the near-annihilation of American democracy, Erickson had a lot of material. New York publishers had turned down *American Stutter*, Erickson told us. One apparently told him it was too ferocious to print.

Here is an excerpt from *American Stutter*, first published in Journal of the Plague Years, and now available in book form.

American Stutter

STEVE ERICKSON

Labor Day Weekend 2021

I live at the end of one of the most famous boulevards in the world. I've been here six months. If you told me six years ago I'd be here, I'd have been astonished, but as we all know, it's been that kind of six years. It was six years ago this summer that a Manhattan faux-billionaire & "reality" TV star began his successful campaign to become the 45th President of the United States.

Anyone who comes to L.A. walks up & down this stretch of road reading stars engraved in the sidewalk. I've walked this boulevard many times never supposing someday it would be my address. When I was four, my Mom & Dad brought me to the theater across the street, designed in its world-famous Chinese style, to see *Lady and the Tramp*, and even had I been old enough to ponder such things, it wouldn't have occurred to me that someday the empty window across the street would be mine. Ignorantly all of us cross, tens or hundreds of times, life's significant coordinates. All of us blithely pass places where later our lives take irrevocable turns, where later we create or destroy something of those lives. Any number of times we may stumble thru that place where we'll die. I'm old enough now that it's not out of the question this is the last place I'll live.

America wearies of democracy was the opening line of something I wrote once. It was eight months ago today that the country's worst attempted coup since 1861 took place, when the national Capitol was pillaged by thousands of domestic terrorists & white supremacists & anti-Semites in "Camp Auschwitz" T-shirts, killing six people & wounding scores of others. In Congress, one of the two major political parties means to cover up the details of this rampage so as to protect members complicit in treason & so as to revise a reality that was broadcast to the world & witnessed by billions. Since spring, virtually every state in the Union endeavors to deliver to a bankrupt Republican Party control of the counting of votes that it may then choose to reject.

This is done in the name of no principle but power, in the name of no hope but the rest of us forgetting. It succeeds because an exhausted people allow it to; authoritarianism abides not by instigation but inertia. More than any time in our lives, men & women of bad faith & bad conscience who have been betrayed by math too often—losing seven of eight national elections in three decades—seize the only recourse left to them which is to betray math back. Due process is slandered. Objective truth is subverted. Like a gasping man beneath the knee of a Minneapolis cop, democracy chokes beneath the knee of a peculiarly American fascism.

If it's true that, more than any other country in history, America has succeeded as a grand overarching idea rather than a mass of traditions, then it may be inevitable that America always has been in a state of civil war. It may be inevitable that its overarching idea could never reconcile what were profoundly competing visions from the outset having to do with race & class, freedom & justice. In any case, now the American Idea is cleaved more painfully than any of us has known. Let's disabuse ourselves of the notion that the last four years were about our previous President. The last four years were about us. Donald Trump didn't happen to America. America happened to America.

I began this journal two years ago at the intersection of manifesto & confession. Notwithstanding fearful New York publishers advising that "its ferocity stands in the way of attracting readers," I figured I might as well tell this as anyone. Other testaments bring you facts. I come bearing the W-W-Word, stuttered but not broken.

∿

March-April 2020

The ideal subject of totalitarian rule is people for whom the distinction between fact and fiction, between true and false, no longer exists by Hannah Arendt

March 01

Biden has won huge in South Carolina & saved his candidacy. African Americans went to the mat for him. In all the primary contests thus far combined, Biden now has more total votes than any candidate. Sanders remains the frontrunner, maintaining a slim delegate lead, and is poised to win day after tomorrow on Super Tuesday. Meanwhile I have to figure out my Super Tuesday vote....

Super Tuesday

It's Biden. I know, I'm slightly disappointed myself. It's strange to have started out with Biden eight months ago while flirting with other possibilities from

Harris to Warren only to end up back at Joe, to whom my head's been faithful as the heart has wandered. In other words I've been an electoral slut ready to sleep with any of them, Barbara Stanwyck to any Fred MacMurray who'll just climb in my backseat & smash in Donald Trump's fucking head at the signal of the honked horn, with me all orgasmic in closeup. After months of Joe's botched debates & lackluster performance, as of this morning's polls he still runs better than any Democrat against Trump, and I'm still having a hard time coming up with more than a dozen states that Sanders has any chance of winning in the best circumstances. And now that you've taken another look, Biden's a stone-noir killer if you've ever seen one, am I right? Shades, slicked back hair, even the name is right out of Cain. Honk the horn & let him have it, Joe.

March 05

Blowout. Entirely unforeseen, Biden has swept 10 states of 14 including some where he didn't spend five mins campaigning. Six days of frontrunner scrutiny on Sanders appear to have taken some toll. Warren is out. I didn't vote for her but I'm sorry to see her go....

Terrence Malick's *A Hidden Life* is the true story of an Austrian farmer who wouldn't swear loyalty to Hitler even as his refusal had no potential of changing anything. One of the agonies watching the movie is how we, the audience, keep trying to find a way out for him. We keep trying to get him off a hook that he won't let himself off, when a hastily & inconsequentially scribbled signature on a piece of paper will save his life. Just sign it, for God's sake! we silently plead. In its hushed murmurs Malick's depiction forgives us—dread rising from rapture, the collapse of sense before the majesty of an MIA god....

March 07

We shouldn't be too glib in our comparisons of what's going on in this country now with what went on in Europe in the '30s. It cheapens the consequences. But besides the exaltation of cruelty & pitilessness as "virtues" that render more human virtues contemptible, constants of fascism include a cult of personality in which people surrender sense & rationale to a single charismatic figure; the abdication of truth & an acquiescence to lies that, in their temerity, overwhelm not just specific truths but the notion of truth generally;

state-sanctioned supremacy of one class or race over others; and a commonly held sense of public helplessness so deeply felt as to result in widespread lunacy. Check, check, check, check.

March 08

I begin paring life down. Part of this is the coming split with Viv, and part is the clarifying impact of the fire evacuation a few months ago. I don't want to unduly clutter my mile-high Dubai penthouse with more possessions than it has room for. I make midnight trips to the canyon library where I leave bags of books at the door till finally one night there's a sign: "Stop leaving bags of books at the door." What remains are dream books, books of secrets, *The Arabian Nights* & *Ozma of Oz* & the selected Emily Dickinson, *Journey to the End of the Night* & *Labyrinths* & *The Book of Disquiet*, *The Zoo Where You're Fed to God* & *The Adventures of Huckleberry Finn* that I last read 40 yrs ago. No writer does himself any good reading *Huckleberry Finn* too many times. It's a novel by which he can count on being humiliated. Now on the verge of a dark & mean America 3.0 that will negate the country's two preceding versions, it's well to remember that the writing of *Finn* began around the time Frederick Douglass published his autobiography, little more than a decade after the Civil War & the death of Slave America—an historical novel then, of the earlier enslaved America that a newly free republic meant to kill, the America of the Asterisk whose death throes the current America still shakes off.

If *Huckleberry Finn* remains the great American novel, it's because not only its voice remains radically American but its subversions. In Huck & his flight for freedom with Jim can still be seen the aspirational America, the America in pursuit of an uncharted self lost in the dark never-healing heart whose bruise is distilled in the lexicon's single most vile word, the word that refers to Jim's color & explodes like a bomb every time it's read or said or heard. Nothing attests to the book's power like its capacity to unsettle & remind us who we are, which is both Huck & Jim on the run and also the ravenous & despicable nation that runs them down and, all this time later, runs down the rest of us....

March 09

When nothing astonishes anymore, an astonishing poll reveals that more than half of Republicans believe Trump is a greater President than Lincoln. So I'm not overly ruffled by Congress' single most spectacular display of nitwittery in human form, Texan Republican Louie Gohmert, talking of civil war if Trump is removed from office. For once Gohmert gets it right. This civil war—albeit a cold one—has been going on at least a quarter century unless, of course, the last 150 yrs have been a Civil War that never ended.

Another lunch with my Mom. Try as I do to avoid politics, halfway thru the meal she says, "I don't want to get into politics, but — " at which point we get into politics. I'm reminded that the Fox "News" she watches barely acknowledges laws of the molecular universe let alone facts of the President's corruption. Soon I'm ranting at her in the restaurant which no one deserves at the age of 92. She allows that the President can be unseemly at times but insists he doesn't get credit for "accomplishments" she can't name. She lets slip—in a manner more regretful than reproachful — her conviction that going to UCLA is where I went wrong. This is her maternal way of absolving me and I admit it accounts for all the strange dreams over the decades of clandestine Marxist professors breaking into my dorm room as I slept & installing this chip at the base of my skull. It also explains the migraines. Startling how badly the job was botched in typically soviet style, with some shoddy transistor picked up back in the day at Radio Shack for $7.98. Programmed to bolt upright at dawn singing The Internationale, I roll over & go back to sleep.

June 10

The hand in the pocket. It's midnight & I'm tired but my brain keeps going round & round as to why now, as to what it is about the Floyd video that's different after all the other videos of police barbarity going back to Rodney King...and it's the hand in the pocket. Not just the act of murder but the gesture of contempt, of hubris, of an officer who's done something like this, if not as lethally, 100 times before. A cop for whom this is as routine as Starbucks in the morning. His hand in his pocket as he kneels on Floyd's neck unperturbed by passersby asking him to please stop—this is what finally became too much. Of course it should have been too much long ago. It should have been too much centuries ago. It should never have taken this long. But this time it's not just the act but the manifest attitude, like a hunter casually crouched on a still thrashing animal he's just shot in the woods, with Floyd's pleas for breath no more than the strangled sounds the animal makes at the end. Whether some significant change comes of all that's happened, there will be consequences either way. This will be one of our indelible images, one of our important pieces of tragic footage for however much longer our history lasts, like the Zapruder film or the towers falling.

June 14

Today I take Zema & a friend to a Black Lives Matter protest march in Hollywood. It's a good Sunday for a march, warm but breezy. The crowd is large enough that, in the middle of it, there's no sense of where the beginning is or the end. Along the march bystanders cheer from the sidewalks & the windows of apartments. The marchers are as everyone's been saying, sprawling & diverse, people of all races & orientations wearing masks. We pass the Comedy Club on Sunset & cut down Crescent Heights to Santa Monica Blvd where everyone turns west, a guy with a bullhorn leading chants. Everyone seems to have backed off "Defund the police."

August 20

Watched tonight the conclusion of the virtual Democratic Convention that ended with the nominations of Biden for president & Kamala Harris for vice president, and an array of ordinary people offering testaments. Some thoughts. First, while in western cultures stuttering is regarded as idiocy, in others it's considered the sign of a savant. Second, you never outgrow a stutter. What you learn is how to stutter as well as possible. The vowels you have to take a running start for. The consonants where you know your larynx locks up like a machine gun stuck on the same artillery round. Third, no one stutters when they sing. Fourth, I'm unaware of any stutterer who can remember any time in his life when he didn't stutter. So your most apparent flaw does indeed become defining from the first moment of self-consciousness. Fifth, stuttering comes more naturally to you than not stuttering, which means that the rare moments when you don't stutter—when you "overcome" your stutter—are your least authentic. The disordered relationship among your mind & mouth & lungs is your natural order of things, an epilepsy of transmission. Sixth, your speech is gripped by a physicality in which the most casual hello bursts from a knot in the pit of your gut & a constriction of your chest, and with the most perfunctory yes (oh those y's!) comes the feeling of trying to touch something on a very high shelf barely out of reach. Finally, by its very nature a stutter isolates you. From the outset it cuts you off from other kids who tend to be merciless about such things, and people draw conclusions about you that may not be accurate. Surmounting isolation is what the rest of your life is about. You might become someone who locks himself in rooms & writes weird novels. Or more impressively you might have the good humor & courage to go on national TV as a 13-yr-old kid from New Hampshire named Braydon Harrington where you employ your battered young voice on behalf of an important man—maybe the next President of the United States—who bothered to make a connection with you when he didn't have to. Or you might be the man himself giving the speech of his life, acknowledging the minefield & continuing to cross, b/c in this life one Word is worth the humiliation & it is d-d-democracy.

September 12

A week that was. Temperatures of 120+ degrees, hottest in recorded L.A. history, comparable to Death Valley. So where's Oklahoma Senator Jim Inhofe with his fucking snowball now? Laws of climate unravel with the laws of men. The Attorney General assigns himself the President's case pertaining to rape charges. While trash talking vets who have died for their country, the President dismisses wholesale the current racial reckoning. Released tapes reveal Trump knew how bad the pandemic was seven months ago & concealed it from the public even as doing so killed people. More indications of his financial Russian connections come to light. In the cities 17-yr-olds with AR-15s are driven across state lines by their moms to shoot BLM marchers. Most stunning: Nothing changes. Polls barely register a tick. My friend Ventura is briefly in town and we lunch outside today at the local bistro for as long as the heat allows. "Those who America has wronged most," he says, "are the only ones who can save it." He makes the outlandish prediction that not only will Trump lose but be impeached again before leaving office.

September 13

My Mom turns 93 in two months and we all should have such a remarkable run. I've decided to stay at her place part-time not b/c she needs taking care of, particularly, but for her peace of mind. She's happy to have me here so I'm trying not to be a baby about it, but at this moment I swear I hear a particular "news" network coming from so many TVs in the house it's quadrophonic. As Fox has it, every city in America run by Democrats is now in flames, peopleoid masses of suspicious hues rage in the streets, and cops are slaughtered by "anarchists" faster than they can breathe. My Mom hasn't a doubt in the universe Trump is going to win handily.

November 07

Wake at 5:30. A little past six there's a cloudburst, forceful & lasting no longer than 10 mins. Toss & turn in bed till seven when I dress & head to the local café to get coffee for me, Viv, the kids. First day of 2020 that feels autumnal—cool & sharp. Back home I build the first fire since the early spring of the pandemic. I'm slightly disappointed the girl at the café got my order wrong—a latte instead of an effete cappuccino in honor of Mark Levin. I sit by the fire & am just settling into work when, at 8:24, the announcement flashes across my laptop that Joe Biden & Kamala Harris are President- & Vice-President-elect.

[later that afternoon]

Church bells across Paris ring in the waning twilight. London night skies fill with fireworks. Covid or not, the world has a block party. Planetary reaction to Trump's defeat is euphoric—relief that America isn't quite terminal after all, just critical. American streets explode joyfully all day & into the dark with international correspondents comparing it to countries where dictators fall. Conspicuous in the interviews with random celebrants is how often her name comes up, how often she is the image on the signs people carry.

Of course everyone loves Joe. He had the savvy & largeness of character—after she skewered him in early debates when she was still a presidential contender—to choose her. But if the only instance in vaguely recent history of a vice-presidential nominee making a difference to the final result is Lyndon Johnson in 1960, anecdotal evidence to any honest pair of ears & eyes is that, for a significant number of voters, Kamala sealed the deal. Seeing Biden & Harris together this evening onstage, anyone would be struck by how much sense it makes, the senior statesman with the experience to set aright the ship of state, side by side with the future. Of course I'm getting ahead of myself, but who can persuasively rule out the possibility we're seeing not just the 46th President but the 47th?

November 08

Listening to Biden last night give his first address as President-elect, I wondered if Make-Do Joe—who we all sort of settled for—might be exactly the right guy in the right place at the right time. Now under the new President it's up to all of us to leave aside rancor & show generosity of spirit. We need to learn how to listen to each other. With malice toward none & charity for...oh screw this. Fuck your feelings, trumptards. When Trump concedes, or when one of these Republican hacks offers Biden a simple congratulations, then I'll drag my magnanimity out from the bottom drawer of my soul. Till then, little kids in cages still won't see their parents again.

January 07

Thirty-six hours since my last entry. Went to bed late last night—about 4½ hrs ago—and woke 30 mins ago to widespread calls for the President's impeachment, immediate resignation, or constitutional removal by the Cabinet. Yesterday was one of those days that swallows up months & years around it. People will write whole books about yesterday. Other major news like Biden's selection for Attorney General—Merrick Garland, cheated out of a Supreme Court seat 5 yrs ago by McConnell—will be footnotes, and the unexpected capture of the United States Senate by Democrats thanks to Georgia, of all states, will wait its turn too....

Upon the ceremonial occasion of Congress certifying the clear electoral victories of Biden & Harris, yesterday the Congressional rotunda was seized by thousands of goons, criminals, hoodlums & terrorists. They stormed security, smashed windows, battered down doors, overwhelmed police, ransacked offices, trampled the House & Senate floors & desecrated history, pissing & shitting on the grounds. Dressed in fatigues, camouflage, militia gear & sweats emblazoned Camp Auschwitz, carrying QAnon & MAGA signs and armed with automatic weapons & molotov cocktails, the marauders streamed thru the Capitol searching for the Speaker of the House ("Where's Nancy?") as well as the Vice President, who just had stated his intention to formally announce from the Senate podium, per tradition, Biden's victory. Now the mob chanted "Hang Mike Pence!" as a noose swung from the porticoes of the outer plaza. Senators & representatives desperately hurried to clandestine security spaces & huddled under desks with the lights off, from which they texted goodbye messages to loved ones & instructions where to locate their final wills. The last time such a threat was posed to Congress was September 11, 2001, with United Airlines 93 commandeered by al-Qaeda & bound for the Capitol as a bomb, before passengers gave their lives to bring the plane down in Pennsylvania.

Televised round the world, the rampage went hrs at the incessant instigation of the President by way of tweet & video for the past two months & with a morning rally at the Ellipse that partly circles the White House's south side. There the congregation carried signs reading BRING DC TO ITS KNEES as assorted Trumps & Rudy Giuliani exhorted the assembled troops to "trial by combat." Following the release of taped presidential threats to the Georgia Secretary of State if 11k votes weren't "found" to overturn November's verdict—the desperation in Trump's voice is evident—the President insisted to the crowd he actually won by a landslide. "They rigged it like they never rigged an election before," he went on, "we'll never give up, we'll never concede. We fight. We fight like hell. We'll never take back our country with weakness. If you don't fight like hell, you're not going to have a country anymore. So we're going to walk down Pennsylvania Avenue to the Capitol and I'll be there with you...I love Pennsylvania Avenue," after which he went nowhere but home to watch on TV with satisfaction what he wrought, even as he was increasingly & futilely beseeched by staff & pols & even some family to call off the melee. Law enforcement roused itself with somewhat less enthusiasm than it brought to the President's Bible photo-op outside the White House seven months ago.

The Congressional certification process recommenced after six hrs once the bldg was finally secured. Five people died & two bombs were found & dismantled. As the i was dotted & the t was crossed in democratic, opposition to the United States Constitution was distilled to Republican congressmen & a White House that literally went dark, disappearing into the night like an evil Brigadoon. Since then, one social media platform after another has cut the President's accounts. This morning the salient images from yesterday involve flags, including the parading of the American swastika otherwise known as the Confederate banner thru the people's house in the nation betrayed by that banner, and new confederates scaling rotunda walls to replace the Stars & Stripes with a flag reading TRUMP in case anyone has any confusion about the priorities. One thing you can't accuse these people of is duplicity. They keep telling us who they are even as Biden, in an address of indisputably presidential sobriety, insists, "This doesn't represent who we are." Is he sure?

January 20
At noon, which is to say nine in the morning my time—following a somber-ly gorgeous ceremony on the promenade last night honoring the plague's

victims—Joseph Biden & Kamala Harris become President & Vice President in an inauguration that clings to hope. Lady Gaga gives a defiant rendition of the national anthem. A 22-yr-old black woman named Amanda Gorman knocks out the country as its young poet laureate; as it happens, or maybe it's not happenstance, reportedly she's a stutterer, and b/c no one stutters when she sings, her reading has a mesmerizing musicality about it. If she's the voice of America to come, we may make it after all. Harris is the first woman & person of color to assume the second most powerful position in the land & be a heartbeat from the Presidency. Biden gives a speech that doesn't aspire to be Lincolnesque or Kennedyesque or Rooseveltian or Obamanian but Bidenesque—perfect for the moment b/c it means not to soar but tell things straight & true. Obama is in the audience, George W., the Clintons, even Pence. A minuet of sun & clouds casts shine & shadow on all the faces. No one storms the Capitol or any of the state capitols.

It all makes me so happy as to almost wipe out four years—almost but not quite, of course, because it's all postscript to the day's true event for which I set my alarm early but sleep thru anyway. I wanted to wake in time to see him go. I wanted to wake in time to see him get on that chopper or plane & never come the fuck back. I wanted to watch the wretched man lumber toward his fate and to imagine prosecutors on the other end waiting to take him into custody, tho I know that won't happen, to imagine INTERPOL seizing him on the other end of an international flight & hauling him off to the Hague, tho that won't happen either. Have I become my own Mark Levin? Whatever else I've been over the course of my life, I've not been a hateful person, and I hate that the now ex-President made me one.

This is the 10-year anniversary of so-called "birtherism" as not just a slander but a strategy. It was 10 yrs ago on a morning talk show that this faux-Manhattan-mogul offered the baseless & racist-to-its-core theory that the first African American President wasn't a real President & wasn't a real American, subsequent to which some months later that President—who might have been on an auction block on the Mississippi River 170 yrs ago—made a laughing-stock of the fuming mogul at a correspondents' dinner & subsequent to which a quarter century of growing Republican authoritarianism was fused with one humiliated man's quest for vengeance. In the Republican refusal over the last decade to quash birtherism lies trumpism's inevitability & the Republican Party's bankruptcy & everything that happened these last two weeks & these last four years. So yet again...yet again everything comes down to a white racism so blindingly livid we would nearly welcome the asterisk's red blot of blood just for distraction.

Is anyone still paying attention, or has it become impossible to know anymore what to pay attention to? Surely by now, if nothing else, at long last we can finally set aside discussions of "norms." At long last we can set aside bloodless laments for what's normal & what's not, what's "normalized" & what isn't. Maybe now is neither nearly too soon nor quite too late to argue instead what's right & good. We could argue not whether white supremacy is normal but whether it's right & good. We could argue not whether mockery of the weak is normal but whether it's right & good. We could argue whether Arab princes murdering American journalists is right & good, whether the state kidnapping kids from terrorized families seeking asylum is right & good. We could argue whether indifference to assaulted women for the sake of a Supreme Court seat is right & good. We could argue whether suppression of the Native American vote in North Dakota or the African American vote in Georgia is right & good. We could argue, with greater intensity every passing moment, whether we are a nation right & good. Fuck normal. It's time for focus & ferocity, realism & resolve, perspective & priorities. Enough with Kanye's mental disorders. Enough with messages scrawled on the back of the First Lady's coat. Enough with toilet paper stuck to the President's shoe. Enough with all that when we should be saying enough with kids taken from families, enough with white supremacists running a woman over in Charlottesville, enough with old men with four centuries among them blithely dismissing the grace & heroism of a woman recounting before the country her experience of rape by a nominee to the United States Supreme Court. The last four years weren't about normal. They weren't even about abnormal. They weren't about an abnormal President or his abnormal political party that's worse than he is. They're about us. Enough with us? Enough with who we are & what we've become? The long slog toward America v.3 was never going to be settled by a knockout blow or electoral wave, b/c one man was never the enemy. We're the enemy.

Let's ponder a concept strange: Let's cut Donald Trump some slack. This isn't to dispute he's the most malignant American in 150 years. This isn't to dispute his treason, the violence he's inspired against fellow Americans & democracy itself. Rather it's to argue that while it's a prevailing rule among politicians

& journalists alike that in a democracy the people are never wrong, that's horseshit. It's not Trump who made America half-stupid. He's not that smart. He's not that charming. Rather it's the America "selfish and proud" that made Trump. The question was never whether Trump was unfit for office, which he himself established beyond anything to which anyone could add. The question is whether the rest of us are fit to be Americans. He's a poor excuse for a man let alone a President, and every moment that we tolerated his presidency, the more we became a poor excuse for a people. Whether we originally selected him for explicitly racist or sexist reasons, at the least we chose to overlook—as sufficient reasons for opposing him—the racism & sexism in which he openly trafficked. We overlooked toxic comments about people of other ethnicities, cultures, religions, genders, orientations, physical challenges. We overlooked mockery of the afflicted, we overlooked his decades of exploiting the poor & dispossessed. We overlooked clear authoritarian impulses & enthusiastic endorsements by the Ku Klux Klan & their fellow travelers. On the world stage we allowed America to be the fat, rich old white guy pushing little countries out of the way to get to the front of the photo op, straightening his tie as he does. So-called progressives who couldn't or wouldn't see the difference between all this & alternatives however imperfect or compromised became their own kind of sociopaths. Trump didn't dishonor us with his election four years ago, we dishonored ourselves. Biden's victory notwithstanding, we must still redeem that dishonor if there's time. Democracy is still at the wall. We're still left to resolve not who he is—we know who he is. We're left to resolve who we are. We're left to resolve the fuliginous rank venom that flows thru some deep blistered vein of our body politic. Long after Trump has departed, his America is still here. It's going to be a long fight lasting years if not decades assuming we haven't already run out of time. If Trump was a President who saw not himself in the context of his country but the country in the context of himself, then we're left to resolve whether we see ourselves in the context of our country or see the country only in the context of our worst selves where no America deserves to exist.

Have I become my own Mark Levin? Maybe I should ground that airplane, the one in my sleep-worn fantasies where I've loaded up the likes of Trump & McConnell? No. Prepare for take-off. Don't bother buckling your seatbelts. Do you think I came all this way & all these words to be edifying? Fuck edifying when you're done fucking normal. Because damned if Levin isn't right. I hate his America b/c I love my America. Damned if Hannity isn't right, damned if Laura Ingraham isn't right, damned if "Judge" Jeanine Pirro isn't right, damned if crazed-gerbil-on-crack Lou Dobbs isn't right, damned if Bow-Tie Tuck the Pot Pie Prince isn't right. In Fox's America proudly I'm a traitor b/c in my America humbly I'm a patriot. Both halves of the country betray each other—we're a nation of traitors & I remain the Patriot of Elsewhere, where my America blasphemes theirs, where my America spits in the face of theirs, where my America is heresy to theirs of the white hood & swinging noose, of the dead stare & false witness borne, of profligate players & the discarded homeless, of the frightened immigrant & native peoples ground to dust, of sweating bullyboys & the are-you-now-or-have-you-ever-been, of auction-block shackles & Black backs latticed with scars, of the Salem stench & the Jesus of "Come to me the little children so I can lock you away in your loveless cage." I hate their America in the name of my America of the eternal pursuit & memory's mystic chord & our natures' better angels & the promise God loves no matter how often we break it. The American civil war goes on. Don't yet lay down your arms.

THE WORLD WON'T WAIT

The word pandemic, of course, means a disease that spreads throughout a country or the world. In the time of Covid, a few places escaped, most of them remote atolls. Tuvalu, for example, three reef islands and six atolls, approximately ten square miles combined with a population of slightly more than 10,000, was still reporting no Covid cases at the end of 2021. Others, like Turkmenistan, may have simply refused to admit the virus was there, like certain Americans.

But as the pandemic roiled the rest of the world, historical events seemed to take on an added poignancy, and sometimes a sense of tragedy deepened by our newfound helplessness.

The Ghosts of Balkh

DAVID WEIR

WHEN YOU ENCOUNTER A FRIEND IN A VILLAGE in Afghanistan, you both stop where you were headed to embrace, hold hands and inquire about each other's heart, body, mind, family, and onward. It can be a long list and if you've not met recently, these greetings may take a while.

In America such an encounter starts with "How are you?" and ends with "Fine." It sounds flat, unsatisfying. In Dari you are able to say "my heart loves your heart" in a way that does not necessarily imply romantic love but does connote how much you truly care for each other. It doesn't sound odd at all.

This week for me and many others who love Afghanistan has been a struggle. It's difficult to express our feelings about the situation in English; it would be much easier in Dari. There are reports on Taliban efforts to convince the international community that the group has fundamentally changed. I doubt that. It's true that Taliban leaders are pledging to extend amnesty to government workers, respect the rights of women, and preside over a peaceful transition of power, using social media to spread their message of the "new" Taliban. As the *New York Times* reports, their audience isn't Afghans. It is "global elites."

There is historical precedent for what happens when military forces assume power, and that record is soaked with the blood of innocents. There is no reason to assume that anything will be different now. As media savvy as the Pakistan-trained Taliban leaders may be, rank-and-file Taliban soldiers are usually 19 or 20 years old. Many grew up in refugee camps after the Soviet invasion. They know nothing but war.

Stories are emerging that suggest the past is, indeed, prologue. Amnesty International reports that in July Taliban fighters tortured and killed Hazara men, members of an oppressed ethnic minority that had made progress during the last 20 years of liberalization. In the weeks since the U.S. pulled back, there are reports of demonstrators killed, along with journalists and their relatives. A woman who told Taliban fighters she had no food to cook for them was beaten to death in her home, according to CNN.

Millions of Afghans are now trying to flee. President Joe Biden suggested that between 50,000 and 65,000 Afghans might be at risk. I suspect the real number is much higher. It's not overblown to say the majority of the country's 38 million people now face danger and suffering.

Such pain is not only written but, in a visceral way, imprinted on the country's historical record and in the psyches of its people. Afghanistan has been criss-crossed by conquerers throughout its recorded history: Alexander the Great and his Macedonians, the Greco-Bactrians, Kushans, Indo-Sassanids, Kabul Shahi, Saffarids, Samanids, Ghaznavids, Ghurids, Kartids, Timurids, Hotakis and Durranis.

In their oral histories, Afghans most often bring up the Mongol invaders, starting with Genghis Khan in 1221. They talk about him and others as if they are still around the next curve of the road. For example, just north of the town of Taloqan is a magnificent mountain known as کوه زب سیاه, which translates as Black Goat Mountain.

∿∿

I was in my twenties, a Peace Corps volunteer like so many others. When riding in the back of a truck packed with people, goats, and chickens, I spoke with a man who recounted stories of the Mongols that have been passed from father to son over the past thousand years or so.

"When they rode in last time, they cut off the heads of a million people," he said, repeating a version that I had heard many times. He said "last time" as if it were a few months ago, or a few weeks. "And they will be back," he added. "Just on the other side of Black Goat Mountain there are hundreds of thousands of Mongols waiting to strike." He was referring to the Uzbek population of Takhar Province in what has long been a largely peaceful agricultural area.

This was when I learned that history, in Afghanistan, as well as many other parts of the world, is not linear. A few hundred miles to the west of Takhar, during a visit to Mazār-i-Sharīf, where the tomb of the brother-in-law of the prophet Mohammed stands, a monument to a man many believe was cheated by assassination of his role as Shia Islam's leader, much the way we regard Bobby Kennedy, I heard similar tales about the Hazara population living in a nearby isolated valley. "They will ride in here soon, so watch out."

Nearby are the ruins of Balkh, a legendary city in the pre-Mongol era, with some of the most ghostly remains I have ever visited. Somewhere in my boxes in storage may still be the shards of pottery I collected at the site, which appeared to be many centuries old. Balkh is where historians confirm that Mongol hordes did in fact decapitate many residents when they struck, and if the eerie winds whistling through the area are not the voices of those long dead, my ears must have betrayed me.

Among Afghanistan's intractable problems is the stark reality that it is less an actual country than the cobbled-together homeland for at least seven major tribal groups. Besides the Uzbeks and the Hazara, there are the Tajiks, Pashtus, Turkomans, Baluchis, and Nuristanis, plus four or five smaller groups, including the nomadic Kochi. Each has a long and often troubled history.

The Hazara, for example, once held autonomy in their region. Bringing the Hazara under control of the Afghani emir in the late 1800s resulted in 60 percent of the population being exterminated. As the history repeated by the man I met on the way to Mazar-e-Sharif shows, they didn't go down without a fierce struggle.

The name of the country means "Land of the Afghans," which is what the largest ethnic group, the Pashtuns, call themselves. That name leaves every other group out, which complicates matters politically. My point here is that Afghanistan has plenty of internal problems without outsiders like the British, Russians and Americans getting involved. No foreign occupier ever stays for long anyway, because the local people simply won't tolerate that.

And once the foreigners leave, the Afghans get back to normal. What this means is that they have to sort out their internal differences now that they are not under the nominal control of any foreign power, unless you count the influence of Pakistan, which armed, and, some say, created the Taliban to head off the possibility of a threat from the border they share with Afghanistan.

After decades of operating mainly as a guerrilla army, the Taliban now must figure out how to govern what many believe to be an ungovernable land. Not only are the traditional tribal loyalties an issue, the big cities, especially Kabul, have modernized over the past 20 years and millions of women are now educated.

Like centuries of would-be conquerers, the Taliban may find themselves prey to forces outside their control. Taliban leadership faces threats not only from their own weaknesses, but from radical Islamists who bear them no loyalty, like ISIS-K, believed to have orchestrated the suicide bombing that killed 11 Marines and a U.S. Navy medic at the Kabul airport during the U.S. withdrawal.

Will the Taliban be able to miraculously transform from a guerrilla army into a government? Will Afghanistan move forward or back? Or will it forever trace the circles of time?

The ghosts of Balkh have been waiting a thousand years for answers to those questions.

Things Left Unsaid

SARAH CHAYES

I've been silent about Afghanistan for too long. I'm breaking that silence now because too many things are going unsaid. I won't try to evoke the emotions, swirling and yet leaden: the grief, the anger, the sense of futility. Instead, as so often before, I will use my mind to shield my heart. And in the process, perhaps help you make some sense of what has happened.

I COVERED THE FALL OF THE TALIBAN FOR National Public Radio, making my way into their former capital, Kandahar, in December 2001, a few days after the collapse of their regime. Descending the last great hill into the desert city, I saw a dusty ghost town. Pickup trucks with rocket-launchers strapped to the struts patrolled the streets. People pulled on my militia friends' sleeves, telling them where to find a Taliban weapons cache, or a last holdout. But most remained indoors.

It was Ramadan. A few days later, at the holiday ending the month-long fast, the pent-up joy erupted. Kites took to the air. Horsemen on gorgeous, caparisoned chargers tore across a dusty common in sprint after sprint, with a festive audience cheering them on. This was Kandahar, the Taliban heartland. There was no panicked rush for the airport.

I reported for a month or so, then passed off to Steve Inskeep, now NPR's *Morning Edition* host. Within another couple of months, I was back, not as a reporter this time, but to try actually to do something. I stayed for a decade. I ran two nonprofits in Kandahar, living in an ordinary house and speaking Pashtu, and eventually went to work for two commanders of the international troops, and then the chairman of the Joint Chiefs of Staff.

From that standpoint—speaking as an American, as an adoptive Kandahari, and as a former senior U.S. government official—here is the key factor I see in today's climax of a two-decade-long fiasco.

The reason our mission never had a chance was Afghan government corruption, and the U.S. role enabling and reinforcing it. The last speaker of the Afghan parliament, Rahman Rahmani, is a multimillionaire, thanks to monopoly contracts to provide fuel and security to U.S. forces at their main base, Bagram.

Is this the type of government people are likely to risk their lives to defend?

Two decades ago, young people in Kandahar were telling me how the proxy militias that American forces had armed and provided with U.S. fatigues were shaking them down at checkpoints. By 2007, delegations of elders would visit me—the only American whose door was open and who spoke Pashtu so there would be no intermediaries to distort or report their words.

Over candied almonds and glasses of green tea, they would get to some version of this: "The Taliban hit us on this cheek, and the government hits us on that cheek." One old man serving as the group's spokesman physically smacked himself in the face.

Too many others to count spent years of our lives trying to convince U.S. decision-makers that Afghans could not be expected to take risks on behalf of a government that was as hostile to their interests as the Taliban were.

Note: It took me a while, and plenty of my own mistakes, to come to that realization. But I did.

For two decades, American leadership on the ground and in Washington proved unable to take in this simple message. I finally stopped trying to get it across when, in 2011, an interagency process reached the decision that the U.S. would not address corruption in Afghanistan. It was now explicit policy to ignore what would determine the fate of all our efforts.

A decade ago. That's when I knew today was inevitable.

Americans like to think of ourselves as having valiantly tried to bring democracy to Afghanistan. Afghans, so the narrative goes, just weren't ready for it, or didn't care enough about democracy to bother defending it. Or we'll repeat the cliché that Afghans have always rejected foreign intervention; we're just the latest in a long line.

I was there. Afghans did not reject us. They looked to us as exemplars of democracy and the rule of law. They thought that's what we stood for.

And what did we stand for? What flourished on our watch? Cronyism, rampant corruption, a Ponzi scheme disguised as a banking system designed by U.S. finance specialists during the very years that other U.S. finance specialists were incubating the crash of 2008. A government system where billionaires get to write the rules.

Is that American democracy?

On the Front Lines

HERB RANDALL

FIRST, THE NAME: IT'S KYIV, NOT KIEV, which is a Russian transliteration, and never "the Ukraine" which denotes the region when it was controlled by the Russian empire, not the independent nation.

The confusion over the name of Ukraine and its capital can serve as shorthand to the current crisis, which has a long, echoing history as if Catherine the Great and Adolf Hitler are shouting imprecations in an unhumorous version of Bill and Ted, only the adventure is not theirs, but Russian president Vladimir Putin's. And the Ukrainian people's nightmare.

A shudder ran through the world yesterday, when Putin signed the long-expected decrees recognizing the so-called Donetsk and Luhansk People's Republics and directing the Russian Defense Ministry to deploy troops in those regions to carry out "peacekeeping functions." A full attack on Ukraine is widely expected in the next hours or days. I remember thinking: February 21, 2022 will be remembered as the exact date when war became inevitable.

I visited Ukraine for the first time in 2013 and fell in love with the country and people, their rich, too often tragic history, and the feeling of being not quite in the East, not quite in the West. Recalling it nine years later, I can almost feel the cold wind that whipped down through Khreshchatyk, the main boulevard in the center of Kyiv the first time I walked through the city. The street's wide lanes and grandiose buildings were once the backdrop for many a Soviet military parade. Now Khreshchatyk is lined with trendy cafés, European luxury shops, and at one end, the huge Bessarabian Market where insistent sellers hawk every kind of Turkish sweet and dried fruit, next to babushkas selling pungent pickled, well, everything. Despite the brutal wind that day, I found myself unaccountably happy.

An archetypal tension between the push toward the West and the ancient pull from the East was the backdrop for the 2014 uprising, called the Maidan Revolution, or more poetically, the Revolution of Dignity, that unseated the Russian puppet president Viktor Yanukovych and his corrupt pro-Russian party. You may remember Yanukovych's name from the news coverage of Paul Manafort, Donald Trump's disgraced former campaign manager. Manafort was, essentially, the fixer on behalf of the Russian oligarchs who made up

Yanukovych's shadow cabinet.

Since he was beholden to Russia, it is not surprising that Yanukovych refused to sign a political association and free trade agreement with the European Union in 2013. This agreement would have brought Ukraine closer to Europe and further from Russia's influence.

Yanukovych's refusal to allow Ukraine to join an agreement that would have transformed the country's economy brought Ukrainians into the streets. After he ordered a massacre of protesters, street violence threatened to get out of hand, and Yanukovych called on Russia to help him flee the country. In his absence, Ukraine's parliament declared that Yanukovych was relieved of duty in a 328-to-0 vote, out of 450 members.

Russia took advantage of the chaos to annex Crimea, a peninsula that was an autonomous republic of Ukraine. Emboldened by silence from the international community, Russia instigated and led a separatist movement in eastern Ukraine, where ethnic Russians make up a sizable chunk of the population. The Russia-backed rebels declared Donetsk and Luhansk independent "people's republics." Independent of Ukraine, that is. Not so independent of Russia, which has continued to supply cash, arms, and actual boots on the ground to keep a pro-Russia insurgency going, though, until now, never declaring them to be independent states.

In 2015, Russia and Ukraine participated in negotiations that were supposed to formalize a structure that would take into account the disputed status of Donetsk and Luhansk: the Minsk Protocols. According to Russia's interpretation of that agreement, it would have required reintegrating Luhansk and Donetsk into the Ukrainian government, handing Russia a veto over Ukraine's domestic affairs and foreign policy. This would have spelled the end of Ukraine's orientation toward Europe, which had brought tangible benefits to its people in recent years despite the many imperfections in its fledgling democracy. Ukraine refused to implement that interpretation of the agreement, insisting instead that Russia withdraw from the Donbas region before elections conforming to international standards could be held.

For the past several years, as the conflict simmered, Russia has been strengthening the insurgencies in Donetsk and Luhansk. While still nominally part of Ukraine, they became full-on puppet statelets dependent on their patron's cash, arms, and sometimes active intervention from regular Russian troops to stay afloat.

Perhaps this is why, during the latest build-up of tensions, most of my Ukrainian friends seemed hardly moved by the renewed threat of war. Part of this is what I call the cult of *all will be fine*: the stock phrase usually offered for any misfortune, large or small. It's a charming cultural affirmation that often things will work out on their own and it's up to God or fate in any case. But press them, and invariably Ukrainians are quick to remind you that they have been at war with Russia for the last eight years.

It is not news to people that their eastern neighbor makes unreasonable demands, wants more territory, and generally seeks to impose its will on Ukraine. Quietly they prepare their "anxious bags," usually a backpack full of important documents, passports, warm clothes, and medicines, easy to grab at a moment's notice. Once that ominous task is complete they go on, enjoying Kyiv's many fine restaurants and chic shops, strolling in Lviv's charming European city center, and taking selfies at Odessa's Langeron pier against a wintry Black Sea backdrop.

These photographs could turn out to be keepsakes for their children, or their grandchildren, in the event that familiar landmarks are bombed into oblivion, relics of a life that will exist only in memory if they are forced to flee. "What else can we do?" they reply to my anxious questions, and life goes on.

I worry but also take some comfort for Ukraine's future. Again, words are important. The Maidan Revolution, named for Maidan Nezalezhnosti, which translates as Independence Square, the central square of Kyiv, sparked a flowering of civic society, particularly in younger generations. There is an infectious spark of creativity, volunteerism, and optimism that will seem familiar to Americans. While going on with life as usual in recent weeks, Ukrainians have also been attending self-defense training and first aid classes, and many are volunteering for territorial defense units.

Last month, as the U.S. Congress debated aid to Ukraine, some politicians expressed concern that funding and weapons could fall into the hands of groups like the Azov Battalion, a particularly effective unit in the Ukrainian National Guard with ties to the country's far-right, ultranationalist National Corps party and Azov movement. Congress has passed measures aimed at preventing aid from going to the battalion, which has negligible political support in Ukraine, anyway. Nonetheless, satellite groups associated with the far-right movement are believed to be slipping past those prohibitions.

There is also opposition expressed by left-wing media outlets contending that the U.S. is representing the oil and gas industry's interests. They believe that U.S. energy companies want to stall the transfer of Russian oil and gas via the 767-mile long Nord Stream 2 pipeline that cuts through Ukraine to enhance sales of U.S. fracked natural gas to Europe. Energy and geopolitics are inextricably linked. Within hours of Putin's move into Ukraine, German's chancellor Olaf Scholz halted certification of the $11 billion pipeline, completed last year, citing security reasons.

While the U.S. has both economic and geopolitical interests in Ukraine, it's not naïve to take the Biden administration at its word. The immediate concern is holding the line on old-fashioned democratic liberalism and human rights in the face of a full-scale invasion by Russia. That seems to be the position of many Ukrainians, as well, including the Jewish community in Odessa. In *The New York Times*, reporter Michael Schwirtz wrote:

> Pavel Kozlenko, the director of the Museum of the Holocaust, who lost 50 members of his family at the hands of the Nazis and their allies, accused Mr. Putin of betraying the memory of the "common victory" of World War II. Then he told a joke, as Odessans often do in dark times, about two Jews standing on the street speaking in Yiddish.
>
> "A third comes up and says, 'Guys, why are you speaking in Yiddish?'" Mr. Kozlenko said, "to which one of the Yiddish-speaking men replied, 'You know, I'm scared to speak in Russian because if I do Putin will show up and try to liberate us.'"

This week, as the world watched Putin carve out another slice of their country, Ukrainian Twitter was raising funds for charities to help their soldiers and encouraging one another to "break through" anxiety while they waited until the early morning for President Volodymyr Zelensky's address to the nation. If Putin goes all in, the Russian army will meet a Ukrainian populace determined to resist. Moreover, with eight years of wartime experience, not to mention Western training and weapons, the Ukrainian army is not the ragtag collection of poorly outfitted, disorganized volunteers and militias it was in 2014. Ukraine will put up a prodigious fight, and it will last as long as necessary.

Like it or not, Ukraine's fight is ours as well. Putin's rabid speechmaking on the eve of Russia's military incursion made it clear that Ukraine's accession to NATO or the European Union (both distant prospects) is not his true grievance. Ominously, he seeks to re-litigate the entire aftermath of the breakup of the Soviet empire, what he has previously called the greatest tragedy of the 20th century.

With Russia flush with cash from its natural gas exports, Putin appears to be aiming for his place in history as a great Russian leader bringing home his country's people separated by accidents of history. He's done the math, and according to the calculations, it's now or never for his gamble that no one will truly go to war for Ukraine.

The echoes of world war are disturbing, as they should be. Ukrainians like to say that for the last eight years, they have been holding the front line for the West. Let's hope that they can continue to do so, for their sake and ours.

Fatal Geographies

STEPHEN PAIN

WHEN I WAS STUDYING AT HEREFORDSHIRE ART College I would often pop into the city cathedral and look at the medieval *Mappa Mundi*. This map is more of a "salvation geography," one which is not empirically correct but meant to symbolize the union of the spiritual and the earthly realms. Unlike our maps, the East was at the top. At the center was the spiritual and terrestrial capital of the Christian World, Jerusalem. In successive maps we find that new knowledge of the world thanks to explorers like Ferdinand Magellan and cartographers such as Gerardus Mercator informed the artists. These earlier religious maps were above all works of art and meant to be read "spiritually."

As the world became more known, it was difficult to situate Paradise in a way that made sense. In the XVI century, Paradise was located at the source of the Nile; poetically justifiable, perhaps, but theologically questionable. Nevertheless, there was enough belief in the old ways of looking at the world to justify the continuation of recognizable spiritual and mythical features often at the expense of accuracy, for example sea monsters and mermaids in nautical maps. The science of cartography would have to wait a couple more centuries before it became practical.

When you stand in front of the *Mappa Mundi* it pays to have read something about these maps and their symbolism. It is very similar to looking at an ordnance survey map and trying to figure out the legend, the box that displays the symbols and their meaning—I remember doing that in Northumberland on a school orienteering course: I looked at contours and the symbols as I tried to figure out the geographic and existential question "Where was I?"

Both the Mappa Mundi and ordnance survey map are representations of the world, ones that help us navigate it; however, the former is also a representation of a faith, a belief system which reinforces the status quo of believer and her god. When you "read" a *mappa mundi* you are entering another space, another "world."

In some ways our contemporary world is full of mental bubbles or *umwelts*. Ethologists have adopted the word *umwelt*, a German word for environment, to denote an organism's unique sensory world. The *umwelt* of a male yellow mosquito (*Aedes aegypti*), for example, differs sharply from that of a human, or a cat. On the personal level we have mental and motor maps that help us navigate and relate to our world, such as the one cognitive scientists talk about, an internal mental map that helps the organism "mind map" and engage the outer world.

Then there are community maps, whereby we attach meaning and significance to topography that is local. There are the ordnance survey maps (based on national surveys and available in different scales) and of course Google Maps which are government and corporate representations of our environment.

When I was at school I remember the old atlas had Britain in a central position and it still had many countries in pink representing the nations in the British Commonwealth. Note this business of centering the world according to the nation. China quite literally means the "Middle Kingdom." Each tribe or nation has its own geography. Sometimes this geography is stolen. I recollect a Sri Lankan friend telling that all his nation's geography text books had been written by the colonialists. Once Ceylon became independent it recovered its geography and became Sri Lanka. Which is correct: Florence, Florenz, or Firenze? The Falkland Islands are called the Malvinas by Argentina.

By naming you make a claim. Imperialism was all about naming, in the same way a dog marks its territory by urinating on a tree. When you look at the *Mappa Mundi* found in the Hereford Cathedral, you will see a wealth of detail. One does time traveling as well as wandering about in space. Felicitas Schmieder has helped us understand the method of reading these *mappae mundi* in her article "How to Read Medieval Mappae Mundi: Geographies of Salvation" (*Peregrinations,* 2018). Schmieder examines how the map was read in the medieval times. Firstly there was the "sense of writing," the *sensus scripturae,* in which the reader processed the map. Here it was recognized that there are different levels according to the Christian tradition: the Christian moral reading of the figures in the text, then the interpretation of allegories, and finally the reading of what pertained to the ascent to heaven and the final judgment.

The complexity and relations in the different planes of referentiality in Christian exegesis of maps are something akin to how we should read what I term "fatal geographies." These are geographies that pose a real existential threat to us and our planet, because they involve players who have the means to totally destroy our "worlds." We can of course include the Western corporate geographies that have supplanted the older colonial geographies.

McDonalds, Disney, Coca Cola, Google, Facebook, Amazon, et al., have their own competing geographies, their own levels. Then there is NATO and the European Union, etc. They all have their dangers.

But, for immediate dangers I would suggest that the geographies and belief systems of Vladimir Putin, Xi Jinping, and Recep Tayyip Erdogan represent the best examples of fatal geographies. These geographies have a *telos* that does not end well! Imagine placing maps on the table and they overlap. For the viewer it means nothing, but wherever they overlap there is suffering and death. For a better analogy in those *mappae mundi* that had paradise in terrestrial form, those overlaps are hells. In Charlie Chaplin's *The Great Dictator* he masquerades as Hitler contemplating a globe as if it is a tray and he is deciding which hors d'oeuvre to pluck.

Maps and power go together. Maybe there is a form of map mania? When we look at how two people argue over a map and directions, then consider the international disputes over territory. There are numerous territorial disputes many that have arisen from Fatal Geographies. While very rarely do ramblers in the countryside come to blows and fisticuffs over maps, there are unfortunately millions who have died over territorial disputes.

While an undergradiuate at the University of East Anglia, I wrote a long essay on the concept and theory of what constitutes a village. Basing my ideas upon a Polish sociologist (whose name I have sadly forgotten) and others, I concluded that until there is a threat or a natural catastrophe, a village is a collection of heterogeneous buildings. What makes a village is the common bonds between peoples and their combined reaction to, say, a fire or in the case of Ukraine, a war. We see courage and identification with the land and the neighbors. The same is true of quasi-sovereign states such as Taiwan. Here one should apply the law of equity to territory and construct a nation status from the fact that the island has acted as a nation for a considerable period.

This is very different from forceful occupation and illegal constructions of suzerain states such as Tibet and Mongolia where the original peoples and their sovereign wills and wealth have been subsumed under imperial meta states.

Resolution of disputes should not involve warfare. We are in the 21st century! Imagine neighbors arguing over a hedge and eventually arming each other! Then firing indiscriminately. It is absurd. War is absurd.

Zonal

MAXINE CHERNOFF

While signs proclaim the madness of the king,
the world spells its name in summary

summer of woes
and nature's worldly
face: how fledglings enter seasons rich
with song, first notes the ear has

never heard or failed to hear: We found you,
world, when we were new, and you were
snow on roof, black branch of unfilled space,
absence to which we lent a listening ear.

Days painted green within a globe
that also holds the song. Only amber
colors world's past display of how we
lived before the map was red with death:
eyes peer out from story's unknown end.

THE LARGER SCHEME

Historian Frank Snowden wrote: "Like all pandemics, COVID-19 is not an accidental or random event. Epidemics afflict societies though the specific vulnerabilities people have created by their relationships with the environment, other species, and each other."

By the pandemic's third year, it was clear that the conspiracy theories about a lab leak in China unleashing a genetically altered virus were implausible. We couldn't escape the knowledge that our heedless relationship to the natural world ensures the coronavirus would not be the last plague. We might expel a would-be dictator and develop vaccines in record time. But the destruction of the environment is perpetrated by our daily lives: where we live, how we live. These hydra-headed problems we cannot solve.

Nature is where it all began and, almost certainly, where it will end.

Shock the Monkey

WILLIAM THATCHER DOWELL

ON THE ROAD FROM THE THAI BORDER back to Cambodia's capital, Phnom Penh, we used to stop at a restaurant that displayed a monkey's corpse crucified to a wooden frame. The monkey, along with body parts of other unidentified animals, made up the lunch menu.

We called it, of course, the Endangered Species Restaurant.

"Looks mummified, doesn't he?" said my companion.

"Or maybe a very devout Christian?" I offered, eyeing the splayed corpse.

I'd first gone to Cambodia in the 1970s when I covered the Vietnam War. By the 1990s, Pol Pot had been driven out and while there was an ostensible government, its reach was limited to the capitol. The countryside was a free-for-all. You never knew if a band of mercenaries would attack you on the road, or whether you'd find a village you'd once known reduced to ashes.

When I say an ostensible government, I mean barely functioning. Thieves were ripping off pieces of the Angkor Wat temple complex to sell to smugglers. The national museum was infested with bats. Not all bad, since the curators were selling the guano as fertilizer to finance the museum. With Cambodia in disarray, bandits and Khmer Rouge irregulars intermittently shooting up the place, a restaurant serving monkey was barely worth remarking on.

I was *Time* magazine's Southeast Asia bureau chief in those days, and what qualified as news was war and, less frequently, peace. When I look back at those trips, I realize that another war was going on, the war ecologist Raymond Dasmann called World War III, industrial man's war on nature. The casualties were all around us.

By the 1990s, conservation biologists recognized that extinction was accelerating, largely because of human population growth. Despite the emotional response to cute animals, extinction is a hard sell to the public. Yet it is a threat equal to climate change. In fact, extinction and climate change act synergistically, and scientists worldwide agree that their combined effects threaten global ecological collapse.

Covid-19 alerted people to a more present danger: 75 percent of all emerging infectious diseases are "zoonotic" which means they are transmitted from animals to people—Ebola, HIV, SARS, and most likely, Covid-19. These diseases spread when humans intrude into wild areas, coming into contact with animals that had once lived their lives undisturbed, or relatively so.

The things that kill you are never what you expect them to be. While the Ebola virus means almost certain death, it is so virulent that it kills the host that it depends on for its own survival, ultimately triggering its own extinction. Covid-19 is more subtle. So many of Covid's early victims were elderly or infirm, the illusion was that if you were young and healthy, there was not much to worry about. That was a false assumption. To date, the global death toll from Covid-19—not to mention the worldwide economic disruption—stands at nearly seven million, and the pandemic is not over. In contrast, the Centers for Disease Control and Prevention reports that total deaths from Ebola stand at slightly more than 11,000.

It almost seems as though evolution is experimenting until it finds the perfect weapon to level at human beings. The vector that carried the Covid-19 weapon—you could say, the gun that fired the fatal bullet—was wildlife, the endangered species that so many people expressed concern over but did little or nothing to protect. It was this wildlife that I had regarded with only the mildest interest on my trips as a foreign correspondent. As Americans debated the origin of Covid-19, I thought about why it is so difficult to stop that war against nature, the one I'd encountered all those years ago, even though I hadn't recognized it.

〰

In 2001, *Time* laid off a lot of us at the foreign bureaus. Still living in Hong Kong, I talked my way into an assignment from *Talk* magazine, the short-lived publication headed by Tina Brown.

I had heard through contacts at the United Nations that the Uruguayan Navy was about to dispatch a peacekeeping force to clear the Congo River of pirates. Some years before, I had met Paul Kagame, the narrow-faced bespectacled general who had ended the 1994 Rwandan genocide at the head of a Tutsi army.

The price of peace was externalizing the remnants of civil war. Rwandan Hutus had spilled into the eastern Congo, which had become a battleground between Rwanda's warring factions, as well as Congolese tempted to seize power from the relatively weak government in Kinshasa.

Talking to my contact at the UN, I had flashbacks to *Heart of Darkness*, reviled by Chinua Achebe and others as racist and colonialist in recent years, yet still possessing an archetypal power. The novel, I was to find, was firmly based in Joseph Conrad's four months as a merchant seaman in Congo. He had gotten the geography right, according to my source.

"The Congo is so vast," a friend at the United Nations explained, "that the river is the only way you can move supplies. There are no roads, and if you fly, you need to carry enough fuel with you to get back to Kinshasa."

He added, just in case I didn't know, that the Congo had played a far more strategic role in world affairs than most people realized. "The uranium that went into the atom bomb that destroyed Hiroshima and Nagasaki came from the Congo," he said. "If you've got a cell phone, chances are that the rare earth minerals that make it work came from the Congo."

"Go for it!" the editor at *Talk* said.

Malcolm Linton, a *Time* contract photographer who had more experience and knew Africa better than I did, came with me. He liked the fact that Africans still had a sense of humor. In light of the general atmosphere of depression that had descended on the Time-Life Building, the Congo, despite its perennial troubles, looked pretty good.

In addition to scaring up freelance work in the wake of our layoffs, I had personal reasons to take the trip. My wife's father worked as a bush doctor in the Congo in the 1950s and I had been immersed in the stories of her childhood and their rushed departure from the country.

Michèle was born in Kivu, in Manguridjipa, a tiny village in Eastern Congo where her father, a Belgian national, had worked as a bush doctor. When the war for independence began to take shape in the late 1950s, the tribal chiefs had gone to Michèle's father. They explained that they planned to kill all the whites in the province except for two families, hers and one other.

"But we will have to take you as a hostage," the chief added, rather apologetically.

The family's rapid move to Europe proved to be a jarring cultural shift that Michèle never really got used to. I was interested in seeing the land of her childhood, and the Congo promised a brief chance to get back to the field. The Congo had a certain magic, one of the legendary blank spots on the map romanticized both by Conrad, and later, the American conservationist Aldo Leopold ('What avail are forty freedoms without a blank spot on the map?')

This was an all-expense-paid way, I thought, to explore a place where nature still had a chance.

When we got off the plane in Kinshasa, I noticed an African in a dark blue suit talking animatedly on a cell phone. A number of other phones dangled from his belt. I guessed this was intended to project an image of technological sophistication in darkest Africa. "No," Malcolm said, "The reception here is lousy. You never know which phone will actually work."

Kinshasa, formerly Leopoldville, looked like a dystopian ruin. Homeless people had moved into abandoned government buildings and were managing cooking fires in the hallways. The window frames no longer had any glass and the edges were charred black from the smoke. The streets were spotted with potholes that looked pretty much like bomb craters. Next to each, you'd see a middle-aged black man dressed in T-shirt and boxer shorts. "They ask passing cars for money and then they agree to fill in the holes," Malcolm explained.

At a few intersections, we spotted motorcycle policemen in blue and yellow uniforms wearing motorcycle helmets and directing traffic. They had no motorcycles, but at least they had the uniform.

We checked into the UN compound, had some iced tea, and watched a tennis match on the compound's courts. We weren't going to spend a great deal of money, so we checked into a hostel run by an evangelical Christian sect. The other guest at the hostel was a Belgian who explained that he was here to buy diamonds. Why else would anyone come to the Congo?

The UN arranged a flight to Mbandaka, halfway up the river. The town had been known as Coquilehatville when it was still a Belgian colony. "The Uruguayans are stationed there, and they'll be clearing the rest of the river from that point," a UN officer explained. The flight was on a nearly empty Soviet-era Antonov transport plane. A crew member, I guessed from Chechnya or some other former Soviet satellite, sat sphinx-like in a chair next to the cockpit door. Next to him was a nearly life-size pin-up of a blonde in a bikini.

Kinshasa spreads out from its tumultuous waterfront as far as the eye can see. Its sibling, Brazzaville, on the opposite bank is much the same. In contrast, Mbandaka resembles a rash from a mosquito bite, or more probably, a tsetse fly. A gathering of 20 or so houses cling tenuously to the riverbank.

The first thing that struck me after seeing the river was that to try to reach the shore, you had to cross 10 or 20 yards of tangled, half-submerged roots. Given the gnarled wood and dense vegetation, my guess is that you would never make it. Islands of floating vegetation passed by. The river was not only imposing, it seemed limitless, the shore inaccessible.

Malcolm and I ventured forth. In the market, we noticed, the locals happily wolfed down live caterpillars doused with red pepper. A woman held one out for me to try, but I shook my head.

UN headquarters was in a white hotel that had most likely been built by Belgians before independence. The Uruguayans seemed determined to convert their patch of jungle into a little Uruguay. They had set up their own FM radio station and were broadcasting Latino songs out over the jungle. The officers wore starched blue UN uniforms, and every one of them seemed to have his or her own thermos full of maté. They clutched the thermoses close to their bodies as though they contained life-giving oxygen. Maybe it was just a memory of home, I thought. In Conrad's account, when you lose those moorings, madness follows.

Malcolm and I checked into what had been described as a sort of local motel. In fact, it was a long building with a number of concrete cells. Each cell had a cement basin holding water, a bed, and mosquito netting. It could have passed as basic prison accommodations for any convict serving a life sentence, but it offered a certain protection from an onslaught of insects and other wildlife ready to eat anyone who might be foolish enough to venture outside at night. The trick was to get under the mosquito net before four or five of the micro-beasts could slip in with you.

I asked the white owner if he were Belgian or Congolese. "Belgian!" he snapped. I later discovered that he was pretty much a man-of-all-trades and was also the local agent for Air Afrique (formerly known as 'Air I Freak'). He lived in an impressive villa with a Congolese wife who was quite beautiful. He had created a tenuous paradise for himself and seemed determined to keep a low profile, lest anyone try to take it away from him.

On the way there, I'd run into a UN delegation from New York, being led by the then-Secretary General, Kofi Annan. A number of the group clutched copies of Adam Hochschild's book *King Leopold's Ghost,* which recounts the horrors of the colonial period. I gathered that the team from New York was striving for an instant understanding of what they were looking at during the whirlwind trip. In Mbandaka, out of curiosity, I asked a number of ordinary Congolese what they thought of the Belgians.

"We wish they'd come back," was the answer. I understood what they were trying to say. No one wanted a return to colonialism, but what had followed that period had been considerably more violent.

On the second day, we tracked down the Uruguayan Navy commander, who bore a striking resemblance to Kevin Spacey. After explaining that the Congo was a chance to up his résumé and experience a little adventure, he assured me that he was eager to talk to the press. "We'll go out on the river, tomorrow," he promised.

On the river, whatever romantic ideas I might have had about nature were rather quickly un-romanticized. The boats we hitched rides on were crammed to the gills with refugees. Pigs rooted in the garbage at the riverbank. As we traveled along the river, the pirogue's crew feasted nightly on bits and pieces of a small crocodile, smoked until it was pitch-black and twisted into a scaly ring so that it appeared to be biting its own tail.

I remember flinching, recalling that one of my father-in-law's tasks was to inspect meat in the local market with a sharp eye for anything that looked vaguely human. No cultural snobbery here. It happens. As one might recall, it happened in California, when the Donner Party was stranded.

Returning to the Covid outbreak for a moment, it's worth noting the extraordinary breadth of the wildlife trade. In Latin America, between five to eight million people rely on bushmeat as a primary source of protein. In Asia, the number is harder to determine but thought to be even larger. In Central Africa, including Congo, where Malcolm and I traveled, more than two million tons of bushmeat are consumed each year, causing Empty Forest Syndrome: forests that look normal but are devoid of wildlife. INTERPOL estimates the illegal wildlife trade at $20 billion annually, just behind guns and humans.

The Covid-19 crisis brought attention to this problem. In the short term, conspiracy theories aside, scientists are fairly certain that the coronavirus outbreak started in an outdoor food market in Wuhan, China. These "wet" markets are where poor and working-class Chinese often get their food. But they are also where rich Asians, not only in China, but Vietnam and Korea, obtain illegal wildlife.

As news of the pandemic broke, China issued a temporary ban on wildlife markets where animals such as civets, live wolf pups, and pangolins are kept alive in small cages while on sale, often in filthy conditions where they incubate diseases that can then spill into human populations. The National People's Congress issued rules against trading in wild animals and limited, but didn't ban, their consumption. President Xi Jinping emphatically declared, "We can't be indifferent anymore!"

That was mostly public relations. The rules are there, and international restrictions on trading in wildlife and endangered species have been on the books for decades. Enforcing them is a different story. Consider the pangolin. Early reports indicated that Covid-19 was spread by a pangolin in the Wuhan market, although the latest thinking is that a rare species called a raccoon dog acted as a middle creature. Nevertheless, the illicit trade in this exceedingly rare creature shows how ineffective and inadequate efforts to control the wildlife trade have been.

All eight species of pangolin are considered critically endangered. China outlawed the sale of pangolins in 2007, yet TRAFFIC, which monitors the global trade in wildlife, reported that around 90,000 were smuggled into China over the next nine years. The conservation group Wild Aid estimated that a million pangolins were poached over that decade.

If anything, the rules and regulations against trafficking pangolins probably made pangolins more valuable as a semi-clandestine delicacy, promoting the status of anyone capable of offering pangolin meat in a hot pot.

In 2020, it almost seemed as if an international outcry might result in real change. Dr. Anthony Fauci, then chief medical advisor to the U.S. president, called for shutting down wet markets. The United Nations biodiversity chief, Elizabeth Maruma Mrema, also called for a global ban on wildlife markets. But Mrema's statement came with a caveat.

"It would be good to ban the live animal markets as China has done and some countries," she said. "But we should also remember you have communities, particularly from low-income rural areas, particularly in Africa, which are dependent on wild animals to sustain the livelihoods of millions of people. So unless we get alternatives for these communities, there might be a danger of opening up illegal trade in wild animals which currently is already leading us to the brink of extinction for some species."

Science writer David Quammen put it in wider perspective, writing in *The New York Times* about "...7.6 billion hungry humans: some of them impoverished and desperate for protein; some affluent and wasteful and empowered to travel every which way by airplane. These factors are unprecedented on planet Earth: We know from the fossil record, by absence of evidence, that no large-bodied animal has ever been nearly so abundant as humans are now, let alone so effective at arrogating resources. And one consequence of that abundance, that power, and the consequent ecological disturbances is increasing viral exchanges—first from animal to human, then from human to human, sometimes on a pandemic scale.

"We invade tropical forests and other wild landscapes, which harbor so many species of animals and plants—and within those creatures, so many unknown viruses. We cut the trees; we kill the animals or cage them and send them to markets. We disrupt ecosystems, and we shake viruses loose from their natural hosts. When that happens, they need a new host. Often, we are it."

By 2023, when wet market bans had been all but forgotten, the war in Ukraine had displaced the pandemic as the crisis du jour. Yet the war's less visible toll was a deepening of environmental decline. Russian attacks on Ukrainian harbors where ships departed to transport grain to Africa threatened food supplies. Forty-five percent of Africa is already desert, and climate change is wringing out more land. The demand for bushmeat will follow the curve of scarcity, ironically, in a continent that is rich beyond imagining in natural resources.

The Congo is one of those African countries suffering from what economists call "the resource curse," the instability that accrues when a country with a weak government finds its natural resources in high demand. These days, the hot commodity, as my UN source had reminded me, is coltan, a mineral used in cell phones. But there are also diamonds.

∿

At the appointed hour, Malcolm and I accompanied the Kevin Spacey lookalike commander in an inflatable rubber Zodiac. We drifted out into the river. The Uruguayan sailors looked incongruous and slightly ridiculous in their blue helmets and bulletproof vests. The Congolese were wearing cutoffs and were mostly shirtless, which made a lot more sense in the climate. The river was huge, but it was still just a river. The boats circled a few times and then their captains decided to go back. The Uruguayans didn't seem too interested in actually finding any pirates.

"What am I going to do with this?" Malcolm asked in desperation. "There's no story," Malcolm repeated, "and there certainly aren't any pirates." I had to admit that compared to the other stories we had worked on, this one lacked drama.

Back at our concrete bungalow, a contract worker, a tech specialist from India, rushed up. "Did you hear?" he said. "What?" I asked. "The World Trade Center!" he said. "They just blew it up."

I found a satellite phone and called Michèle in New York. "It's terrible here," she told me. I said something to the effect that maybe now Americans would understand what the rest of the world has been dealing with all along. "I'd be careful about saying that," she said. "This is different."

With New York, the Pentagon and most of the U.S. in full panic mode, a bunch of Uruguayans circling the water in a motorboat was, to put it mildly, not much of a story. We decided to keep going, for reasons that now seem obscure.

Malcolm disappeared into the crowd and came back a few minutes later. "I rented a dugout with a motor," he said, "and we have a crew to run it." The crew was a young man, Paté, and an older man whose name I never got, but who apparently knew motors. We threw our packs into the canoe and headed downstream.

In late afternoon, we pulled up to the riverbank in a village named Gombé. Belgian nuns were running a clinic, which consisted of thatched mud huts.

"You had better see the district commissioner," we were told as we arrived. We were led to a ramshackle ruin of a house that might once have served as a villa for a Belgian colonial administrator. We were ushered inside. There was no door and the windows were gaping holes.

The commissioner, however, was a dapper, gray-haired man in pressed slacks and a crisply ironed, white button-down dress shirt sitting behind a wooden desk piled high with papers. A vicious-looking dagger with a handle carved from the bones of some unidentified animal lay next to a pile of papers on his desk. He saw that I had noticed the knife and deftly covered it with a sheaf of papers.

"What do you think of our village?" he asked.

"Picturesque," I said.

"It's a ruin," he said.

"It could be improved," I admitted.

"No, it can't," he said. "That would require money, and we have none."

Sunlight broke through holes in the collapsing roof. Straw had been wedged into the rafters. Feathers floated slowly toward the commissioner's desk. I guessed some birds had stashed their nest there.

The next morning we took off downriver in the canoe. Around a bend, we came across a Congolese Navy post. A plump but seemingly good-natured man in civilian clothes introduced himself as a major, obviously in intelligence.

At Mbandaka, a woman selling an electric catfish, which delivers 300 volts.
Photo by William Thatcher Dowell.

He invited us to breakfast, which we happily accepted. He had heard about the attack on the World Trade Center.

"You Americans must be destroyed," he said. I said that the casualties had been less than 3,000, and the U.S. had a population of nearly 350 million.

"We are shaken," I said, "but I hardly think that we are destroyed." He nodded. "And besides," I said, "the Congo has a population of around 60 million people, and more than two million have been killed in fighting over the last two years. You are not destroyed."

"Yes," he said, "but we are Congolese. We are used to it."

The next week was equally uneventful. We found a barge. The passengers told us stories and hit us up for money. As we docked one night, an evangelical pastor prayed loudly at midnight, leading his followers into the river, a Biblical scene from John the Baptist. *Perhaps God would protect them,* I thought, recalling a woman I had seen in the market. She was selling a huge electric catfish capable of delivering a 300-volt shock. Cowardly, perhaps, but I never got into the water after that, even when it was brutally hot. The river had secrets that I would rather avoid, and the catfish, I assumed, was only one of them. Malcolm snapped a few pictures.

Still, no pirates. The captain's foreman, a pleasant-looking, slightly rotund man in his mid-forties, approached us. Motioning us away from the others, he spoke in a low voice. "Are you interested in diamonds?"

Malcolm and I went through the motions of submitting the story to *Talk*, but for the next six months, no one could talk or think about anything except 9/11. Despite the media frenzy, hardly anyone seemed to spend any time thinking of why someone would want to attack the U.S.

I was asked to work on a film for PBS *Frontline* on the religious implications of the attack. We were tasked with answering the question: How could God let such a thing happen? At a story conference, I mentioned that, in fact, a similar occurrence is mentioned in the Bible. The destruction of the Tower of Babel was a retaliation for man's arrogance against Nature and God.

It was not only the World Trade Center building that resembled the original tower, I said, but it was really the economic system that the building represented. In producing record profits, our economic system had ravaged the planet and encouraged inequality, exploitation, and the destruction of anything that stood in its way. That might have been easy to ignore until now, but to continue along this path was clearly unsustainable, morally, politically, and ecologically. Not surprisingly, the suggestion received a less than warm reception.

I suppose there is a grim sort of hope. In H.G. Wells' turn-of-the-century science fiction thriller *War of the Worlds,* an invasion by seemingly invincible aliens is defeated by the common cold, which is, in fact, a coronavirus. It turns out the advanced aliens have no immunity against the planet's lowliest, single-cell biological entity. As we encounter more animal species previously shielded by impenetrable jungles and rainforests, we may find ourselves in a similar situation, only this time, we are the not-quite-invincible aliens.

As a foreign correspondent, it was easy to become immersed in political squabbles and the senseless carnage that results from man's apparent inhumanity to man, and easy to overlook quieter dangers that are ultimately likely to prove fatal.

I stand by the notion that 9/11 was not exceptional, a word we like to use about America, just another in a long line of attacks and murders I reported on. The attack was a one-time event for Americans, but atrocities in the Congo continue as they have for decades now, largely ignored by the Western media.

The animals? They're still eaten, of course. In places where people are struggling for survival, basic needs must be met. Most efforts to save the environment are just paper, empty policy statements, or, worse, luxuries to make people in the West feel better about themselves.

Nobody seems to be able to stop any of it.

Endangered Species

JAMIE MACARTY

Haze of pink light, desert microburst: pearl hail
pelts human bodies
                              and industrial machinery
             contiguous with meteorologists'
                          beat-liberating weather.

Our bodies pocked   by what surrounds them

A snippet gains no more depth.
In this mecca of erotism: a tiger skeleton
maribates in an aquarium.

                 The dark tonic: said to supply
                              tiger stamina.

For thematic coherence: follow the grail of wine bones.

The liquer affects.   desire, not ability.

With undainty haste,   always yes and no.

              The illicit thing: partial.

To pull together certain themes: the new century's new

couple enters late.

                              Zinfandel on their cheeks.

Accretion of context,   not meaning.

The division flimsy, connected
                              to other such moments
             implicated in the world's disgraces

Dénouement at the serial killing
              of rhinoceros and seahorses
                              owed to the demand
             for aphrodisiacs and medicine
                              no stronger than aspirin.
Lifestyles keep the demand infinate.

From the grid of structure, the last gesture
                              toward the body.

A burning fragment

              in the menagerie of the surviving world.

Located at the disturbing interface of endangered species, animal poaching, and aphrodisiac hawking, the poem "Endangered Species" brings focus onto illegal wildlife traffic and trade: tigers, rhinoceroses, seahorses, and pangolins (although unnamed), whose body parts are extolled, consumed, and worn for their sex-enhancing, infertility-curing, body-building, and disease-fighting powers.

Though these claims of curative powers lack scientific basis, the belief in them, and the consumption of animal parts based in those beliefs, persists. These medicinal claims come from traditional cultures and medicine practices in Latin American, African, and Asian countries. The venues for procuring these animal parts, so-called "wet markets," also exist in these countries.

However, since the novel coronavirus, now called Covid-19, likely originated in China, let's focus on markets there. Not all wet markets in China are the same. There's a range of types and product availabilities, along with gradations of risk associated with buying and consuming. A typical market sells perishable foods such as fresh produce, filleted fish, and slaughtered meat at indoor and outdoor stalls. Other markets sell commonly eaten, live domesticated animals—chickens, ducks, pigs, and such—bought and butchered on the spot.

The variety of wet market at the apparent origin of the coronavirus pandemic is one that allows the sale of live, often endangered and poached, wild animals. At such a market, the conditions are horrid for animals, such as bats, peacocks, turtles, cobras, badgers, pangolins, and other "exotics." Confined to cages stacked one atop others, animals are subjected to the urine, feces, blood, pus, and saliva from those above. Not much imagination is required to grasp how animal-to-animal disease is spread.

Now, introduce humans. Chinese wildlife wet markets are a chock-a-block bustle of human, live animal, and bloody flesh. In other words, disease-incubating, 24/7 experiments in the transmission of zoonotic pathogens. Animal-to-human diseases are especially dangerous because humans have low or no resistance. We've not had the the chance to develop antibodies—hence the "novel" coronavirus.

Scientists think the new pathogen responsible for our global pandemic started with animal-to-animal spread, followed by animal-to-human spread, followed by travel and communal transmission. Because bats carry coronaviruses, current thinking is that a bat, possibly a horseshoe bat, common in live wild animal wet markets, defecated on another animal in a cage below it, then that animal, possibly a pangolin (one of the most hunted endangered species in the world) was slaughtered and sold, creating an animal-to-human, then human-to-human link in the virus chain.

The Huanan Seafood Wholesale Market in Wuhan, China, where the first 20 people diagnosed with the disease were linked, along with all other Wuhan wet markets, was shuttered while the city was under quarantine. Now, as Wuhan emerges from quarantine, the wet markets are said to be reopening.

On the surface, a complete elimination of wet markets may seem warranted, but doing so is complicated by socioeconomic and cultural considerations. Closing wet markets altogether would affect poor and working-class Chinese for whom the markets are a daily source of affordable food, subsistence income, and local community. The markets that include the sale of wildlife or wild meat are a different story. At these markets, impoverished people who come to buy cheap bushmeat mix with affluent buyers, searching for tinctures and talismans, such as tiger claw necklaces to improve virility.

To further complicate the matter, it turns out that traditional Chinese medicine has been leveraged to bolster commercial trade in wildlife products, from which wildlife traders and the Chinese government profit mightily. You see, the industry and its markets are not based solely in the demand of Chinese consumers, but also in the influence of the wildlife traffickers, traders, and breeders.

Even with this complex of factors, there's a way to ban the sale of wildlife in wet markets and reduce the risk of disease, while also maintaining income and food security and cultural and culinary practices. Doing so would require the Chinese government to check the power and greed of wildlife traffickers, traders, and breeders, while emphasizing the health and safety of its citizens, and all denizens of our human-dominated world.

The Secret Life of Peter Beard

SUSAN ZAKIN

One of the penalties of an ecological education is that one lives alone in a world of wounds. Much of the damage inflicted on land is quite invisible to laymen.

— Aldo Leopold, *Sand County Almanac*

ONE YEAR AGO TODAY, THE BODY OF 82-YEAR-OLD photographer Peter Beard was discovered a few miles from his home on Montauk, Long Island. Not long before his death, an editor had slapped this headline on a story about him: "Peter Beard Might Actually Be the Most Interesting Man in the World." If there is such a competition, Beard would certainly be in the running.

After his corpse was discovered obituaries stressed Beard's *louche* side: the partying, the models, the drugs. In recent years, those proclivities had caught up with him. Suffering from dementia after several strokes, he had wandered off from home into the nearest forest as if he were an animal knowing it was his time.

Beard's friend Graham Boynton published an obituary in *AirMail* called "The Ladies' Man Vanishes" comparing the handsome preppie photographer to polo-playing Tommy Hitchcock and Porfirio Rubirosa, the Dominican diplomat fictionalized by sex novelist Harold Robbins in *The Adventurers*. Beard deserved better.

An artist who reinvented forms of photography and a true adventurer, Beard tried with every iota of charm and intellect he possessed to stop the mass die-off of the world's plants and animals. He died before coronavirus became widespread but of all people, he would have understood what it meant, the poisoned gift of wild creatures reduced to small bands of survivors carrying diseases once safely hidden in the forest.

Beard attracted so much attention while he was alive it's difficult to imagine there could be anything left to discover after his death. Yet one mystery remained. After Beard had pretty much given up on saving the world—one never does, not completely—he became obsessed with unusual objects carved from the horns and bones of wild animals. Used by the Maasai in his adopted home of Kenya, these pipes, amulets, and staffs became, in Beard's mind, *memento mori*, aesthetic objects that act as a reminder, or a warning, of death's inevitability. And death was the ultimate subject of Beard's art.

Why had none of the anthropologists who studied the Maasai seen these sculptural objects, so strangely beautiful? One man had unlocked the mystery. Because of a scandal that surrounded these mysterious artifacts, for 25 years he refused to make his research public.

Sometimes being a reporter is a matter of timing. When I called him in 2013, he was ready to talk. His name was Roderic Blackburn.

In the summer of 1990, Rod Blackburn set out for Kenya. It was his first visit to this region in more than 20 years. He had arrived in 1968 as a gangly anthropology student. Now he was a man nearing 50.

Blackburn had grown up in New York's Hudson Valley. The son of wealthy but distant parents with Victorian notions of child-rearing, Blackburn had been happiest hunting with his father in the forest surrounding their enormous house in Selkirk, near Albany. When he showed up in Nairobi, a Ph.D. candidate looking for his dissertation topic, an old Africa hand told him to look into a band of hunter-gatherers believed to be extinct: the Okiek. Someone had reported seeing forest people fitting their description along a dirt track in the Mau forest. The largest mountain forest in East Africa, the Mau contained the headwaters for rivers that provided much of the country's water. In those days, the Mau was still largely undisturbed.

Blackburn headed into the forest. Using the skills he'd developed as a boy in the woods of upstate New York, he found the Okiek. For the next two years, he and his wife DeGuerre lived with them. His dissertation established him as a scholar respected in the U.S. but even more so in Kenya.

Rod Blackburn's research was important for many reasons, not least of which was the disregard in which hunter-gatherers were held in Kenya. Called *dorobo*, a word now considered derogatory although it is still in common use, the country's hunter-gatherers were seen as "a dying-out remnant of thieves, outlaws and other degenerate undesirables," in Rod's words.

Starting in the 1960s, the more powerful ethnic groups in the newly independent country had disenfranchised hunter-gatherers. Like the *dorobos*, Rod's culture was going extinct. Marked by the reserve associated with the culture of old-money WASPs, he'd eschewed a conventional academic career. He shrank from the theatrical aspects of teaching. The brutal nature of academic disputes was anathema. A first-rate field man who could repair his Land Rover and live off the land if necessary, Rod kept meticulous notes and journals. But where he truly excelled was as a listener.

One colleague described Rod Blackburn as unsuited for academia in another way: he was more interested in observation than theory. Anthropology, like many academic disciplines, had become mired in theoretical debates, and Rod was a throwback to earlier anthropologists: Franz Boas, Bronisław Malinowski. Like many 19th-century scientific pioneers, Rod Blackburn possessed a trust fund that allowed him to follow his interests when they led to unexpected byways.

In 1990, Rod's enthusiasm for photography had led him to Hog Ranch, Peter Beard's compound in the Ngong Hills outside Nairobi. Rod had returned to Kenya to research the medicinal plants used by the Okiek, an aspect of their culture he hadn't thought to ask about in the 1960s, before Westerners became aware of ethnobotany.

He expected the visit to be purely social. Instead, Beard and his friend Gillies Turle showed him a vast array of objects—pipes, amulets, staffs—carved from bone and horn. Acting in Rod's words "like eager schoolboys" they told him about Maasai diviners called *laibons*. Turle had been participating in their ceremonies, Beard often traveling with him, making portraits of the *laibons* and their ceremonies.

Beard and Turle described an intricate tradition akin to what Westerners would call shamanism. The practices often involved pipes carved from bones through which the *laibons* blew smoke made from certain herbs to cure madness, bronchitis, or any number of ailments. Amulets protected livestock. Certain bones from an elephant or giraffe could lead to achieving wealth in the form of cattle. Alternately, these same herbs could speed death in a terminally ill person. *Laibons* could foretell the future, smite enemies, or heal wounds suffered by a *moran*, a young Maasai warrior, when he participated in the ritual killing of a lion.

Their stories, if true, were astonishing. None of the literature on the Maasai, one of the most-studied ethnic groups in the world, mentioned this mystical tradition.

There was no question in Rod's mind that the pipes, amulets, grinding bowls for herbs were beautiful. Beard and Turle considered them akin to the work of Picasso, Brancusi, and Noguchi. Given the African influence on 20th-century artists like Picasso and Modigliani, the Maasai objects, while they obviously hadn't influenced the Westerners, were redolent of the archetypes that mythologist Joseph Campbell would later describe, symbols and stories that recur across civilizations.

Would Rod be willing to go out and research the objects? The Maasai *laibons* were concentrated in the Loita Hills, not far from the Okiek. Intrigued, but not necessarily convinced, Rod agreed to make side trips to investigate. He needed a research permit from Richard Leakey, not just to look into the Maasai artifacts, but for his Okiek research. The meeting turned out to be awkward, and a little bit frightening.

Second Sons

It was Beard's friend Gillies Turle who unwittingly set the collision course between Peter Beard and Richard Leakey. Rod and Gillies were merely caught in the crossfire.

In British novels, second sons are feckless boys sent to the colonies to manage the family's plantations or forced to join the military. Turle fit the archetype so perfectly that if this story were fiction, there would have to be some sort of wrinkle, a reversal of expectations, the revelation of an expected

The Gentleman Scientist

aspect to his character. Perhaps there is one.

Turle's father was an admiral in the British Navy, an heroic figure who returned to active duty in his forties when World War II broke out. Wounded in Greece, he was made a Commander of the Order of the British Empire. Turle's elder brother Arish did well in school and followed the family tradition by joining the military, where he would have a storied career. His younger brother was an unremarkable student, rebellious, but in harmless, mischievous ways, engaging in boarding school pranks. After an indecorous stint in the British Army, he set off for adventure. He wrangled livestock as a jackaroo cowboy outside Sydney, mined for opals in Cooper Pedy where he learned about dreamtime from an Aborigine girlfriend, sheared sheep in New Zealand, and wound up among the bohemian set in Greenwich Village.

Returning to London, Gillies discovered the gangster-run casinos of Swinging '60s London. He soon gambled away his trust fund. Arish managed to get his feckless younger brother hired by a private security company to guard Kenya's first Minister of Lands after independence. Bruce MacKenzie was the only white minister tapped by Jomo Kenyatta in his first administration, a canny effort to avoid intertribal strife.

Land means everything in Kenya, and thanks to his proximity to MacKenzie, Gillies became a Zelig character. Black, white, East Asian, everyone showed up

Gillies Turle's father,
British Navy Rear-Admiral
Charles Edward Turle,
C.B.E., D.S.O., R.N.

at the land minister's door. What kicked over a change for Turle, as he tells it, was meeting Kenyatta himself. "The way I describe it is that when I came to Kenya, I wore lace-up boots," Turle said. "I had all the attributes of an English schoolboy: racism, isolationism, superiority, arrogance."

The strapping young ex-Army officer was introduced to Kenyatta at a garden party. Calling a black man "Mr. President" and "Your Excellency" was difficult, he remembers. But he managed. He recalls Kenyatta admonishing him, in avuncular tones: "You look after my minister."

A simple enough exchange, but Kenyatta's sheer presence, his obvious depth and intelligence, the man's undeniable gravitas, all of these made an impression on the newcomer. After Kenya became independent in 1963, Turle decided to stay. He married an English girl whose family had money and they bought a coffee plantation. Seeing an opportunity, he bought up art and household décor left by the departing British and used them to stock Nairobi's first antiques shop. These were artifacts, too, in retrospect—a preview of Turle's fate.

In the late 1970s, Peter Beard wandered in to Turle's shop looking for a Zanzibar chest, one of the antique wood and brass chests used by Omani rulers of Zanzibar to transport their possessions. The men bonded over old books about Africa, a shared passion for the outdoors, and the aesthetic sense that Beard had always possessed and Turle was cultivating in himself. After Turle was divorced from his proper British wife, he moved onto Hog Ranch.

Beard's compound was no more than a hyped-up safari camp: a smattering of canvas tents visited by giraffes and warthogs (hence the name, although it's said that Beard was cracking wise about the famous Nevada brothel, Mustang Ranch). The humans who visited were a who's who of the era: Jacqueline Onassis and Lee Radziwill, David Bowie and his wife, Iman, and a constant stream of fashion models. Beard's trust fund wasn't as large as some imagined so he hustled work for big magazines: *Vogue, Esquire, GQ, Elle*. Like Beard, Turle was handsome, with impeccable manners and a taste for the good life. Unlike Beard, he had a car and a modicum of organizational ability. He fit right in.

By the late 1980s, the left-behind British silver was running low. Turle was segueing over to African art, and one day a Maasai man came to the shop. "I have something that will interest you," Turle recalls the man saying. Refusing to elaborate, he insisted that Turle meet him at a Maasai village located several hours' drive from Nairobi.

Still an adventurer at heart, Turle couldn't resist. At the village, the man led him into a *manyatta,* a hut made of sticks and dirt and cattle dung that is the traditional Maasai dwelling. Digging in ashes that looked as though they were the remains of a campfire, the man pulled out a stained staff called a *rungu.* While staffs like these were commonly wielded by leaders, the only ones Turle had seen were carved from wood. This *rungu* was rhino horn.

Thus began an obsession that would derail the lives of both Turle and Peter Beard. Turle was not an artist himself, but he had an eye for beauty and the compulsive drive of an art collector. He kept buying these objects. Not just *rungus,* but all of them: horn and bone pipes, arm bands, amulets, the carved splints young Maasai warriors used to pry open a lion's jaws in the ceremonial hunts that were their initiation to manhood.

Turle's sources explained that the sons and grandsons of *laibons* were no longer interested in these objects. For traditional people, objects tend to have value through their use, not as contextless objects mounted in a museum. Turle remembers spending about $150 for each piece, sometimes a little more, sometimes less.

As the Maasai became a larger part of Turle's life, Peter Beard found a new subject for his photography. The artifacts were truly *memento mori,* aesthetic symbols of the Kenya that had drawn Beard as a young man. That life, guided by the rhythms of the natural world, was ending.

Not to Give a Damn

"I first got to know Peter the best way—not at a party or a club, but through his work," writer Paul Theroux told *Town and Country* after Beard's death. "People are full of stories about his carousing, but the fact is that his intensity as a writer, a traveler, a photographer, and an artist are what stands out for me."

Theroux is on to something, as he usually is. Like his slightly older contemporary, Lucian Freud, Beard located his interests early in life and possessed the means to follow where they led. In 1955, a 17-year-old Peter Beard traveled to Africa with the grandson of Charles Darwin to shoot a film on rhinos. in 1961, barely out of Yale, he traveled by ship around the Cape of Good Hope, visiting the island of Madagascar, remarkable for its rare plants and animals, before landing in Kenya.

Beard had been pre-med at Yale, studying population dynamics before switching to art history. But his real education began after university. On his way back to Africa, Beard sought out Karen Blixen, who had written *Out of Africa* and several other books based on her life in Kenya, under the pseudonym Isak Dinesen. Dinesen had retreated to Denmark after her farm went bankrupt, her lover Denys Finch-Hatton was killed in a plane crash, and her debt-ridden husband infected her with syphilis. ("I had a farm in Africa, at the foot of the Ngong Hills...." was the deceptively simple opening of *Out of Africa,* recited by Meryl Streep in the opening scene of the 1985 film adaptation.)

Blixen is derided as a colonialist now, but her writing remains impressive. Chiseled and burnished, her descriptions reveal a profound understanding of the place and its people. Through her offices, Beard bought 45 acres in the Ngong Hills, not far from the grave of Finch-Hatton. After her death, Beard hired Blixen's majordomo, Kamante (Kamadi Gaturo). Gaturo's drawings on Beard's photographs helped gain him recognition as an artist in his own right.

Beard had read a book about Francis Bacon as a secondary school student in England, and in London, he sought out the painter. Bacon's art was steeped in dissolution, raw and unsettling but masterful—half-realist, half-surreal renderings of the psyche. Over the course of their friendship, Bacon painted Beard 30 times, and Beard photographed Bacon. Some said the painter was in love with the young photographer.

Who wouldn't be gaga over Beard? Preternaturally handsome, quick and bright, someone who used himself hard but somehow remained delicate, Beard was becoming an artist in his own right yet, as Bonn noted, he shared Bacon's preoccupations.

"Bacon was probably secretly in love with Peter, and maybe not so secretly," said Guillaume Bonn, a photographer who became friends with Beard and made a film about him. "They were very close. He connected with the work that Peter was doing, particularly with the carcasses and the dead elephants that Peter photographed. I think that spoke to Bacon's work—they were both interested in the dialogue between life and death."

It's not difficult to see Bacon's influence on Beard's work, but Beard's influence on Bacon is less easy to spot. Yet Bacon acknowledged it. Bacon wrote: "Over the years, Peter Beard has given me many of his beautiful photographs. For me the most poignant are the ones of decomposing elephants where, over time, as they disintegrate, the bones form magnificent sculpture, sculpture

which is not just abstract form but has all the memory traces of life's futility and despair."

Bacon's generous assessment of Beard's photographs is an apt description of Bacon's own art: realism and surrealism existing simultaneously, flesh decomposing, folding in on itself, evoking the breadth and arc of an individual life. What's remarkable is how Beard internalized and transformed Bacon's influence while managing to develop his own voice. His photographs, and later, his collages—using monochrome images as a canvas for newspaper and magazine clippings, old contact sheets, dried leaves, insects, bones, butterflies, food wrappers, rocks, keys, buttons, feathers, a pocket from a pair of velvet jeans—had surreal elements, yet they were recognizable, much like the characters in Bacon's paintings.

"I like things that don't look like you're in control. It's like life itself. You just learn how to benefit from accidents and chances that you take," Beard told documentarian Derek Peck. It was a variation on something he'd said many times, and the way he lived.

"Here at long last one was in a position not to give a damn for all conventions, here was a new kind of freedom which until then one had only found in dreams!" Karen Blixen had written of her life in Africa. That spontaneity, so different from his prep school background, was precisely what Beard found in Africa, only to lose it after what felt like mere moments.

In 1965, when Beard settled in Kenya, recognition of the extinction crisis was largely confined to scientists. E.O. Wilson would publish his landmark book, *The Theory of Island Biogeography* with ecologist Robert MacArthur in 1967, explaining that animals, particularly large ones like elephants or lions, needed more land than anyone had realized.

The first Endangered Species Act would pass the U.S. Congress virtually unremarked in 1968, the brainchild of two biologists with the ear of liberal Republicans in the Nixon administration. According to contemporary accounts, the politicians who supported it had no idea of the law's far-reaching effects, or the extent of the crisis. When the law was strengthened in 1973, extinction remained a little-known phenomenon.

In Africa, you didn't have to be a scientist to see that the animals were disappearing. Most of America's big animals had been driven to extinction or remnant populations a century before. In Kenya, death was right there in front of your eyes. Peter Beard's eyes. Beard's pre-med studies had not been in vain. He'd reportedly studied population dynamics, and he understood that when a species is winnowed down to a certain number, there's no hope that it will survive.

In 1965, Beard, only 27, published his first book of text and photographs: *The End of the Game: The Last Word from Paradise*. The book was a passionate collage of warnings that the world was facing the Sixth Great Extinction: the loss of at least half the world's mammal species and untold varieties of plants and insects. A genocide, if you will, far in excess of any events given that name, this extinction episode is almost entirely caused by humans.

Art historians see Beard as obsessed with death, and that's not wrong. But that obsession manifested itself in the loss of the natural world. Beard was ahead of his time, a terrible fate for an artist and sensitive people generally. In the last 30 years, successive international science panels were warning that extinction poses a threat equal to climate change; the two operate synergistically, and the forecast is dire. Yet extinction remains largely ignored.

During World War II, Beard's father had served in the military. The family followed him to Maxwell Air Force base outside Montgomery, Alabama. From accounts of that time, the young Peter Beard barely attended school, spending most of his time in the Southern pine woods and bringing home critters he'd found.

Later, Beard would tell talk show host Charlie Rose: "Until we figure out the principles of art and nature, two subjects that we dismiss in kindergarten, we're dead." It was around the time Beard was in kindergarten that he ignored school and hied himself off to the woods.

Into the Wild

When he was out of Yale and free to embark on his real education, Beard didn't confine his apprenticeships to artists. In his twenties and thirties, he worked as an unpaid assistant to Kenya's Great White Hunters, the British outdoorsmen who translated their bush skills to conservation work. The man known for carousing at Studio 54 (and in his seventies, at Nobu and the Sanctuary Hotel) subsisted on Ritz crackers and canned tuna while he studied elephants in Tsavo National Park, tracked elephants and hippos in Uganda, and wrangled crocodiles for the Kenyan government. When he wasn't with his mentors in Kenyan conservation, he would disappear with his African guide, into places where there were, decidedly, no paparazzi.

In his review of *The End of the Game, New York Times* reporter Anthony Lukas noted that Beard had set a new standard for wildlife photography. "These are not 'pretty' Walt Disney shots," Lukas wrote, highlighting Beard's warning about "the remorseless removal of the central symbol of African life, the animal.

"He warns that the continued slaughter could have consequences far beyond the destruction of the great herds of buffalo and wildebeest which once roamed across the East African plains," Lukas wrote. "Eventually, he says, it will bring about 'the final dying, the end of all nature's processes, patterns, cycles and balances.'"

The causes of that slaughter were not easily addressed. In colonial Kenya, when the British realized the game animals were overhunted, their response was to institute a feudal system not unlike Britain's, instituting game laws and excluding Kenya's traditional hunters from the vast swaths of land they controlled.

After Kenya won its independence in 1961, the country faced a different problem. Parks and protected areas were postage stamps compared to the big country that elephants and lions—and Maasai cattle—once roamed. In the 20th century, human encroachment into wilderness—habitant destruction—became the largest driver behind extinction in Kenya, as it was throughout the world.

In 1971, the worst drought in decades was killing elephants in Tsavo National Park. The park's director, a British ex-military officer named David Sheldrick, refused to intervene by culling—shooting a certain number of elephants—the remedy that Beard and his mentors believed was necessary. (That was conservation theory at the time; now more is known, and there are other methods to reduce populations when the food supply runs out.)

Sheldrick refused to allow Beard into the park but the brash American wasn't deterred. Hiring a single-engine Cessna, Beard made aerial photographs that had a timeless quality: grimly poetic portraits of boneyards, misery, and mass death, eerily reminiscent of images by the first photographers to enter Auschwitz. Appearing in the revised 1977 edition of *The End of Game*, they gave Beard a foothold in the art world.

That same year Beard had a solo show at the International Museum of Photography in New York. By then, Beard was a celebrity, touring with the Rolling Stones, hanging out with Andy Warhol. At a party at Warhol's Factory, he sat with *Interview* magazine editor Bob Colacello for hours, talking about Nietzsche and Kierkegaard.

"He was absolutely mesmerizing," Colacello told *Town and Country* magazine, "and when I told Andy about it, he said, 'Oh, you've fallen for him, too.'" He had that effect. As a teenager, I remember reading about Beard in *Vogue*, a dashing, shirtless figure, a character who combined art, adventure, and glamour in the days of Diana Vreeland, before elitism became crass. In those photographs, in my memory, he was always in motion.

"It's Such a Waste, Sleep"

There were, of course, the women. After his divorce from the socially appropriate Minnie Cushing and a subsequent barbiturate overdose landed him in Payne Whitney, the mental institution for genteel maniacs, he married Cheryl Tiegs, the first model to appear twice on the cover of *Sports Illustrated*'s swimsuit edition. The relationship was volatile. Beard disappeared for days at a time, a habit he never lost (his nickname was "Walkabout") but Tiegs later called Beard the love of her life.

"It was the highs and the lows," she recalled in an interview with *People* magazine after his death. "The highs were just the most romantic I've ever [had]. He changed my life in many ways, just by being Peter. But I couldn't put up with the other side."

The list of Beard's lovers is a who's who of beautiful women: Candice Bergen, Carole Bouquet, Lee Radziwill. Yet when asked by an interviewer about the most beautiful women he'd seen, he talked about archetypes from his youth: fleeting glimpses of the Mexican actress Linda Christian and the supermodel of her day, Suzy Parker.

In his fifties, Beard married Nejma Khanum, the daughter of an Afghan judge. A strictly brought-up Muslim, Nejma would stay with Beard despite a well-publicized separation and many infidelities. In a 1996 *Vanity Fair* profile written during his separation from Nejma, Leslie Bennetts describes Beard emerging from his safari tent at Hog Ranch with not one, not two, but four girls. Or was it five?

"Did they all sleep in your bed?" Beard nods, grinning. "Wasn't it crowded?" "We were very cozy." "Aren't you tired?" "It's such a waste, sleep," he says dismissively. "You're just lying there."

It all sounds so offhand. Gillies Turle admiringly described Beard staying up all night making collages and drawing at Hog Ranch. When I asked if Beard might be bipolar, Turle scoffed in his veddy British way. But after his death, Stacy Stowe reported in a *Vanity Fair* article that Beard was diagnosed with bipolar disorder in 2013. Sleeplessness, priapism, intense creativity: textbook.

The dry terms of a DSM diagnosis distract from what often distinguishes bipolar people: the ability to see past the ordinary to the profound. Beard once described his sensibility as "debonair morbidity." That isn't a bad way to characterize some of his work: the photographs of the model Veruschka, arms akimbo, standing over a massive rhino, Iman mirroring the predatory gaze of a leopard. Most of all, the Tsavo photographs. Watching the natural world disappear took a toll. As the years went on, Beard became increasingly angry, frustrated by the failure of conservation in Kenya. Any pretense of debonair morbidity evaporated when he talked about extinction.

The mass death of Tsavo's elephants exemplified everything that was wrong with conservation: the self-serving emphasis on fundraising, the soppy sentimentalism that raised money to "give an elephant a drink" when the loss of habitat was killing thousands of them in a slow agony of starvation. It was easy to blame poachers, but the real problem was people. For Beard, one particular person stuck in his craw: Richard Leakey.

Mr. Leakey

In 1989, Kenya's elephant population had plummeted from more than 160,000 in 1975 to less than 20,000. Under pressure from Western nations and institutions like the World Bank and the International Monetary Fund, Kenya's president Daniel arap Moi had issued a shoot-to-kill order against poachers. To win back the confidence of Western funders, he appointed Richard Leakey to head the Kenya Wildlife Service.

Like Turle and Beard, Richard was the second son of a prominent family. Louis Leakey, his father, had discovered human origins in Africa. Louis ran Kenya's National Museum, while Richard's mother Mary, some said, was the better scientist. Beaten and spat on in his British prep school in Nairobi because he had black friends, Richard didn't have an easy time of it. A classic middle child, he dropped out of high school and completed only one year of university. His real education came from working in the field with his parents, and he made significant finds of early hominid fossils while still in his twenties.

Louis Leakey was a true polymath but the kind of man, according to at least one colleague, who needed to be an authority on everything. Richard carried a lifelong sense of intellectual inferiority. All the Leakey children had become versed in anthropology by doing fieldwork with their parents, but Richard's true talent lay in politics—and publicity.

The Leakeys were, to some degree, outsiders in British Kenya. Never part of the aristocratic White Mischief crowd, Louis was the son of a missionary and grew up among the Kikuyu, the ethnic group of Kenya's first president, Jomo Kenyatta. Louis Leakey, famously, wrote that as a boy, he dreamed in Kikuyu, and during the Mau Mau rebellion, he was tapped to translate at the trial of Kenyatta. After independence, that work would come back to haunt him.

Jomo Kenyatta was gifted academically—he had studied anthropology in London with Bronisław Malinowski—but he was also pragmatic. Unlike some other post-colonial leaders, he did not expel the former colonialists, realizing their expertise was needed to keep the country's economy running. After he became president, Leakey and Kenyatta had a tête-à-tête to iron out any ill feeling, or, one might term it, make a deal. Kenyatta tapped Leakey to run the country's museum.

Like Kenyatta himself, who changed his name and his wife, depending on whether he was studying in Britain or brandishing the mantle of indigenous rights, Leakey was a code-switcher. His son would become a convenient conduit to the white world in the form of foreign aid. Richard Leakey's family history was deeply intertwined with Kenya's, but he talked the talk, and he did it in a tony British accent. Like many countries in the Global South, Kenya was, and remains, addicted to predatory loans pushed by international development banks, so this role was not to be taken lightly.

After his appointment to head Kenya's beleaguered game management agency, Leakey held a public burning of 12 tons of confiscated ivory, a media event to signal the country's commitment to ending poaching. Raising millions from Western donors, Leakey turned the Kenya Wildlife Service into a paramilitary organization tasked with stopping poaching. The remedy harked back to the old colonial days, and betrayed Leakey's ignorance of modern conservation theory. Perhaps it also indicated that Leakey was, not to put too fine a point on it, a bully.

In Pulitzer Prize-winning reporter Raymond Bonner's 1993 book *At the Hand of Man: Peril and Hope for Africa's Wildlife,* he wrote: "Thirty suspected poachers were killed in the next four months—no game rangers died—and the 'enemy's' body count continued to rise, one poacher killed on the average of every four days during Leakey's first year."

In his defense, Leakey told reporters that many of the poachers were Somali bandits armed with automatic weapons. It's quite likely that this is true, so Kenya's rangers would have been vulnerable and outgunned if they had tried to stop poaching without the heavy weaponry and vehicles provided by the West. And it was President Moi who issued the shoot-to-kill order, before Leakey took office.

The reality is that Leakey did manage to stem the poaching epidemic, which didn't resurge until the 2000s. There is one crucial detail: state-sanctioned killing wasn't the only reason he succeeded. According to sources in Kenya, Leakey's reportedly set up a back channel to halt the involvement of Kenya's powerful families in the ivory trade.

The alienation of native Kenyans from conservation had begun during the colonial era. The poaching crackdown only intensified it.

Traditional hunters targeted by Leakey's poaching patrols weren't the only ones unhappy with transforming the KWS into a paramilitary organization. Peter Beard had known Leakey slightly, but now the swaggering politician was becoming an obsession. Beard understood that Kenya's traditional hunters had evolved a system of game management over thousands of years, and the West's meddling had been largely counterproductive. He considered Leakey's ivory burn an empty publicity stunt.

"Leakey's basic problem is that he simply doesn't tell the truth," Beard told his biographer Jon Bowermaster. And that was the least of it. One of Beard's nicknames for Leakey was "Leaking Faucet." After Leakey's lower legs had been amputated after a plane crash, Beard started calling him "Stumpy." Leakey was no kinder. His nickname for Beard was "Weird Beard," according to Nairobi gossip.

Leakey has acknowledged, with regret, that a tendency to overreach was his fatal flaw. After wooing funding from the West, $140 million from the World Bank alone for his anti-poaching efforts, Leakey went after corruption in the Kenya Wildlife Service itself. He didn't go for half-measures, firing 1,640 agency employees. President Daniel arap Moi reacted categorically: Leakey was out.

More accurately, Leakey was back at Kenya's National Museum. The pattern would be repeated. After starting his own political party and winning a seat in Parliament, President Moi persuaded Leakey to become head of Kenya's Civil Service, making him the country's second most powerful politician. Once again, Leakey attacked corruption. Instead of going after a handful of unpopular ministers, he went for broke, presenting Moi with files detailing corruption of 12 of the president's 15 ministers. They stayed. Leakey left.

The failure must have rankled. At least in the museum Leakey had absolute power. To this day, museum staff resent Leakey's high-handedness. Even long after he left the museum, fear of his retaliation shaped decisions made by museum staff.

Gillies Turle didn't seem worried that the artifacts he was collecting were made from rhino horn and other animal parts that were illegal to buy or sell. Just as he had doubled down in the London casinos, he kept expecting, somehow, the arrival of good fortune.

Memory Made Tangible

By the late 1980s, Turle was deep in his collecting mania. Channeling his British schoolboy rectitude, he started applying for permits for his burgeoning collection. As antiques, they should be exempt from the bans on trading wildlife. One certificate he received authenticated 240 objects. He also donated pieces from his collection to national museums in Kenya and Tanzania.

Like Beard, Turle was increasingly aware that Kenya was changing as human population grew. By 2016, researchers found that Kenya's most common wild animals had dropped by two-thirds. The media loved covering elephants, but less iconic but equally valuable species were verging on extinction: wildebeest, giraffe, Grévy's zebra, and the delicate hirola, a type of hartebeest living in proximity to the similarly endangered Boni people, hunter-gatherers on the Kenya-Somalia border.

America was captive to Wall Street's new credo: Greed is Good—or, one might argue, Greed is God. Kenya was no different. Corruption, which had started with Jomo Kenyatta, grew deeply entrenched.

Beard was feeling bitter and pessimistic, according to his biographer Jon Bowermaster, when he landed an assignment that brought him to southern Africa, where conservation efforts were more successful. In Namibia, he met Garth Owen-Smith and Maggie Jacobsohn, a couple who had spent decades working with the Himba people to protect desert elephants and lions.

Owen-Smith hadn't started out as a professional conservationist. Arriving from South Africa in the 1960s, he had simply seen work to be done. Jacobsohn arrived to interview him and stayed; her anthropology background stood her in good stead with the locals. Thanks to their efforts, poaching halted

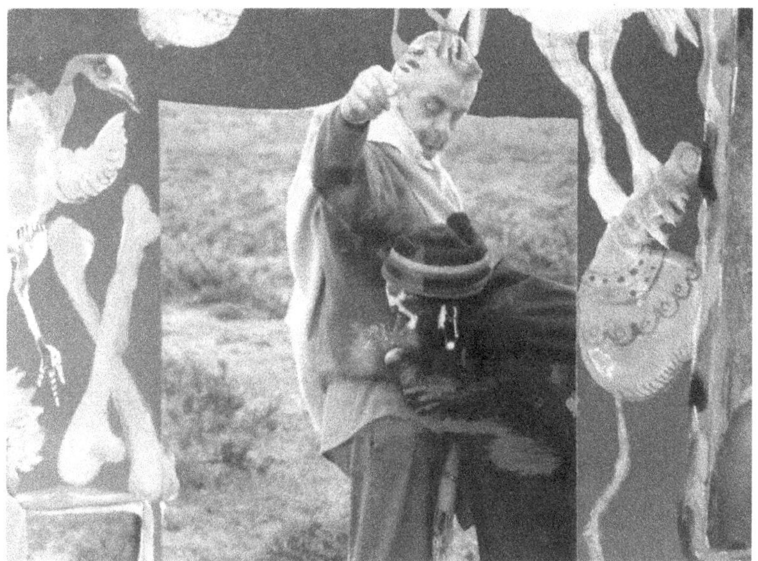

Gillies Turle with the
Maasai *laibon* Ole Kiapi

without bloodshed. Later they would start a safari company run by locals. The profits gave them a stake in conserving wildlife.

Back in Kenya, Beard found refuge with people whose lives were intertwined with the animals whose presence made the landscape alive. Traveling with Turle on his trips to Maasailand, he shot photographs of the carved bones and horns, tools of the *laibons*. They embodied his aesthetic. Andrea Whittle described it in *W* magazine as "memory made tangible."

Turle and Beard found it strange that the Maasai ritual diviners didn't show up in scholarship by Western anthropologists. Turle found one reference in a 1905 book, *The Maasai: Their Language and Folklore*, by British colonial administrator Alfred Claude Hollis. "Old men amongst the Masai make pipes of goats' bones, rhinoceros horns, or pieces of wood," Hollis had written.

Hollis described "medicine-men" who cast stones in buffalo horns, adding this note:

"Lastly, if a rhinoceros is killed, its horn is taken and carved into clubs, which are used for beating the he-goats and bulls with. The counsellors' clubs arc also made of rhinoceros horn."

This explained the rhino horn *rungu*. But unless Turle could prove that every piece in his rapidly growing collection—and Beard's—were genuine antiquities, it was almost certainly illegal to buy or sell them. Perhaps it was even illegal to possess them. Rhinos were endangered, and protected under the CITES treaty, the Convention on International Trade in Endangered Species. Under CITES, it was also illegal to trade in ivory.

The two "eager schoolboys" were skirting Kenyan law, too. In the 1970s, animal rights groups had convinced the Kenyan government to ban hunting and the buying or selling of wildlife parts. The bans did little or nothing to help Kenya's animals; in fact, they may have made the situation worse. Hunting groups point out, not without justice, that since hunting was banned in Kenya in 1977, wildlife populations had dropped 70 percent.

A fluffier version of British colonialism, interference by Western animal rights activists, and international banks turned traditional hunters into criminals, leaving the field clear for poaching operations run by the country's elite in the 1970s and into the 1980s.

Beard was well aware of this colossal blunder. Decried as an elitist because of his insistence that overpopulation was going to destroy the world, Beard had spent much of his young manhood in the bush with African guides. He understood the inequities of Kenya's targeting of traditional hunters, the latest iteration of the cultural genocide started by the British.

"Most of the elephants in Tsavo depended on traditional hunters, people we labeled as poachers, to keep their numbers down so the trees didn't completely go and they had that woodland cover to take them through the drought," Beard told documentary filmmaker Lars Bruun in 1996.

"But of course poachers had to be eliminated in our way of thinking. We eradicated traditional hunters. The population went up and ate the habitat. We saved the game! We were saving the game, buying an elephant a drink, water for wild animals. All of our do-gooder causes destroyed the balance, the equilibrium and the age-old systems of a dynamic mosaic, a rich, diverse habitat.

"And we ended up with a desert and 35 to 45,000 dead elephants in the biggest national park where you're supposed to be saving them. We gave it the human touch," he wound up, more sadness than bitterness in his voice.

Louis Leakey's Son

Convinced the Maasai *laibon* tradition had enormous aesthetic and anthropological value, Beard persuaded a United Nations official to include the artifacts in an exhibit of indigenous art at UN headquarters in New York. Turle landed a book contract with Alfred A. Knopf. The two men were, as they say, stoked.

They had reason to be optimistic. In early 1990, Turle had received a letter from Andrew Cheptum at the National Museum in Nairobi thanking him for donating 144 artifacts to the museum. Cheptum noted that an expert at the Institute for African Studies had determined the objects were used between the 1850s and 1940s, "for practicing medicine and divining purposes."

Turle needed additional certificates to send pieces to United Nations' headquarters in New York. When he arrived at the National Museum, he didn't anticipate problems. But Andrew Cheptum's letter had been sent before Leakey's return to the museum.

"I took in a bunch of artifacts and I sat in front of him," Turle recalls. "He had a huge desk, big enough to play ping-pong on. I was pulling things out of my bag, saying, 'Hey, look at this.'"

As Turle remembers it, Leakey said, 'We know who killed, carved and smoked your last five rhinoceros *rungus*. He had your name and address in his pocket.'"

"My mouth dried up," Turle recalls. He rallied, asking Leakey why he hadn't arrested the man. More to the point, why would a poacher sell rhino horn to Gillies Turle for $150, roughly what he was paying for these objects, when rhino horn was considered an aphrodisiac in China and Vietnam and fetching $60,000 a kilo? "Who on earth is going to kill a rhinoceros, and shave the horn down to a thin, artistic, incredibly elegant medicinal pipe?"

Leakey acknowledged that part of the collection might be old, according to Turle. Turle asked if Leakey had any idea which would qualify as antiquities and which might have been carved by an imitator. There was no answer, according to Turle. The meeting ended without a resolution.

Not long afterwards, the Kenya Wildlife Service raided Hog Ranch. Agents confiscated 15 *rungus* made of rhino horn, but left behind the bone and horn objects, Turle recalls. While Leakey was working at the museum rather than the KWS at that point, it seemed clear that Leakey had instigated the raid.

Nobody was arrested. Not that time. The raid might have been the end of it. But Beard wasn't letting go of his criticisms of Leakey, and Leakey didn't let go of Beard. For his part, Turle couldn't stop collecting. Over the years, he had developed into an aesthete not unlike Bruce Chatwin's obsessive collector, the fictional character in the eponymous novel *Utz*. Turle knew he was being reckless, but he couldn't stop himself.

Leakey was a formidable opponent. His long-running and highly publicized disagreement with Donald Johanson, director of the Institute of Human Origins at Arizona State University, over human origins had been a fixture of paleontology since the Seventies. (*New York Times* science reporter John Noble Wilford called their televised debate a "brawl.")

Johanson had discovered the 3.2-million-year old "Lucy" skeleton in Ethiopia in 1974, while Leakey, in his youth, had found the 1.6-million-year-old "Turkana Boy" skeleton in Kenya. Johanson proposed that Lucy's species, *Australopithecus afarensis*, was the oldest known ancestor of human beings as well as Australopithecus, a branch of "ape-men" that would become extinct. If this were true, Johanson would displace the Leakeys as the discoverer of humanity's origins.

In 1989, Wilford wrote: "From Mr. Johanson's telling of the quarrel, its basis may now be less professional than personal. It reached a nadir in pettiness when he and Richard Leakey had an explosive confrontation in 1981 while taping a television show with Walter Cronkite. Recalling the argument, Mr. Johanson attributes Richard's unyielding stance to the burden he may be bearing as the son of the famous Louis Leakey."

When Leakey finally capitulated, the ultimate showman managed to turn defeat into hagiography. The two men appeared on stage together, Leakey acknowledging that Johanson had been right, in a live-streamed event at the American Museum of Natural History in 2011.

Leakey may have been wrong about Lucy, but there was one area in which his hegemony was unquestioned: publicity. To one anthropologist, Leakey's obdurate refusal to admit error had unacceptable consequences: "Leakey set back paleoanthropology decades," he said about the nearly 40-year feud.

In the less well-publicized case of what Rod Blackburn called "The Bones," Leakey was equally obdurate. He believed—or convinced himself—that the artifacts were fakes and that Turle and Beard were selling them to fund their indulgences: travel, women, and in Peter's case, self-medicating with weed and coke, plus the odd magic mushroom. The two were perennially short of cash but Leakey, too, had found himself in straits at times, and there were rumors that he was not immune to the corruption that was rampant in Kenya. It may seem petty and implausible for a man of Leakey's stature to take a personal grudge to the lengths of what happened next.

The real problem may have been Beard's other art form: the rant. For Beard, Leakey represented the two things he detested most: authority and the phoniness of white savior conservation. Beard admired Graham Hancock's 1994 book debunking international aid organizations, *The Lords of Poverty: The Power, Prestige, and Corruption of the International Aid Business*. Later, he would cite *Dead Aid*, Dambisa Moyo's 2009 book critiquing foreign aid. He laid it out in the Bruun documentary, sounding particularly bitter.

"The environmentalists are like the do-gooders, the Lords of Poverty, the alms race, the clichés...The whole industry of doing good. It's a huge cliché and to be an environmentalist is to be a joke," he said.

Later, Leakey himself would talk of regret at one aspect of Western interference with Kenyan conservation: the bans on hunting and the trade in wildlife objects.

"Hunting has never been stopped in Kenya, and there is more hunting in Kenya today than at any time since independence," Leakey said in a 2006 speech at Nairobi's Strathmore University. "(Thousands) of animals are being killed annually with no control. Snaring, poisoning, and shooting are common things. So when you have a fear of debate about hunting, please don't think there is no hunting. Think of a policy to regulate it, so that we can make it sustainable."

Polite as Beard usually was, he didn't mince words once he got going. According to Gillies Turle, Beard railed endlessly about Leakey, not caring who was listening. Later Beard would say that Leakey was a perfectly decent companion on a safari. He couldn't understand why Leakey had it in for him. Could it have been the fact that Beard was bad-mouthing him to anyone who would listen?

Beard's arguments made sense, in a purist way. By brokering funds from the World Bank and other institutions with their own ideas about poaching and conservation, Leakey had enabled Westerners to determine Kenyan conservation policy.

Countries like South Africa and Namibia were using a more homegrown approach and succeeding in keeping wildlife populations viable by giving Africans an economic stake in conservation. In some cases, this meant not only low-wage, unreliable ecotourism, but controlled hunting and "harvesting" (yes, that word) of wildlife by Africans themselves. Conservation was supporting itself, at least to some extent.

By contrast, Kenya, the Westerner's dream image of Africa, was foundering. It wasn't just mythology that attracted Western dollars. Kenya had a common border with Somalia and other nations whose weak civil societies made it easy for Islamic extremists to gain a foothold. Over time, a system had developed, not just in Kenya, but in Africa generally, that balanced the West's need for military bases with a lukewarm desire to curb corruption. Corrupt politicians skimmed funds from development loans into their Swiss bank accounts, but cracking down was dicey, involving geopolitics as well as delicate questions of national sovereignty. Evidence of effort, or, in plainer terms, window dressing, was usually enough.

Back in the 1990s, Leakey still thought he had a chance to make inroads against corruption. As head of Kenya's Civil Service, he might even be in line to become the country's first white African president. To accomplish anything, though, he had to continue being the crucial pipeline to international funding. Beard's rants about Leakey's incompetence, or worse, his alleged corruption, could ruin everything, especially if Beard was hosting a fellow Yalie who worked for the World Bank or the International Money Fund.

Or it was simply ego. It's certainly possible that Leakey genuinely believed Beard was a con man. Perhaps he was, a little. Weren't they all, except for Blackburn? But that didn't mean Beard was wrong about the artifacts.

Maasailand

In this tale, is Beard the villain or is Leakey? When Beard urged Rod Blackburn to apply for a permit to research the *laibon* artifacts, he gave Leakey credit for knowing his way around the East African bush. According to Blackburn's journal entry, he also called Leakey a "thief" who had diverted funding from the Danish government earmarked for the Karen Blixen Museum, part of Kenya's system of 22 museum facilities and monuments. Beard had been on the board of the Blixen museum, so he was in a position to know, and Blackburn had found the accusation worth noting. There is no documentation for this charge, but it demonstrates the inflammatory nature of Beard's rants. Blackburn wrote this detailed account of his meeting with Leakey.

06.22.90: 1 June 22

Nairobi Appointment to see Richard Leakey. Go to R. Leakey's office at entrance to Nairobi National Park. Purpose is to acquaint him with my current research on hunter-gatherer tribes in East Africa and that I [am] now about to do a survey of those in central Kenya…

He indicates that he knows of my research on the Okiek. He sits on the edge of his chair wanting to finish up our conversation before it has hardly begun by responding in short answers. He gives no response to some leading political questions. So I explained the survey I was doing of the Okiek and gave him a copy of it. Showed him my travel route.

He acted like he didn't have specific information on areas or Dorobo. But he gave me names of three people in his department to see…

I mention that I had been shown some unusual Maasai things belonging to a Mr. Gillies Turle. He responded "I am very suspicious of that man, I don't know what he is up to. he had an appointment with me and canceled saying he was sick. But maybe he was just avoiding seeing me about these things. I am very dubious about their authenticity. I think they are new and faked with smoke to look old. I know the rhino rungu is new. I have traced a rhino kill to it. That is a very serious matter. I have never heard of these things, some of the early settlers collected from the Maasai and they would have some of these if they were real. How do you know this Turle?

I was given his address in Nairobi as a contact to meet Peter Beard.

Oh, I didn't know they knew each other.

I guess they must if the address is the same.

Do you know Peter Beard?

No, only met him for the first time when I just arrived in Nairobi.

Well I am very suspicious of him. He is a great faker [i.e. don't believe what he shows or tells you]. He is an artist, you know.

According to the notes he scribbled as soon as he returned to his car, Blackburn mentioned that Turle had donated part of his collection to the National Museum. Leakey responded that he thinks this was a clever ploy. Leakey ordered him to wait while he went into another room. Returning with a cardboard box, Leakey turned it upside down, dumping a pile of carved pieces on his desk.

Leakey told him to take the objects into the field and figure out where the "fakes" had come from. Worried about having contraband items in his possession, Blackburn refused, telling Leakey he'd rely on photographs.

Blackburn had spent his career avoiding conflict. He didn't want to take on Leakey. But he, too, was curious. Carrying Beard's photographs and some of his own, he headed out to talk to the Maasai.

At the end of June, Rod interviewed Taiyanna Ole Ol-onana. Taiyanna was the last living son of the Maasai's most famous diviner and leader, Ol-onana. Ol-onana, whose name means "the gentle one" in Maa, had been the principal *laibon* and paramount chief of the Loita Maasai until his death in 1911. Rod estimated that Taiyanna, one of his younger sons, was about 85 when they spoke in 1990.

The two men sat under a wizened little acacia tree for four hours "in the course of the conversation...during which a cow gave birth to calf which was nursing by the time we left."

"The *dorobo* [hunter-gatherers] cut these things and bring them to us," Rod wrote that Tayianna told him. Taiyanna explained that a certain bone pipe in one photograph had been brought to his father by the *dorobo*.

Not only had Taiyanna identified a specific piece from the collection, he had provided the missing link. The Maasai were not hunters; their taking of wildlife was confined to initiation rituals. And they were not "makers." How had *laibons* obtained the raw materials for these pipes and fetishes? Who carved them?

According to Taiyanna, it was the hunter-gatherers who lived nearby. Like a good reporter, Rod wanted a second source: confirmation from the *dorobo* themselves. Realizing that his little side trip was turning into a full-fledged research project, he drove his Land Rover to the places that Taiyanna had mentioned.

His Okiek sources denied making the objects. Rod wasn't sure if they were telling him the truth. Secrecy is part of the mystic tradition in virtually all traditional cultures. But the strictures that bound them to silence went deeper. British colonialists had severely punished Africans thought to be practicing witchcraft. And the hunting ban had intensified the fear.

But small-town gossip was a remarkably efficient way to circumvent all that. When Rod stopped at his usual gas station for fuel and supplies, the young man behind the counter asked about his work. He had heard that Rod was looking for someone who knew about certain kinds of objects.

The young man's name was John Lonkushu. He was Saleita, hunter-gatherers who, along with the Okiek, inhabited the area Taiyanna had identified as the source of the objects.

Rod Blackburn described their meeting this way:

I told him of my trip there and how no one knew about these objects, to which he calmly said "Oh, I know about those things."

I stared at this bright-eyed young man who could hardly have been more than 25 thinking, how could he at this tender age know what his elders do not? I showed him the photographs and he, to my great surprise, began to tell me what the objects were, generally confirming what Taiyanna had said about them.

How is it you know so much about these, I asked? He went on to explain that his grandfather had been a kind of *laibon* for the Saleta, and had been very knowledgeable about medicines and curing, and had made and used these bone objects himself and traded them and medicines to the Maasai *laibons* in the Loita Hills. Even, he said, his father knew a lot about these things.

Is he alive, I ask? Yes, he said, and he will be in Narok in a couple days and you can talk with him.

I shook my head in amazement at this accidental meeting. Finally, I exclaimed, the one person among the Dorobo who knows about these things, his father, and he is about to be dropped into my lap by pure chance.

John, for that was his name, smiled and glanced at me askance, softly saying "Maybe not by chance."

Rod Blackburn's lucky encounter with John Lonkushu could have been a simple story. But what happened next was anything but simple. The Bones became a screen onto which Westerners projected love, ambition, jealousy, and, deepest of all, grief.

Carved from rhino horn, ivory tusks, and the bones of giraffes, antelope, and wildebeest, the Bones seemed to possess power, even if it was only in the minds of the people who fought over them, Rod half-jokingly remarked.

And just as it did in Maasailand, that power, whether real or imaginary, might cure and protect, but it could also destroy. They harmed Beard and Rod Blackburn, but those men went on with their lives. They almost destroyed Gillies Turle.

High Crimes or Misdemeanors?
In 1992, Alfred A. Knopf published *The Art of the Maasai*, the book about the

artifacts and Turle's experiences with the Maasai, with Beard's photographs and Turle's text. What comes through is an evocation of a way of life that was disappearing, a life offering transcendence and a sense of proportion and the peace that comes from connection, in contrast to the modern dilemma of constant anxiety. It is not just the animals who suffer when the landscape dies. Or rather it is, because we, too, are animals.

There was a flurry of attention, much of it negative. A virtual bar fight broke out in the pages of *African Arts*, a quasi-academic journal published by the University of California Los Angeles. According to one anthropologist, the general reaction was that Beard and Turle were in it for the money.

Turle freely admits that he had hoped to sell much of the collection to museums; he still would like to produce replicas of the artifacts like the turquoise hippopotamus and jewelry sold at the Metropolitan Museum of Art. He estimates that he spent about $200,000 on the collection, and with court fees, even though Beard pitched in, his compulsion practically bankrupted him.

If Turle's doggedness in the face of legal jeopardy is any indication, the objects meant far more than a business proposition. For the second son, they were a chance to do something valuable with his life. The collection was a validation both for his reckless streak and his aesthetic. And like any aesthete, petty concerns paled in relation to the Absolute.

"I was there with the money, the connections, and the nerve to pick these pieces up, knowing it was gray territory," Turle said. "You couldn't put this collection together again. I was going around with the Maasai in those days. I was going to the ceremonies. My friend was the circumciser. I knew it was the end of things."

American journalist Bill Kurtis went on the road with Turle, visiting *laibons* in Kenya and Tanzania for a PBS documentary called *Secrets of an Ancient Culture*. Kurtis, a respected TV anchorman in Chicago and winner of the William Allen White Award, hired safari guide Peter Jones to make arrangements for the film crew.

Like Richard Leakey, Jones was the son of a scientist who possessed little formal schooling. Coincidentally, he had a connection to the Leakey family. As a young man, he had worked on the field crew of Mary Leakey, Richard's mother.

Jones was dubious about the provenance of the objects. After the video shoot, he and his wife, an American heiress named Margot Kiser (then

Kiser-Jones), asked Turle to introduce them to the *laibons* in the Loita Hills. According to Turle, the couple insisted on bringing their own interpreter, who created tensions. The visit did not go well.

Kiser aspired to be a journalist. Scenting a story, she contacted Leakey about the objects, hoping for a "scoop" on Peter Beard. She had visited Beard at Hog Ranch, according to her Instagram. Yet, apparently convinced of his guilt, she papered the Internet with comments like these on the *Vogue* magazine website:

"Peter Beard does NOT spend his time between Kenya and NY. The Kenyan gov relegated him PNG [persona non grata] for eight years after it was discovered that he was had been laundering and smuggling ivory and rhino horn out of Africa. He now lives mainly in France."

She contacted Rod Blackburn by email, but after a few exchanges he ended the correspondence. His last email was uncharacteristically severe.

"Margot, it is increasingly evident to me from this and prior communications that your inquiry about these objects is not a productive approach to understanding them. You, as have some others, focus on personalities and relationships when you should focus on Maasai and Dorobo ethnography."

Not long after Kiser contacted him, Leakey ordered a second raid of Hog Ranch. This raid involved not only Kenyan police, but also agents from the U.S. Fish and Wildlife Service.

Turle was at an ashram in India, using his still-extant military training to help with logistics at a camp treating the poor for eye diseases. The same ashram, he notes wryly, that Elizabeth Gilbert wrote about in *Eat, Pray, Love*.

"Beard and Tunney [Peter Tunney, Beard's gallerist] were at Hog Ranch and this raid came on. I was in my ashram sort of holier-than-thou," Turle recalled. "I got a telegram saying there was trouble. Beard left as quick as he could after that."

In Turle's account, Beard kept his smaller collection of objects in a suitcase. As the agents arrived, he quickly dispatched it to his friend, the artist Tonio Trzebinski, like Beard a notorious bad boy whose talents matched his appetites. Then he headed out of the country.

By the time the agents reached his tent, there was nothing to confiscate, no evidence to charge anyone. Not that night. But there was a slip of paper. When they rifled Turle's files, the agents found a receipt for a storage locker. Inside the locker were 17 tin chests containing nearly 3,000 objects.

When he returned from India, Turle was thrown into jail.

While the melodrama played out in Kenya, U.S. Fish and Wildlife Service agents were questioning officials at the American Museum of Natural History. At Hog Ranch, the raid had yielded a letter from one of the museum's curators expressing interest in the objects. And in Chicago, agents showed up at the office of documentary filmmaker Bill Kurtis.

Kurtis said that the agents confiscated a single *rungu* that he had brought home as a souvenir. In the documentary, he had carefully hedged on the question of authenticity, because of the lack of experts who could validate Turle's collection. Personally, after talking to the *laibons*, he had no doubt that many of the objects were antiquities that had been ritually used by the Maasai.

When I interviewed him, Kurtis said that he found the episode faintly ridiculous. Although he'd felt obligated not to take a stand in his documentary, the veteran journalist had no doubt that the artifacts were genuine.

Turle felt the same way about the absurdity of it all, only he had more at stake.

"The '99 raid was that they wanted to catch Peter. Peter was the big fish," Turle said. "These agents, together with Kenyans looking for the team of poachers that I had trained and armed. It was a massive delusion."

After more than a year, the court dropped Turle's case without reaching a verdict. Turle didn't know why. Much later, it appeared that Maasai Kenya Wildlife Service agents had interviewed several of his sources and reported that the whole thing was a farce.

Many questions remained. Could Peter Beard, the artist manqué of wild Africa, have secretly been involved in the smuggling of rhino horn and ivory? Beard had been known to pull a prank or two. He had launched the career of the model Iman by satirizing Western views of Africa: Beard touted Iman, who would later marry David Bowie, as a simple Somali herd girl when he knew perfectly well that she was a well-groomed, well-educated diplomat's daughter.

That prank was harmless. But Beard was fond of the *épater le bourgeois*. He'd boasted about smuggling some of the artifacts into the U.S. Beard and Turle were both chronically short of money, so it's hardly outside the realm of possibility that a few pieces might have been sold to discerning friends.

People are complicated. Like sports figures whose bad habits still manage to shock us, the character of people who think far enough outside the box to discover something new (or old) may require scrutiny of their discoveries, but does not preclude authenticity. Heinrich Schliemann, the dodgy German businessman who discovered Troy, was genuinely obsessed with Homer and completely unscientific in his methods, yet managed to find the long-sought city of Troy and the mask of Agamemnon. Beard and Turle are veritable saints compared to Schliemann.

But a vast smuggling ring? Leakey was accusing Beard and Turle of far more serious crimes, including working with poachers. Wildlife is the fourth-largest smuggling trade behind drugs, humans, and arms, and the illegal trade is estimated at $20 billion annually, according to a report by the United Nations Environment Program and INTERPOL.

For anyone who knew them, the idea that Beard and Turle were running a poaching operation was laughable. Not only were both men passionate about wildlife, they were terrible businessmen. Certainly, Peter Beard was the antithesis of an international crime kingpin, an artist who often left home with no cash and traded photographs for dinners. Turle had done slightly better, but given the compulsive nature of his collecting, it's hard not to believe him when he says that the ledger was firmly in the negative.

Does any of it matter now? The enduring tragedy is the disappearance of the artifacts and, in a larger sense, the way of life they represent. For years, it seemed that this shard of African history, culture, and art had been forgotten. The nearly 3,000 objects collected by Turle, ostensibly locked away at the Kenya Wildlife Service, might be gone. Nobody dared ask Leakey about them.

The Chronicler of Bones

In 2011, I was living on Lamu Island, where Gillies Turle ran a hotel and Richard Leakey has a vacation home, when I received an odd text message from a woman I'd met briefly on the island. She was asking me for information about Turle. I had found her rude and peremptory. This is hardly how you cultivate a source, I remember thinking. Besides, I didn't know what she was talking about. I didn't respond.

Not long afterward, I interviewed Richard Leakey for a profile that later appeared in *Sierra* magazine. We'd enjoyed a delightful lunch on his rooftop terrace. Our interview had been relaxed, and far-ranging. As I was headed down the stairs to the first floor, I casually asked about the obscure gossip she had mentioned. Some dark secret about Gillies Turle?

Leakey's eyes hardened. He told me that he had nothing against Gillies. A decent fellow, he called him. It was Beard he was after. Leakey told me that he regretted that he had been out of town when his agents arrested Gillies. I

Peter Beard and his daughter Zara
at Hog Ranch. Photo by Rod Blackburn

paraphrase, because I'd put away my notebook by then, but what I remember is Leakey saying: I could have broken him. He would have "persuaded" Turle to give up Beard. Based on what was generally known about Kenyan police, it was a natural assumption that this meant having him beaten.

The change in Leakey's demeanor was striking. I didn't know Gillies Turle well, other than taking his yoga classes, but when I returned to Shela village, on the other side of the rather small island, I contacted him. Turle had always struck me as reserved, but when I asked him about this episode in his life, the story poured out.

I had no intention of writing anything. The woman who had contacted me turned out to be Margot Kiser, the heiress who had traveled with Turle and Bill Kurtis for the TV documentary. She seemed to consider it her territory and I was concentrating on fiction.

But when I had returned to the U.S., missing Kenya, I did an Internet search for Peter Beard. In a *Vanity Fair* profile by Leslie Bennetts, a glancing reference to the controversial objects contained a reasonable-sounding quote from Rod Blackburn. I searched the name. Blackburn lived a few miles from my house.

I called him, and to my surprise, he was willing to talk to me. "I'm not going to try to influence what you write," he told me. "Look at the evidence and make up your own mind."

It was clear that Blackburn's systematic research among the Maasai and Saleita had yielded a storehouse of information about the practices of *laibons*, men he describes as "ritual experts, diviners, prophets, shamans and, sometimes, sorcerers."

His notes provided a fascinating window into a way of life that, according to the estimates of museum officials like Andrew Cheptum that were borne out by Rod's notes, existed until around the 1940s.

Miniature ivory and bone spears were used to put enemies to sleep before warriors raided their cattle enclosures. *Laibons* used certain objects to bless the Maasai warriors called *morans*. They used others to "empty the mind" of anxieties. Still others were the means to cause someone's death.

The sheer number of objects the informants recognized was striking. One or more of them recognized 58 out of the 60 objects shown in the photographs. More than a dozen Maasai *laibons* identified the types of objects in his photographs. Several recognized not just types, but, like Taiyanna, identified specific objects that had belonged to people they knew.

Blackburn left Kenya for the final time in 1993. In the seven years following his departure, Lonkushu continued showing photographs of the artifacts to Saleita elders, always asking the same series of questions, and carefully recording the answers in slanting schoolboy cursive.

In his unpublished manuscript, Blackburn noted that his research was augmented by nearly 3,000 pages of testimony collected by John Lonkushu. He sent some of the material to Gillies Turle and myself with this comment: "What is really new are the richly detailed interviews with the Saleita who were once a virtual factory for these objects, mostly to the Loita Maasai but also to other Maasai, even into Tanzania."

I asked Blackburn why generations of anthropologists drawn to Maasai, Kenya's most iconic and most-studied tribe, hadn't found evidence of these practices. "They didn't ask," Blackburn said simply.

He had experienced a similar cultural disconnect. In the mid-Sixties, when he lived with the Okiek, he hadn't thought of asking about medicinal plants. In the 1990s, when he and his wife returned to research Okiek ethnobotany, it turned out that their use of medicinal plants for traditional medicine was extensive.

Rod wrote about his humbling revelation when interviewing the *laibon* Taiyanna.

> As Taiyana [*sic*] droned on, occasionally sipping beer, my mind was abuzz with what else I had missed years ago. I had all but ignored the subjects of forest medicines yet apparently the Dorobo were experts

in this area, supplying the Maasai. I had little information on witch-craft, how it is practiced and cured, yet on this matter the Dorobo and the Maasai loibons [*sic*] apparently have a close relationship.

I had always been proud of the rich quality of my field notes but now began to realize that the subtlest incident could have opened a whole area of inquiry if I had been just tuned into its significance. A word here or there that I did not understand and so ignored may have been the key to what I now see I missed.

Blackburn was too hard on himself. His sources had good reasons for not volunteering information: the harsh penalties for practicing "witchcraft" and the bans on hunting, trading, or possessing animal parts.

By the 2000s, several anthropologists had begun to interview *laibons*, including Elliot Fratkin, a professor of African Studies at Smith College. But Rod had not kept up in the field, and his health was starting to fail. He didn't know of their work. When he wrote to the British anthropologist he regarded as the expert, the man had recently died.

But in Kenya, a new generation of African anthropologists were rushing to preserve their heritage. I contacted a friend at Kenya's National Museum, and she gave me the name of Mercy Gakii Kinyua, an anthropologist who specialized in the Maasai. (Mercy herself is Meru, not Maasai.)

Rod sent her his manuscript and she promised to look for John Lonkushu. It took her 18 months to locate him. It was another year before I managed to get back to Kenya.

From Maasailand to East Egg

Before I returned to Kenya, I tried to contact Peter Beard. I had made overtures before. Phone messages weren't returned. Peter's wife Nejma answered my emails, telling me that Peter had health problems and it would be better if I sent questions in an email. I balked at the idea, a terrible way to interview someone. I was afraid that as soon as I brought up the artifacts, Nejma would shut me down and I wouldn't get another chance. She had taken over the management of Beard's career, creating a market for his photographs that earned $2 million in 2020, the year of his death. She had a reputation for zealously controlling access to her husband.

We all knew there was a deadline. I'd heard that Beard was bringing up the subjects with reporters and friends, but nobody had followed up except in a cursory fashion. None had access to Blackburn's research. Until recently, none, to my knowledge, contacted Turle. If they had, they might have access to the information that I received from him over a period of years.

Around this time, Gillies Turle found among his files a 52-page account by an anthropology student named Sheena Gidoomal. In 1991, Gidoomal traveled to neighboring Tanzania to ask about the artifacts collected by Turle. Her results were almost identical, statistically, to Blackburn's. Anecdotally, they contained their own eureka moment.

Two *laibons* named Laitayioni and Birrika possessed ivory pipes similar to those in Turle's collection. Birrika told Sheena Gidoomal that the objects were used between the 1850s and the 1940s—the same time period specified by the National Museum's Andrew Cheptum. The time period tracked with what Taiyanna had told Rod Blackburn.

The key moment for Gidoomal was when Birrika pointed to the photograph of an ivory pipe in Turle's collection, saying that he had seen the pipe—not a pipe like it, but the identical one—used to cure madness. When I had this in hand, I was even more determined to talk to Peter Beard.

Beard rarely went to Kenya anymore. He had retreated to New York: an apartment at the Osborne on West 57th Street that he'd owned for years, and his place on Montauk, the "End of the World," a wild seascape where he had once hung out with Andy Warhol and the Rolling Stones. When I heard there was an opening for a show of his photography at an East Hampton gallery, I did something I had never done in 30 years as a reporter. I ambushed him. Or I tried.

This ambush stuff wasn't my style. I remember being unbearably nervous as I waited outside for the gallery to open. Finally, the doors swung. The gallery-goers looked affluent, but East Hampton still had the ambience of the old Hamptons, mercifully free of hedge fund vulgarians. Beard hadn't arrived.

Then the crowd parted. There he was, a blurred version of the lithe young man of my teenage *Vogue* reading, still handsome but visibly battered. He wore sheepskin slippers and shuffled. As Nejma had written in her email, there had been health problems. A stroke, maybe more than one. I introduced myself, mentioning Rod Blackburn. Beard asked after him with evident affection. His manners were effortless, his accent almost imperceptibly upper-class WASP.

I told him that I'd tried to contact him before but Nejma didn't want him interviewed. "I don't care," he said bitterly, almost shockingly visceral after the almost tender politesse. He'd let that anger slip in interviews, I remembered, calling her "a terrorist." Yet they had remained married. He couldn't have been easy; I remembered the regular coverage on Page Six when Beard was well into his seventies, affairs with models that never ceased, the story of Nejma signing him in for psychiatric evaluation after he trundled home in the wee hours with Russian hookers in tow.

I handed him a signed copy of my first book, a history of the environmental movement, with a letter from Rod tucked inside. An enormous bodyguard instantly snatched it out of his hands. Other people came up to talk to him. The bodyguard imposed his bulk between us.

It all went so fast. I talked to Nejma, awkward and tongue-tied, surrounded by that glossy crowd, telling her I wanted to interview Peter. I mentioned Rod Blackburn's name, which elicited grudging respect, but she was immovable.

Later I thought of the silky long dresses that Nejma and Zara wore that day, and remembered the scene from *The Great Gatsby*: "Daisy and Jordan lay upon an enormous couch, like silver idols weighing down their own white dresses against the singing breeze of the fans."

Were these people merely rich? I wondered. Was that all there was to it? No. In an interview, Beard had called a book tour "my prostitution trip."

"I cannot stand these parties, because I'm really a pathetic person. I have a hard time talking with one person, and two people make it impossible. But," he added, "I have the ability to adapt to things very easily when I come back to this rat race. I can force myself, in a phony way, to enjoy this life."

The Objects Collect Us

As I prepared to leave for Kenya in 2018, I tried to persuade Rod to come with me. He refused, saying that he preferred to remember it as it had been. He spoke of weeks spent camping with DeGuerre and the Dorobo in the forest. I had seen a photo of DeGuerre holding a rifle from those days with the prey she had bagged. The land is empty now, he told me.

He gave me several tasks. One was to get John Lonkushu's contact information so the two men could speak again, after an absence of more than a decade.

The Loita Hills, a three-hour drive from Nairobi and not far from the famed Maasai Mara, is a region famous for the *laibons* who live there. Mercy

Lenana, the most famous Maasai *laibon,*
born in the 1870s

and I went to visit Kirriapa ole Simel, someone Mercy had known for years, a kindly-looking old man with spindly legs encased in Wellingtons. His brother is the chief *laibon* of the Loita Maasai.

On the night we arrived, he launched a spiel about the cosmology and history of the Loita Maasai. It sounded practiced, as if he had given it before to visiting scholars. Mercy's laptop was running out of battery life. Rod Blackburn's photos of the artifacts were on the laptop and we had no paper copies. I started to panic.

Interrupting the old man, I asked if he would look at the photographs. Our interpreter, Henry Saitabau, a young Maasai anthropologist who grew up in the Loita Hills, flashed me a look that told me I was being rude. The *laibon,* unruffled, acquiesced. We showed him the photographs, one after another.

Yes. No, not that one. Yes. Yes. So these are used by *laibons*?

He looked at us quizzically.

Yes, he said in Maa, the Maasai language. Would you like to see mine?

His tone was so matter-of-fact he might have been asking if we wanted to see his mother's collection of Hummel figurines. Rod Blackburn had written about the same experience when he visited Taiyanna, mentioning his shock when the old man had simply asked if he wanted to see his tools of the trade.

Early the next morning, the *laibon* disappeared from the house. He came back carrying a leather bag. Carefully laying out a piece of red fabric on the grass, he unpacked the tools, and placed them on the fabric. Two were pipes made from delicately curved antlers, spiral edges circling like corkscrews. Others were smooth and resembled gourds. They looked like some of the pictures we'd shown him.

He packed herbs into a pipe and smoked. Then he shook a gourd that had been worked into a canteen with a top. He threw stones out. He answered our questions about our futures. Our interpreter and I asked about our marriages. Mercy begged off, saying she'd rather not know.

He asked if we were going to visit the chief *laibon*, his brother. We said yes. He predicted that his brother would be drunk. We did. He was. No points for that one.

After 18 months of searching, Mercy had located Rod Blackburn's research assistant, John Lonkushu. We all met for lunch at a restaurant in Narok. It was market day and red *shuka*-clad Maasai *morans* thronged the stalls. John showed us the pages from Rod's ethnobotany research, smoothing them out on the table's oilcloth. He had kept them all these years.

I returned from Kenya jubilant, but when I told Rod that we had found John, Rod looked baffled. He no longer remembered John. His son Logan told me later that Rod had been diagnosed with brain cancer. He had left it untreated.

As I write this, Rod Blackburn is still alive. He has lucid flashes, but fewer now. John has tried to contact him several times by email. When he was well into his seventies, Rod built his own websites, researched university databases, producing full-color catalogues, maps, and illustrated book manuscripts. He is no longer is able to use a computer to answer John's messages.

Camp Hero

All three of these men, Beard, Turle, and Blackburn, were nagged by the unfinished business of The Bones. As I researched the story over the span of a decade, I watched them age before my eyes.

Leakey was slightly younger than the others, but battered by health problems that would have felled a less determined character: not only the damage to his legs from the plane crash, but two kidney transplants, a liver transplant, skin cancer.

When I contacted Leakey for this article, telling him that I knew a Kenyan anthropologist interested in the collection, he wrote that he was "disinclined" to get involved. He did say this:

It's important for the young anthropologist to be aware that the objects were fabricated in a homestead on the Ngong Hills and a good deal of video was shot showing all plus some rather incriminatory audio.

The objects are fake and I saw some of the video. I retired years ago from KWS. Sorry but on this I cannot help. R

If Blackburn and Gidoomal's research is right, then Richard Leakey is wrong. Or at least partly wrong. Some of the objects that Turle collected might have been "fakes" made by people who got wind of his compulsion. Turle himself acknowledges this. But according to many testimonies from the *laibons* themselves, at least part of the collection is genuine. In that case, Leakey did not just wrong Blackburn, Beard, and Turle. By making the collection inaccessible to scholars, he did a disservice to the Maasai and the world's storehouse of cultural knowledge.

Whatever his flaws, it almost makes me sad to say it. Because Leakey, too, grieved. In the 1996 book he wrote with Roger Lewin, *The Sixth Extinction*, he wrote that he was an ardent naturalist as a child, "more interested in living things than old bones," which were, of course, his parents' stock in trade. The way of life, surrounded by animals, is the death all of these men could not accept. Can any of us?

That does not excuse the missed opportunity to follow up on Rod Blackburn's research with the *laibons* and Saleita elders, or the disappearance of nearly 3,000 objects. Is Turle's collection still in the possession of the Kenya Wildlife Service or have the pieces been sold off on the black market?

Corruption in Kenya is threaded throughout society, from petty bribes to low-level government officials to multi-billion-dollar scams, and there has been little or no progress since Leakey's numerous attempts to root it out. It's likely that at least some of Turle's collection is gone. Still, hundreds of *laibon* tools remain, scattered throughout the country. But they are hidden, largely because of Leakey's ire.

Beard is gone. At the time of this writing, Rod Blackburn is in hospice, cared for by his son Logan. Gillies Turle is in his eighties. Once he dies, will anyone re-assemble his voluminous notes, photographs, documents, and diaries? What about Rod Blackburn's research?

Blackburn's Legacy

For nearly a decade before he became ill, I often found Rod Blackburn working late into the night in his Kinderhook, New York, office. He assembled a book of maps of Kenya's indigenous lands and a memoir of living with the Okiek.

After I contacted him in 2013, Blackburn revisited his research on the Maasai objects. He was surprised at the amount of material in his files, especially John Lonkushu's notebooks. Eventually he assembled a detailed spreadsheet and a book manuscript. I have begun circulating these to reputable academics, something Blackburn started but was unable to finish before his illness.

Richard Waller, Professor of African History Emeritus at Bucknell University and author of a seminal work on the Maasai, wrote this:

> I was peripherally involved in the controversy years ago and remember some of it. The general view, I recall, was that the objects were probably fakes, artificially aged. For some reason, they were not properly examined for signs of ageing or use. Part of the difficulty was that Turle and Beard were thought in some quarters to be rather dubious characters, and it wasn't difficult to see that they had a financial interest. They were certainly very reticent about the exact circumstances of acquisition. My own view was, and is, that the verdict should be Not Proven, certainly in the absence of proper forensic examination.
>
> The argument that artefacts like these had never previously been reported is not a very strong one. There are a number of good reasons for their apparent absence. (a) *Laibons* are usually quite secretive about the tools of their trade, for good professional reasons. It would be difficult to get access to things like these without permission and it would be very dangerous indeed to try without, let alone to steal something from a *laibon*. (b) During the colonial era, *laibons* were regarded with some suspicion by the authorities. With some notable exceptions, they tended to keep a low profile.
>
> Many of the objects are far less exotic or esoteric than is made out. *Laibons* do certainly grind ingredients for medicines and the various mortars shown here would be suitable for the purpose—and not

much use to ordinary Maasai. The same might be said of the pipes. Staffs of office are held by spokesmen rather than *laibons* (despite Olonana's "poker") and are quite public.

Usually now, they are of wood but I have certainly heard of rhino horn clubs in the past. Horn containers are used by elders of all sorts, for things including snuff and *magadi*. None of this, of course, proves that the objects are "genuine/authentic," but it does suggest plausible reasons for them. As far as motive/intent and methods of acquisition are concerned I can have no opinion.

I asked Waller if it was time for the Kenya Wildlife Service to release Turle's collection, if it is still in the agency's possession. While it seemed likely that Turle had, in effect, created a market for fake artifacts, based on the research, it was equally likely that some of the collection was genuine.

Waller's answer was unequivocally yes. He wrote that "it would certainly seem sensible to have all the extant pieces examined for (artificial) aging and actual use (traces of medicine etc). It would also be helpful to establish when, where and by whom the photos Rod Blackburn used were taken; and, if possible, link them to actual pieces."

He noted that while rhino horn or ivory objects would be subject to strict controls, "it is difficult to see how a carved wooden spoon or a giraffe vertebra could now be regarded as inherently contraband, especially if pieces are to be 'returned' to the Maasai."

The story might have been simpler if Peter Beard had never wandered into the Loita Hills with his friend Gillies. The battle over The Bones felt so personal, it reminded me less of a scientific argument and more of a dispute over family heirlooms, as if the men were brothers externalizing the loss of a parent onto family keepsakes.

As the dispute fades, the objects take on yet another meaning. *Laibon* artifacts are being sought by the descendants of the people who originally used them: the Maasai. A few months ago, Monicah Nkina Sairo, a 32-year-old anthropology student who is Maasai, began her own investigation of the *laibon* tradition. A Ph.D. candidate at Roehampton University, she has been showing photographs of items from Turle's collection to people in Kenya's Maasai community.

There doesn't seem to be much mystery about them. People know what they are, including, to Sairo's surprise, her own mother.

"My mother has been meeting with the *laibon* himself," Sairo said. "He wore one of these objects around his neck. She told me the name. She was actually flattered that I was asking. She gave me more details than I even expected. She told me how the rituals were done. She said, 'Oh, my God, I had forgotten the new generations are so unaware.'"

While veteran staff at Kenya's National Museum remain cautious, Sairo says she isn't intimidated. At the same time, she isn't trying to get Turle's collection back from the Kenya Wildlife Service. She's smart enough not to engage in a power struggle with Leakey, but she's also determined, a millennial with her own sense of authority on matters of equality and justice.

"There is lots of politics around this, but that will not stop me from trying to understand my own culture," she told me.

Sairo and her colleagues hold the real answer to this mystery. With a new museum dedicated to Maasai culture that opened in 2019, run by the Maasai themselves rather than the National Museum of Kenya, it seems likely that the artifacts will be studied. When traditions of secrecy permit, they will be seen by the great-great-grandchildren of the famous *laibons* that Beard photographed. Perhaps most of Turle's collection will never be found, but there are other pipes and *rungus*, amulets and charms.

I feel lucky to have had my own experience with them, in the bush, unbound by museum rules. On that last trip I made to Kenya, surrounded by Maasai elders, I held a bone pipe in my hand.

While the others talked around me, I clutched it. I didn't want to let it go. This was not some abstract, symbolic notion of extinction or colonialism or misguided wildlife policy. Like Gollum, I wanted it. The object had power.

Mercy, the anthropologist from the National Museum, noticed my reaction. "Put it down," she ordered. I looked at her. She was serious. "You can't take it," she said. "You can't have it."

The bones collect us. We want to hang on, all of us. Perhaps all that will remain of the earth's great and beautiful creatures is art, if that: the caves at Lascaux, rock art in the Namibian desert, a Francis Bacon painting, a Noguchi sculpture. A virus, perhaps.

Sonetos De Cascadia

PAUL E NELSON

16-March-2020

—no heaven is, no earth, and the memory of both extinguished but for the
one ashtree-believing-nuthatch—,"
—Paul Celan

EARTH CLOSED. WHICH WAS THE SKY'S WISH THE birds, trees, un-
spoken mammal wish as if heterotrophs had a vote (& shd) & then do when
they conspire to halt "human progress" for a few weeks, lighten the air,
unclog the cities, add a dash of the duende to the stew we call life without
sports without eating out within no closer than six feet of the average human
germ-spewing capability. Earth closed. As a reset button as in what's in it
besides ratrace for you as in how might you act in prison but still cooking
your own meals as in get to enjoy, really enjoy brown rice. Earth first.
Finally. We had it coming, we stable geniuses knowing humans have all the
answers, all the technology, all the gear except for face masks, hand sanitizer,
toilet paper & ventilators. Duendification of life resynchronizes us with
the nuthatch and redwing, the coot raft and seagulls and there is no panic
buying by the lake, there is no hoarding (except for squirrel) there's nothing
but these last three days of winter and a slight sense of the new normal
in late capitalism.

All the Paintings

BRIAN CULLMAN

BACK THEN, I LIVED ON 16TH STREET AND Third Avenue, near Union Square. Big Joe Turner and Mrs. Big Joe lived there. So did a dominatrix with steely eyes and a bulldog jaw. And a South African art dealer who specialized in interracial pornography. There was a club kid who lived in the apartment next to mine. He had a beautiful German shepherd named Echo that he kept in a cage inside his apartment. The kid would go out to clubs and not come home for days at a time. The dog would whimper and bark, then whimper some more, sometimes all night.

I approached the kid in the hallway once. I like dogs, I told him. I often work at home. If you gave me the keys to your place, I could walk him at night sometimes when he's barking.

The kid leaned back against the wall. He folded his arms and shook his head.

"Yeah," he snorted. It was a laugh, but not much of a laugh. "Like I'm really going to give you keys to my place!"

I didn't know that he dealt Ecstasy. Among other things.

I lived on the 13th floor. The woman in this story lived on the eighth. I'd see her in the lobby and in the elevator, maybe by the mailboxes, and we probably nodded to each other, though we'd never spoken. She had hair the color of wet sand.

When I came back that day, she was in the lobby weeping hysterically and there were five or six people standing around her, all shaking their heads, trying to comfort her, talk to her. She kept crying.

Someone had broken into her apartment. She hadn't been gone long, a few hours at most, the time it took to go up to Macy's and come back, and in that time someone had broken into her apartment and taken all her paintings, all her artwork. Nothing else. But they'd taken all the drawings and paintings and lithographs from her walls, artwork she'd been collecting all her life, some inherited from family, some she'd bought in London or Paris. Her beautiful artwork.

We had to see, she said. We had to see.

She herded us into the elevator, seven of us, maybe eight by that point.

We had to see, she said.

The apartment looked freshly cleaned. It smelled of pine cones and lavender and lemon flowers, as if, not being able to choose the right fragrance, she'd decided on all of them at once, and the chairs and piano and piano bench were freshly waxed.

Paintings and drawings, most of them carefully framed by the same hand, were hung on every wall and were propped up on the tables and sideboard. There were the sorts of pictures of horses and dressage you'd see in Connecticut drawing rooms, in Greenwich or Darien, sunsets and landscapes and cloudscapes, Victorian portraits, still lifes, and nature and 19th-century ballerinas at rest.

The South African dealer had taken off his glasses and was looking at a pencil sketch of a West Indian girl with bare breasts.

"Boom boom," he said. "Boom boom."

The paintings, someone said.

They're here.

Nothing's gone. You're all right.

They're here.

The woman shook her head. She was crying, but softly, no longer hysterical.

"No," she said. "No. No. No."

She pointed to a canvas of a young woman at a loom, something Vermeer might have thrown away.

"No. These aren't my paintings. They're not. They look like them. They're almost them. They look like them. But when you look, you can see. My paintings, my real paintings are gone."

People nodded in sympathy. Someone tried to correct her, but stopped mid-sentence and cleared their throat and backed away. The South African dealer had put his glasses back on and was looking at his watch. One by one, we all left and went on with our lives.

The next day and for many days after, I'd see her outside the building, standing beneath the awning. She was waiting for the thieves to return. She'd stand there in an old woolen coat, out of the sun and out of the rain, waiting.

Around 9:30 or 10 at night, her father would show up, sometimes with chicken soup or minestrone from a diner nearby, maybe Joe Junior's, and would take her upstairs and put her to bed. The next day, bright and early, she'd be back, standing guard. The thieves, she knew, would be back. They couldn't help themselves. They'd be back. And she'd be there.

Time went by. I moved to 9th Street, but I still had friends in the old building. I'd stop by from time to time, and sometimes I'd see her outside the building in the same woolen coat. Once, last year, I was passing by, and I thought I saw her there under the awning, though it might have been someone looking for a cab.

That was a year ago, though it seems so much longer than that.

For more than six months, we've all been in seclusion. And now, people are stepping out their doors. There are restaurants that are open, and you can sit outside. Not inside. But outside. And you can get your hair cut or your nails done. You can go to the dentist or see your lawyer.

I went into a local bookstore a few hours ago and bought a Brazilian book about the West Village. Afterwards, I sat in the shade outside a small café and had an iced coffee. The waitress who brought it was wearing a mask, and when she got within a few feet of my table, I pulled my mask back up. I nodded. She smiled. Or I think she smiled. It's hard to know.

The city is opening up.

But it's not my city.

These are not my paintings.

The Writers

Beth Alvarado is the author of four books, including the award-winning *Anxious Attachments*. She teaches at Oregon State University.

Blanche McCrary Boyd is a novelist, essayist, and professor. Her most recent novel, *Tomb of the Unknown Racist,* was a Finalist for the PEN-Faulkner Award in 2019.

Michelle Browder is the founder of the youth nonprofit I Am More Than and More Than Tours, a tour company featuring walks that reveal both the well-known history of the civil rights movement in Montgomery, and the secret tunnels used by slave traders along with the stones that once marked the city's water fountains "Colored" and "White."

Michael Brown, an associate professor at the Rochester Institute of Technology, is the author of *Hope and Scorn: Eggheads, Experts, and Elites in American Politics.*

Lauren Camp is the author of seven books, most recently *An Eye in Each Square* (River River Books) and *Worn Smooth between Devourings* (NYQ Books). She is an emeritus fellow for Black Earth Institute and was Astronomer in Residence at Grand Canyon National Park. She currently serves as Poet Laureate of New Mexico.

Sarah Chayes was a National Public Radio correspondent reporting from Paris and the Balkans, as well as covering conflicts in Algeria, Pakistan, and Afghanistan, where she remained after starting a nonprofit employing women. She later served as special adviser to the Joint Chiefs of Staff and worked at the Carnegie Endowment for International Peace. She is the author of three books, including *On Corruption in America.*

Maxine Chernoff is the author of 18 poetry collections, most recently *Light and Clay.* Former chair of Creative Writing at San Francisco State University, she is an NEA Fellow, a winner of the PEN Translation Award, and a former visiting writer at the American Academy in Rome.

Sunnie R. Clahchischiligi is a full-time instructor in the Writers' Studio in the School of Applied Sciences and Arts at Arizona State University. She is a contributing writer at *Searchlight New Mexico* and a member of the Navajo Nation. Her work appears in the *Navajo Times, The New York Times, The Guardian* and other publications.

Kate Cohen is a former *Washington Post* contributing columnist and author of *We of Little Faith: Why I Stopped Pretending to Believe (And Maybe You Should Too)* which chronicles Kate's journey to outspoken atheism and argues that nonbelievers should be more vocal, for the good of the country. The Freedom from Religion Foundation honored her with its "Freethought Heroine" award in 2023. She is the author of two previous books.

Matt Cooper is Executive Editor Digital for the *Washington Monthly*. He was senior editor at *Newsweek*, and is a former reporter for *Time*, where he made national news for refusing to name his sources on the story of Valerie Plame, the CIA agent whose assets were put at risk when Bush administration officials leaked her identity.

Paul Cullum has written for the *LA Weekly, Los Angeles Times, New York Times, Variety, Hollywood Reporter, Los Angeles. Review of Books, Salon, Slate, Daily Beast, Arthur* and hundreds of tiny subversive magazines. He was a songwriter and frontman with the band Wild Blue Yonder.

Keith Donnell Jr., originally from Philly, is a California-based poet and book editor. He is the author of *The Move* (Nomadic Press, 2021) and his work has appeared in journals and anthologies, most recently *POETRY* and *Best American Nonrequired Reading*. His second poetry collection is *supreme night* (Black Lawrence Press, 2025).

William Thatcher Dowell was a staff correspondent for *Time* based in Paris, Cairo, Hong Kong, and New York. From 1993 to 1995, he worked as *Time's* Southeast Asia Bureau Chief. He covered the Arab world and Iran from 1989 through 1993.

Steve Erickson is the author of 10 novels including *Shadowbahn* and *Zeroville,* and has written for *Esquire, Smithsonian, McSweeney's* and the *New York Times*. He is a Distinguished Professor and Chair of Creative Writing at the University of California, Riverside.

Essential Worker Zh43dfC is the pseudonym of a Mississippi high school teacher who wants to make sure she keeps her job. She holds an MFA in creative writing from the University of Mississippi.

David Galef is the author of three novels and three short story collections. His work has appeared in *The New York Times, Inside Higher Ed, The Writer's Chronicle, McSweeney's, The Daily Drunk,* and many more. He is creative writing program director at Montclair State University.

Mikal Gilmore is the author of four books, including the National Book Critics Circle Award-winning memoir *Shot in the Heart,* and the 1960s cultural history *Stories Done*. He is a longtime writer for *Rolling Stone.*

J.C. Hallman is the author of six books, most recently *The Anarcha Quest: A Story of Slavery and Surgery* (2023). "Quagmire Days" was first published in *The Baffler*.

Tom Henderson has been a newspaper reporter and editor in Oregon and Idaho for the past 40 years. He is the former president of the Society of Professional Journalists in those states and has won more than 100 national and regional awards for his work.

Christine Kiessling is an art historian and art acquisition consultant who came to art history through studio experience. Along with the Western tradition, her expertise includes Pre-Columbian Art, African Art, Feminist History of Art, and the History of Photography.

"Endangered Species," by Jami Macarty, is from her book *The Minuses,* part of the Mountain West poetry series. Reprinted with the permission of the Center for Literary Publishing. Macarty is editor of *The Maynard* and teaches poetry at Simon Fraser University in Vancouver, British Columbia.

Gregory McNamee is an author, editor, and publisher who makes his home in Tucson, Arizona. His books include *Gila: The Life and Death of an American River.* He is a contributing editor to *Encyclopaedia Britannica.*

Mike Medberry has served as a senior environmentalist for local and national conservation organizations. His books include *On the Dark Side of the Moon* and *Living in the Broken West—Essays.* He lives in Angels Camp, California.

Alberto Montero is clinical director of the Breast Cancer Medical Oncology Program at University Hospitals Seidman Cancer Center in Cleveland, Ohio. He is an associate professor of medicine at Case Western Reserve University School of Medicine.

Ted Mooney was the author of several prize-winning novels, including *Easy Travel to Other Planets* and *The Same River Twice.* A former editor at *Art in America,* his essays appeared in *Granta* and *Esquire.*

Poet and interviewer Paul E Nelson founded the Cascadia Poetics Lab. He is the author of four books of poetry, a book of essays and a book of transcribed interviews. Among his titles are *A Time Before Slaughter, Pig War: & Other Songs of Cascadia, American Sentences* and *Haibun de la Serna.* He lives in Seattle, in the Cascadia bioregion.

Tim Page won the Pulitzer Prize for Criticism in 1997 for his writings about music for the *Washington Post.* He is the author or editor of more than 20 books, including *Parallel Play* and *Dawn Powell: A Biography.*

Stephen Pain writes short stories, essays, and poetry. His writing has appeared in *New Poetry, Deep South, Black Bear Review, Pen & Sword,* and *Kilometer Zero.*

Stephen Derwent Partington was born in England, but emigrated to Kenya, where he is the principal of a small rural school. He writes academic articles for journals and for the Kenyan press, and acted as poetry editor for what was then East Africa's only creative writing magazine *Kwani?* His most recent poetry collection, *How to Euthanise a Cactus* (Cinnamon, UK), featured poems on Kenya's post-election violence of 2007.

Ben Quick is a professor at the American University in Vietnam. He is a winner of the Pushcart Prize for nonfiction.
Herb Randall's writing has appeared in *Apofenie, Punctured Lines*, and the *Los Angeles Review of Books*. He lives in northern New Hampshire.

Unkonda Rasheda Sawyer has worked for several international aid agencies. She is the author of the children's book *Who Knew New Words?* which tells the story of a little boy sent home from school because of Covid.

Rosemerry Wahtola Trommer lives in Placerville, Colorado. She has 13 poetry collections, most recently *All the Honey; Beneath All Appearances an Unwavering Peace*. Her work has appeared in *O Magazine, A Prairie Home Companion*, and the PBS News Hour.

Thrity Umrigar is the author of 10 novels, most recently *The Museum of Failures*. She is a Distinguished Professor of English at Case Western Reserve University.

Hailey Nicole Warner is a graduate of the San Francisco State University creative writing program.

David Weir is a journalist who has worked and published at *Rolling Stone, Salon, Wired.com, The New York Times, The Nation, Mother Jones, New York, New Times, SunDance*, and many other publications and sites. He is a co-founder of the Center for Investigative Reporting and the author of four books.

Acknowledgements

Not long after we started *Journal of the Plague Years*, we began calling the magazine's writers and readers a tribe. As the world seemed to be falling apart, spontaneous connections built our magazine and the book you have in your hands. Working with talented, brilliant people was galvanizing. More than that, it was comforting.

We thank the writers for their generosity. The legendary graphic designer Roger Black created our logo, including our oddly genial Plague Doctor, and became one of our most trusted advisors. Advice and support came from John Oakes, Lee Pacchia, Walter Shapiro, Steve Wasserman, and David Weir. Artists, illustrators, photographers, and videographers made crucial contributions: Cole Coonce, Georganne Deen, Corinne Dufka, Alexa Grace, Ben Quick, Maranie Rae, Don J. Usner. Poets have been our moral center. Our first poetry editor, Jami Macarty, brought her impeccable taste; Maxine Chernoff took over from her, providing erudite poems of her own, unexpected connections, and solid guidance. Lauren Camp came through in a pinch, Paul Nelson transmitted Beatnik spirit, Rosemerry Wahtola Trommer gave us dailiness and hope. Songwriter and musician Lisa Mednick Powell has been our copy editor and more. Bruce Bauman, Paul Cullum, and Deanne Stillman provided necessary perspective. Steve Erickson supported the magazine in many ways, not least by contributing his extraordinary talent. Mikal Gilmore has been kind and generous throughout. Joan Juliet Buck is always delightful. Blanche McCrary Boyd worked her magic. Tim Page shared his talent and grace in more ways than one can see on the page. Our interns, Hailey Nicole Warner and Jamil Bakar raised our spirits. One of the joys of starting this magazine was getting to know Ted Mooney (1951-2022). We miss him. *Covfefe!*

Editors

Susan Zakin is best known as the author of *Coyotes and Town Dogs: Earth First! and the Environmental Movement*. She has covered politics and the environment for national magazines. In 2001, a Senator John Heinz Fellowship for Environmental Writing took her to Madagascar. Her subsequent articles and essays on African politics and conservation are collected in 2017's *Waiting for Charlie: Mercenary Soldiers, Failed States, and the Love That Means More Than Money*. A novel, *Libertyville*, is forthcoming in 2025.

Brian Cullman is a writer and musician based in New York City. A three-time winner of the ASCAP Deems Taylor Award for writings on music, he is a regular contributor to *The Paris Review*. Cullman has written for *Rolling Stone, Creem, The Village Voice,* and *Details*. He produced the soundtrack to the documentary *Gypsy Caravan*, and scored *Padre Nuestro*, winner of the Grand Jury Prize for best U.S. drama at the 2008 Sundance Festival. His CDs include *Winter Clothes, The Opposite of Time,* and *All Fires the Fire*. He is a founding member of Lisbon-based group *Rua das Pretas*, which he described as a United Nations of talents: "...samba players from Brazil; fado singers from Lisbon; bass players from the world of jazz; singers from Cape Verde; Americans like me who fell in love with the sea and the cool night air..."

BLUE BOOKS publishes high-quality fiction and nonfiction that reveals the friction, as startling as it is inevitable, when people and cultures find they have outgrown their past but can't yet make sense of their future.

www.journaloftheplagueyears.ink

www.journaloftheplagueyears.ink

www.ingramcontent.com/pod-product-compliance
Lightning Source LLC
Chambersburg PA
CBHW040915010826
48978CB00013BB/1298